Number One

Ranji: A Genius Rich and Strange

Letting Rip: The Fast-Bowling Threat from Lillee to Waqar

Simon Wilde

Number One

THE WORLD'S BEST BATSMEN AND BOWLERS

Victor Gollancz
London

First published in Great Britain 1998
by Victor Gollancz
An imprint of the Cassell Group
Wellington House, 125 Strand, London WC2R 0BB

A catalogue record for this book is
available from the British Library.

ISBN 0 575 06453 6

Typeset by Production Line, Minster Lovell
Printed in Great Britain by
St Edmundsbury Press Ltd, Bury St Edmunds, Suffolk

98 99 10 9 8 7 6 5 4 3 2 1

To Freddie, Lily and Eva,
who defy separation
in my affections

CONTENTS

THE BOWLERS

FOREWORD

by Matthew Engel

There is a BBC Radio Four programme called *In the Psychiatrist's Chair*. The idea is that a well-known personality faces a soft-spoken Irish shrink and supposedly gives away his or her most intimate secrets to the listening hordes. These days, most have learned the technique and play everything with the straightest of bats. Years ago, though, Geoffrey Boycott went on and gave what seemed a most uncharacteristic performance, trying to smash the questions everywhere.

The shrink, Anthony Clare, mused that cricket was an odd sport, because it was at the same time both a team game and an individual one. Boycott denied the premise. 'It's an individual game,' he said. I have often wondered in the years since how it is that Geoffrey can talk with such authority and expertise – as he undoubtedly does – on the telly about the details of cricket, when he cannot even agree with conventional wisdom on the object of the exercise. But that I suppose is just one of the game's many glorious mysteries.

Fact: cricket *IS* both a team game and an individual one. But it is the individual aspects of it that give cricket its drama, its character, its fascination. If England beat Australia, that is interesting (indeed, these days, miraculous). But what makes cricket special is how it happens, and who makes it happen. So maybe Geoffrey was making a very deep psychiatric point about the nature of cricket and was, in his way, right too.

Wisden gives more space to the highest individual innings than to the highest-ever team scores. In August 1997 Sri Lanka made the highest-ever total in a Test match, 952 for 6, knocking out the 903 for 7 scored by England at the Oval 59 years earlier. But there was far more interest in whether or not Sanath Jayasuriya would surpass Brian Lara's record for the highest individual score. He failed, falling for 340, short of Lara's 375. But the near-miss created more stir than the record that was broken.

So that's the fascination in *Number One*. Who were the greatest players in the world at any given time? No one can ever know for sure, and I certainly do not agree with all Simon Wilde's judgements, still less those of the computerized rankings system. But anyone interested in cricket history, and how the game's past relates to its present, will appreciate the idea and enjoy this book – by one of the sport's most gifted and best-informed young writers. This is cricket turned into the world heavyweight championship, as it was before it degenerated into farce. One has the sense of the torch of history being passed from one top performer to another. It is a rather noble sort of concept.

There are of course a number of artificialities involved. It is a little misleading even to split the game between its two core skills: batting and bowling. This is partly because so many of the champion cricketers were brilliant at both. And then there are the subsidiary skills: fielding, naturally; captaincy; and that extra something, which takes us back to Boycott's radio interview.

What is the extra something? I suppose one can define it best as a sense of perspective. It is that understanding of when the individual ceases to matter and the team matters more; of when the team ceases to matter and cricket matters more (something understood less and less, as the top players become more bad-tempered and dishonest); and of when cricket ceases to matter and life as a whole matters more.

Sir Neville Cardus once marvelled at an innings by Bradman, and added what I think was the highest praise of all: that on top of all his technical skills, he was 'a son of the game'. The true champions are all sons of the game. I think Simon Wilde has unearthed dozens of them for your delight. Read, enjoy, and have the courage to disagree with him.

Matthew Engel, Editor, *Wisden Cricketers' Almanack*.
Newton St Margarets, Herefordshire, December 1997.

INTRODUCTION

Arguing the relative merits of all-time great sportsmen is fraught with difficulty. How can one compare performers of different generations? Games are conducted differently now to the way they were twenty-five years ago, let alone fifty, seventy-five or a hundred. The players are very different too, and so are many of the laws. The culture of sport has changed, and so has society's. Such variable factors fan the flames of debate at one turn, and douse them with cold water at the next.

This does not mean, though, that meaningful comparisons cannot be drawn between same-generation players – and that is what this book uniquely attempts to do for cricket. Identified here are the world's top batsman and bowler *at any one time*, from the game's formative years down to the present day. Not decade by decade, but champion by champion, each one supreme until he quits the scene or a better performer comes along. Presented here are two lines of sporting monarchs and their reigns.

The method is straightforward. Although many people may have opinions about such matters, some people's opinions are clearly more important than others', and in this case they are those of the leading players themselves. If Don Bradman thought Bill O'Reilly the best he faced, that surely says a lot about O'Reilly's bowling; if Shane Warne thinks Sachin Tendulkar a less forgiving batsman than Brian Lara, that, too, must be significant. Collected here are the views of the great players about each other. The critics also have their say. But the final decisions are mine, and mine alone.

Apart from opinions, there are facts. If a bowler is really worth his salt, he will cause even the most domineering batsmen to think twice; similarly, a batsman with pretensions to be the world's best will have answers to the most cunning of bowlers. These duels-within-duels are rarely focused on by outsiders. They form a central part of this book.

There are only two ground rules and they keep faith with the perennially cautious attitude of players and critics towards new 'stars'. The first is that no one can be considered the world's best without having proved himself against various opponents and in a variety of conditions – witness the reservations held over the young Bradman when he first came to England in 1930. One outstanding season or Test series is insufficient basis for a claim, which accounts for the exclusion here of such briefly brilliant bowlers – at the highest level – as Larwood and Tyson. The second is that if there is any doubt about the relative merits of rival players, the benefit goes to the man in possession. A brief lapse in form – which can strike even the finest player – does not necessarily end the reign of a 'Number One'; nor do absences through injury, or a missed tour.

In the relatively few cases where the evidence is inconclusive – and this is mainly in modern times, where active players are often reluctant to express their thoughts about opponents – the author has drawn his own conclusions. Scoring runs and taking wickets in a meaningful manner, and helping teams to win matches, was marked high; style for style's sake counted for nothing. It goes without saying that anyone who warrants a mention is an absolutely outstanding cricketer and all reservations expressed are strictly relative. I do not expect anyone to agree with all my findings; but I hope many will agree with most of them.

If such an exercise sounds artificial, it ought not, because it belongs to an old tradition. Up until the early nineteenth century, when almost all the leading players batted and bowled as a matter of course, the title of 'champion cricketer' was usually bestowed on the best all-round performer. The fashionable single-wicket contests were commonly one of the ways of establishing who that was. Subsequently, use of the term spread to the leading batsman and bowler in England, bestowed chiefly by the sporting press and popular acclaim. Fuller Pilch and George Parr were successively champion batsman; William Lillywhite was for many years champion bowler (his nickname was the 'Nonpareil'). Then, as now, the choice was often easier to determine for batsmen than bowlers. Among the latter, the range of techniques blurred the issue.

Alfred Mynn, meanwhile, became known simply as the 'Champion Cricketer' in recognition of his larger-than-life character and all-round accomplishments – a throwback, essentially, to the term's original usage. This title was also readily granted to

W.G. Grace, whose domination of the game was so total and so lengthy that the name stayed with him long after his powers had waned, and even in death: he was to be 'The Champion' for ever. He had made cricket, but killed a custom – and once Grace's game spread its wings across continents, it was no longer a simple matter to compare players.

Resolving disputes is one theme here; another is an examination of sporting greatness. Being the second-best batsman or bowler in the world might be easy but it can only be intensely demanding being the best, as Brian Lara and Shane Warne would confirm. What qualities took these players to the summit and kept them there? One might guess at talent and temperament, single-mindedness and stamina, selfishness, a pioneering spirit. These attributes are duly apparent, but other, less expected denominators also emerge and are outlined between pages 15 to 18. Taken together, these individuals' histories map out the landscape of cricket's entire history.

For the special purposes of this book, Coopers & Lybrand, who sponsor the computer system that rates the performances of players in Test cricket, agreed to run their system for each year since Test cricket began in 1877. The ratings of the Number Ones are given for the years of their reigns (if they achieved top-five positions); if they were not ranked number one, those who were are named.

The system – introduced in 1987 and the brainchild of Ted Dexter, the former England captain and one of the best batsmen of his day – attempts to overcome the inadequacies of traditional batting and bowling averages. It takes account not only of runs scored and wickets taken, but of some of the variable factors that are so troublesome: when the runs were scored and wickets taken (with greatest store placed on the most recent performances), the strength of the opposition and the context of the match.

The ratings are far from faultless but can claim to be at least as revealing, in their way, as conventional averages. They are given here simply as another means of comparison. After all, if it were possible to measure players by figures alone, there would not be much for us to argue about.

Simon Wilde
Clapham, December 1997

NOTES

Note 1: When other Number One players are referred to in an entry, their names are capitalized at first mention.

Note 2: The Coopers & Lybrand ratings published here are those calculated in the September of each year. Only players who appeared in a Test match during the previous twelve months, and had not announced their retirements, are included. The ratings for 1978 and 1979 are distorted by the absence of many of the leading players who had joined Kerry Packer and were ruled out of Test cricket.

Note 3: Statistics dealing with the players' records against Number One batsmen/bowlers apply only to the occasions when they faced each other as the respective Number Ones – i.e. they are not career summaries of their facing each other.

Note 4: A player's nationality, or the place where he learned his cricket, rather than the country he represented, is given after his name at the head of each entry, though cricketers from the Caribbean are given as West Indies.

WHAT IT TAKES TO BE
THE WORLD'S GREATEST

Forty-nine cricketers are listed in the pages that follow – 22 batsmen and 27 bowlers. The batsmen enjoyed reigns that on average lasted just over ten years, bowlers ones of just over seven. The batsmen enjoyed their peaks between the ages of 27 and 37, bowlers from 29 to 36. The youngest 'Number One' batsman was Grace, who was 18 when his reign began, followed by Beldham and Bradman, both 21; the oldest were Beauclerk and Small, respectively 52 and 50 at the end of their reigns. The youngest bowlers were Freeman, Richardson, Gregory, Lillee and Warne, all 23; the oldest Lillywhite at 57 and Clarke at 54. Beauclerk and Grace shared the longest unbroken reigns for batsmen of 20 years, Lillywhite the longest for a bowler of 22.

Among the 49, six used the name William, another six John or Jack. There were three Fredericks (though it is doubtful whether Spofforth or Trueman would have wanted to share the company of Beauclerk) and three players – Trumper, Grimmett and Bedser – appropriately had Victor somewhere in their name. The most common birthdays were in July (eight), September (six) and December (five); no one was born in January. Small and Barnes were both born on 19 April, Grace and Lillee on 18 July, and Freeman and Sobers on 28 July.

Those for whom the information exists were on average one of six children. Shaw was one of 13, Hobbs one of 12, Lara one of 11, Parr, Grace and Shrewsbury each one of nine. O'Reilly and Trueman were both the fourth of seven. Hammond, Barry Richards and Marshall were only children, though Marshall has a half-brother and half-sister. Bedser and Waugh belong to sets of twins.

There is also a modern and unhappy trend for parents not to live to see their sons reach stardom – perhaps the experience made the aspiring cricketers more self-sufficient and determined. Lindwall lost his mother when he was seven and his father when he was 17. Laker's father died when he was two and his mother when he was in his early twenties. Hobbs's father was dead by the time his son was in his early twenties, as was (probably) Ranjitsinhji's. Hammond was about 15 when his father died, Sobers five, Marshall one and Lara 19; Ambrose was a small child. Shaw's mother died when he was ten and May's when he was 16. The absence of fathers suggests that mothers have played larger parts in the formative years of the best sportsmen than previously acknowledged. Martha Grace, cricket's First Lady, may not be such a singular figure after all. Hutton, for one, said that his ability came through his mother's side of the family.

Thirty were born in England, ten in Australia, six in the Caribbean, and one each in India, New Zealand and South Africa. Ranjitsinhji was born and brought up in India but played for England; Grimmett, a New Zealander by birth and upbringing, appeared for Australia. Englishmen, naturally, dominated the game in the eighteenth and nineteenth centuries, but they have produced only one top batsman in the last 38 years (Gooch) and no bowler in 25.

Most grew up and learned the game in an essentially rural environment; few in metropolises. Sydney and its outlying districts can boast Spofforth, Trumper, Gregory, Lindwall and Waugh; the New South Wales country Turner, O'Reilly and Bradman. Nottinghamshire provided six players and Sussex four (all bowlers). Cambridgeshire and Norfolk, regions that have played little first-class cricket, at one time or another nurtured Pilch, Carpenter, Ranjitsinhji and Hobbs, who between them held the position of top batsman for 43 years between 1860 and 1928. The family of a subsequent batsman, Bradman, also had its roots in East Anglia.

Eight played principally for New South Wales, seven for Surrey and six for Nottinghamshire, who provided both top batsman and top bowler between 1850 and 1853 (Parr and Clarke) and 1858 and 1860 (Parr and Jackson). This double was also accomplished by New South Wales between 1932 and 1935 (Bradman and O'Reilly) and Surrey from 1956 to 1959 (May and Laker).

Of the 30 English-born players, only four were amateurs at the time of their reigns – Beauclerk, Ward, Grace and May, all batsmen – and only Beauclerk, Ward and May learned the game in a traditional public-school setting, where the principles of orthodox technique are habitually instilled. A lack of formal coaching is a common characteristic: these champions were either self-taught, or left to their own devices by coaches who understood that genius has no need of orthodoxies. Equally, not many amateurs could spare the time necessary to reach the very top.

The average height among the batsmen was 5ft 10$\frac{1}{2}$in; the bowlers were an inch taller at 5ft 11$\frac{1}{2}$in. The heights of the batsmen varied little, the tallest being Ward and May at 6ft 1in, the shortest Beldham, Parr, Carpenter, Shrewsbury, Bradman and Lara, all around 5ft 8in. The tallest bowler – by three and a half inches – was Ambrose at 6ft 7in; the shortest Lillywhite at a mere 5ft 4in.

No bowler was a left-armer and only two batsmen left-handers: Sobers and Lara, both from the West Indies. There was a trend in the first half of the nineteenth century for the best batsman to be positioned centrally in the order at number four, before Grace showed the advantages of going in early. Since then, and mirroring the growing threat from pairs of fast bowlers wielding a new ball, all the Number One batsmen played at their peaks as openers or in the pivotal number-three position – except May, Sobers and Waugh. Of the bowlers, three bowled underarm, four roundarm and 20 overarm; of those 20, nine were out-and-out fast in speed, five were fast-medium or medium, three were leg-break/googly bowlers and three off-spinners (though Shaw was an embryonic one). The fastest bowlers typically reached the top around their mid-twenties and enjoyed short reigns, Lillee's being easily the longest at ten years; other types took longer but, once there, stayed longer.

Though there were some exceptions, in the main the batsmen encouraged and inspired each other, as did the bowlers, but between the two groups there were some fierce rivalries. Most were just about confined to the field.

Apart from a sensitivity to criticism, perhaps the commonest denominator was an ability to succeed in almost all conditions, whether favourable or not: these were players resourceful enough to constantly adapt and excel. This was especially true of all the batsmen since Parr, and all bowlers since Spofforth. As these players show, the main advances in the game in the twentieth century have been on the mental rather than the technical side.

Outside their playing days, most Number Ones maintained close connections with the game – they coached and umpired, wrote and commentated, managed teams and administrated. Other popular sidelines were running public houses (Beldham, Pilch, Lillywhite, Richardson and Tate) or banking and insurance (Ward, Spofforth, Turner, May and Barry Richards). Lillywhite and Clarke both had spells as bricklayers. Stevens was a gardener, Lindwall a florist. Trumper, O'Reilly and Snow either taught or were trained to teach. Most made money – directly or indirectly – out of their positions, some substantially so; not all, though, managed to hang on to what of it came their way, notably Jackson, Turner, Richardson, Lockwood and Hammond. Four batsmen (Hobbs, Bradman, Hutton and Sobers) and one bowler (Bedser) were knighted.

The 15 batsmen who have finished their innings lived to an average age of 67, the 19 bowlers ten months longer. With the exception of Shrewsbury, who committed suicide at 47, only Trumper (37) of the batsmen died before reaching 60; of bowlers, only Richardson (41) and Harris (48). Shaw and Shrewsbury were buried in the same graveyard. The longest-lived batsman was Beldham at 95, the longest-lived bowler Barnes, 94.

The Players

EARLY CHAMPIONS

In cricket's pre-history, it was a long time before the individual contributions to the team cause were routinely recorded. In the game's formative years, the outcome of a fixture was perceived to be its only point of interest and few details of anything but the results of matches survive from before 1770. However, reputations were won by the best players, of which some records exist, if only in the briefest terms.

The first player known to have achieved widespread renown was William Beddel, born in Bromley in 1680 and living later in Dartford. He was described at his death as 'formerly the most expert cricket player in England'. By the 1740s, Richard Newland, one of three brothers who helped make Sussex the strongest county, was the most famous player in England and heavy bets were laid on his personal scores in 'great' matches.

One of the few of these for which extensive details survive is Lord John Sackville's challenge match in 1744 between Kent and All-England at the Artillery Ground in Finsbury, hailed by James Love in his celebrated contemporaneous poem as 'the greatest match ever known'. It is in fact the oldest match for which detailed scores survive and also the first recorded in *Cricket Scores & Biographies*, the seminal work of Arthur Haygarth, who, as a Harrow schoolboy in 1842, began collecting the scores of every significant match ever played (Haygarth later became a batsman of note himself). Newland made the two highest scores in the game and claimed eight wickets, and Love referred to him as 'The Champion', perhaps the first time that title was bestowed in print on any cricketer.

By then, Kent had inherited Sussex's mantle and soon one of their number, John Bell, was being referred to as 'the most noted cricketer in England'. Later, one of Lord John Sackville's sons, the third Duke of Dorset, maintained on his estate a man called Joseph Miller, 'of England's cricketers the best'. Miller was a batsman, but it is noticeable that the reputations of these early heroes were not as batsmen or bowlers but as 'cricketers', an indication that players had yet to specialize in one discipline. In any case, for many years statistical comparison between bowlers was hampered by the practice of only crediting them with a batsman's dismissal if they bowled down his wicket. Catches went down in the first scorebooks as the sole work of fielders.

Newland, a surgeon by profession, also taught the game, and one of those he tutored was his young nephew Richard Nyren, who rose to become the most influential figure in cricket's first great club, Hampshire, or 'Hambledon' as it is better known to posterity.

It was with Hambledon's golden age, during the second half of the eighteenth century, that cricket reached adulthood. By then, it was played in a manner recognizable – if in some respects still primitive – to the modern eye and was popular across a wide range of society. It was fashionable in the well-to-do circles of London, where the Laws were published in 1744 and the Marylebone Cricket Club had become suzerain; practised at the leading educational establishments and patronized by the noble landowners whose estates dominated the rural areas of an agricultural society. Matches were often staged on the private grounds of the aristocracy, and huge sums wagered on the outcomes. Gambling was an integral part of the game until the 1820s and resulted in many corrupt practices – and near-terminal decline for the game – before action was taken to bar bookmakers from Lord's in 1817. But the most important fixtures, or 'great' matches as they were known, were an attraction to the 'disinterested' spectator as well.

By comparison with today, pitches were bone-threateningly rough and scoring low and slow. For someone to score a hundred runs off his own bat was an astonishing feat in 1770 and still a rare one in 1820. As batting techniques developed, the lbw law was introduced and the size of the wicket increased on three occasions, while bats gradually evolved from the long, heavy, curved implements first designed to deal with a ball trundled along the ground and began to resemble the straight, shouldered instruments of today. Bowling was underarm until 1828 when, after several attempts to gain acceptance for a roundarm method, one was finally accepted. Bowlers had exerted control by mastering the arts of pitch, break and speed, but as batsmen adjusted to these developments, bowlers ran out of initiatives and were clamouring for change for years before it finally came.

Significantly for the advancement of the game, patronage and payment led to the creation of a small school of technically sophisticated cricketers capable of performing – and teaching – the game to a high level. Among this band of men there developed lively rivalries for the plaudits and the purses and these were not entirely confined to the rapidly growing ranks of professionals. They were the kind of rivalries which essentially survive to this day among the world's best.

JOHN SMALL (England)

Number One: 1768–87

Born: Empshott, Hampshire, 19 April 1737; died: Petersfield, Hampshire, 31 December 1826. Career: 1755–98.

Though the scores of many of the matches in which he played are lost, John Small was indisputably the first batsman in England for most of the quarter-century that Hambledon were at their height. Two things set him apart from his contemporaries: concentration and defence, cornerstones of every great batsman's game.

He once kept up his wicket for three days against All-England, and when STEVENS bowled down his wicket during a match between Hampshire and Kent at Bishopsbourne Paddock, near Canterbury, in 1772 – a match that reportedly attracted an attendance of more than 15,000 – it was said to be the first time Small had been so dismissed 'for several years'. Three years later, Small helped V of Hampshire to a narrow defeat of V of Kent by scoring the last fourteen runs they needed. It took him almost three hours.

During the course of that innings, Stevens bowled the ball through Small's two stumps without dislodging a bail, an injustice that contributed to the introduction of the middle stump. After that, 'straight' play became even more essential but Small, who was also a batmaker, not only maintained his position at the head of the field but remodelled his bats to make them more suitable for the purpose. He was reckoned to be the first stealer of short singles.

When Hampshire beat Kent in 1768, Small 'fetched above seven score notches off his own bat'. Four years later he scored 112 of Hambledon's 225 runs against England and in 1775 reached 136 not out against Surrey, after which the *Kentish Gazette* described him as 'the best cricketer the world ever produced'. These were astonishing match tallies, but they were comfortably eclipsed in 1777 when James Aylward, another Hampshire man and Small's chief rival, set a record for 'great' matches with a single innings of 167 against an England attack containing Stevens. Aylward was the first outstanding left-handed batsman in history.

Though born in Empshott, Small lived for all but six of his eighty-nine years in Petersfield. He is said to have taken part in his first 'great' match in 1755, when he would have been eighteen years old, and gave up his first trade as a shoemaker to play cricket. Around this he eventually managed to fit a new career as a game-keeper, regularly making the seven-mile tour of his land before setting off for a match. He continued playing until he was sixty-one years old, extending his career in important matches beyond forty years.

As his reputation flourished, Small also started to make cricket bats and balls – and to a high standard. At the time of his death, the balls he made were widely held to be better than those of Duke's of Penshurst, who had manufactured them since 1780 and produce them still. The last six made by Small were purchased by Edward Budd and sold on to WARD.

Apart from his affection for cricket, Small also possessed a profound love and knowledge of music, by no means the last man to combine an active interest in the two pursuits but possibly the first. Small was a member of the Petersfield church choir for seventy-five years, regularly attended evening parties as a violinist and was perhaps as well known in local quarters for his music as for his cricket ('though his name was Small, yet great his fame'). Once, after Small had seen Hampshire to a famous victory over Kent, the Duke of Dorset sent him a fine violin as a gift. One of the greatest measures of Small's cricketing skill was that, on uneven pitches and without the protection of gloves, his fingers were in sufficiently good repair for him to play his instrument.

Small was a popular figure, Pierce Egan attesting in his *Book of Sports* (1832) that 'no man was more remarkable for playful wit, cheerful conversation, or inoffensive manners'. One example of this playful wit survives, for Small is known to have hung a sign outside his house in Petersfield which read:

> *Here lives John Small,*
> *Makes Bat and Ball,*
> *Pitch a Wicket, Play at Cricket*
> *With any man in England.*

Small's son, John junior, who helped run the family business, also played for Hambledon and became one of the leading batsmen of his day. Like his father, he played to the noisome cheering and cajoling of Mrs John Small, a regular attender at their matches on Broadhalfpenny Down and the first woman in this story.

EDWARD STEVENS (England)

Number One: 1770–83

Born: Send, Surrey, 1735; died: Walton-on-Thames, Surrey, 7 September 1819. Career: 1767–89.

Edward Stevens – or 'Lumpy' – was the first cricketer to win fame solely through his ability as a bowler. Although little is known about him, his standing within the game is unquestionable. Famed for his accuracy and stamina, there was a period when he was the most important player in England, the first man to demonstrate the adage 'bowlers win matches'.

Such was his importance, Stevens – a short, stout and genial character noted for his huge appetite – was sometimes the only player named when arrangements of challenge matches were published in the newspapers. In 1774, Kent challenged Hampshire, 'on condition that Lumpy and two other men from any part of England, except Hampshire, might play for Kent'; in 1777, it was reported, Hambledon 'have undertaken to play Lumpy with ten Hampshire men against twelve of Kent and three of Surrey, supported by the Duke of Dorset'. Stevens was the only bowler who was a genuine match for SMALL, whom he engaged in some much talked-of battles.

Like many great bowlers, one of Stevens's main attributes was cunning. He was notorious for choosing to pitch stumps – a decision then left in the hands of the bowlers – on the brow of a hill, so that the ball would shoot through low on the unsuspecting batsman. In doing this, he reportedly paid little heed to the needs of his colleagues; indeed, he is said to have possessed little understanding of or interest in the game, except as it affected him.

Stevens was concerned only in taking wickets and winning large wagers for his patrons. The first of these benefactors was a Mr Porter, a Chertsey brewer; the second, the fourth Earl of Tankerville, who supported Stevens financially during his playing days and, when they were over, employed him as a gardener on his estate in Walton-on-Thames.

'Lumpy' once won £100 for his Lordship by hitting a feather with a ball four times in a row. Tankerville and Stevens were both members of the English cricket team dispatched to play in Paris in 1789 in an attempt to allay anti-British feeling there, only to be stopped at Dover by the news that the French Revolution had started.

Stevens's principal rivals were Thomas Brett, a strongly built farmer from Catherington who was reputedly the fastest bowler in the years up to 1778, and Hambledon's redoubtable general Richard Nyren, slower than Stevens but almost as accurate. When Stevens died, the Earl of Tankerville erected a tombstone over his grave.

◎ DAVID HARRIS (England)

Number One: 1783–98

Born: Elvetham, Hampshire, 1755; died: Crookham, Hampshire, 19 May 1803. Career: 1778–98.

David Harris, like SMALL a Hambledon man, was not only the greatest bowler of his era but one of the outstanding figures in the history of the game. He was described by John Nyren, Richard's son, in 1833, long after his death, as 'the very best bowler, a bowler who, between anyone and himself, comparison was to fail'; in 1862, many years after the introduction of roundarm bowling, Arthur Haygarth wrote that Harris was 'not to be excelled, either in his own day or since'. BELDHAM, whose duels with Harris produced the finest cricket of the day, said that Harris was 'always first chosen of all men in England'.

Harris's relentlessly accurate 'length' bowling set a new standard in his trade and demanded dramatic technical improvements of batsmen. He made forward defence an integral part of their art. 'To Harris's bowling I attribute the great improvement that was made in hitting, and, above all, in stopping,' Nyren wrote, 'for it was utterly impossible to remain at the crease when the ball was tossed to a fine length. You were obliged to get in, or it would be about your hands, or the handle of your bat, and every cricketer knows where its next place would be.' Even those who could block him struggled to score runs and Tom Walker, 'Old Everlasting', once received 170 balls from Harris and notched up just one single.

Harris delivered the ball in a most curious manner, bringing it from high up under his right arm 'with a twist', as though he was pushing it away from his body, but there was no doubting the effectiveness of the technique. 'How it was that the balls acquired the velocity they did by this mode of delivery, I could never comprehend,' Nyren wrote, though Harris's training as a potter, which gave his hands unusual strength, may have been a factor. His speed was no less perplexing than his accuracy, and Beldham described how a ball from Harris 'would grind his [the batsman's] fingers against the bat; many a time have I seen the blood drawn in this way'.

Like STEVENS, Harris had a good eye for where to pitch a wicket, but he was an altogether shrewder operator. He deployed his fielders with great skill, displaying the accumulated wisdom of three generations, having been taught at Hambledon by Richard Nyren, who himself had been tutored by Richard Newland. Harris devoted hundreds of hours to mastering his craft, practising inside a barn when the hours of winter daylight were short.

Harris began to bowl in partnership with Stevens for Hambledon in 1782 and by the following year was starting to outperform him. By 1787, his bowling was frequently deciding the outcome of important matches: that year he shone in Hambledon's match with England and bowled down eleven of Kent's twelve wickets in a six-a-side match at Lord's.

Though he was a greatly admired man, Harris never attracted the benefactors Stevens did and the only prize he is known to have received through the game was a gold-laced hat. Indeed, his career came to a pathetic end. By the time he was in his forties, he was suffering from gout and, unable to give up his obsession with the game, played on despite his crippling illness, finally being transported onto the field in a wheelchair, from which he would rise to deliver the ball. He died, a widower, five years after playing his last match, at the age of forty-eight.

WILLIAM BELDHAM (England)

Number One: 1787–1805

Born: Wrecclesham, Farnham, Surrey, 21 March 1766; died: Tilford, Surrey, 26 February 1862. Career: 1784–1821.

At his peak, William Beldham, or 'Silver Billy' as he was known because of the glint of his hair, set standards in batsmanship that were unmatched for years. Long after he stopped playing – at the age of fifty-five, after forty summers devoted to the game – he was still revered by cricket's earliest chroniclers. He was 'the great, the glorious, the unrivalled William Beldham' to the Reverend John Mitford. John Nyren described Beldham as 'the finest batter of his own, or perhaps of any age'.

Beldham was the game's first great stylist but, like SMALL, made defence the key to his success; he was, in Nyren's words, 'safer than the Bank'. Yet he was also a brilliant hitter. 'He would get at the balls and hit them away in gallant style,' wrote Nyren, 'but when he could cut them at this point of his bat, he was in his glory; and, upon my life, their speed was as the speed of thought.' Mitford praised his composure, eagle eye, strong wrists and fine timing.

For about the last dozen years of the eighteenth century, Beldham averaged 43 runs per match, a phenomenal achievement for the period. Time and again he made scores in excess of 50 when to pass 20 was a boast for others. In 1794 he played innings of 72 and 102 for Surrey against England and seven years later one of 82 – out of a total of 109 – in the same fixture, perhaps the most important in the calendar.

Beldham took to the game at an early age, arrived at the Hambledon club at fourteen and by the time he was twenty-one was effectively established as the best batsman in England (and therefore the cricketing world). The son of a farmer, he would almost certainly have gone into farming himself had he not come across a local gingerbread baker by the name of Harry Hall, who taught him cricket. Hall outlined the fundamentals of defence and implored his charge to 'keep the left elbow up'. Beldham must have been a considerable cricketer by the age of nineteen, because minutes of the Hambledon club in July 1785 stated that he and his brother George were among those ruled members, and therefore eligible to play for Hampshire and draw expenses, even though they lived at Farnham, Surrey. In fact, Hampshire cricket soon declined and Beldham maintained his connection with Surrey.

Two years later, he appeared in his first 'great' match at Lord's, between England and the White Conduit Club – the precursor of MCC – for 1,000 guineas, and by scoring 80 runs in the game showed himself as 'by far the best player on the ground', according to *The Times*. As Small scored 62 in the game and Aylward 108, the quality of Beldham's play must have been exceptional. Two months later, he again outscored Small in a match against England.

In Beldham's prime, only the bowling of HARRIS was a true match for him and they enjoyed some epic duels. Though Harris, who had the advantage of choosing where the wickets were situated, once famously 'laid prostrate' Beldham's wicket, Beldham took the upper hand by going down the pitch to smother Harris's 'length' balls and demonstrate the value of forward play. He may not have been the originator of this technique – William Fennex, a regular member of the England side in the 1790s and a noted single-wicket player, claimed that honour – but Beldham was certainly the most adept at it. His other main batting rivals were the Walker brothers – Tom, an unrepentant blocker, and Harry, something of a dasher. There was also Robert Robinson, a left-hander who played with specially constructed bats because his right hand had been damaged in a fire. He was known as 'Three-fingered Jack'.

Though many match scores have been lost, it appears Beldham went into relative decline after 1801 and by 1805 he had taken second place to the high-scoring BEAUCLERK. He nevertheless continued his long career in 'great' matches until 1821 and occasionally produced an outstanding performance. Even at the age of fifty-three, he was capable of batting brilliantly for 72 against the hostile pace of Brown, who had boasted to him in a tavern the previous night that he would 'bowl him out'; and in his last 'great' match, the Gentlemen–Players fixture to celebrate the coronation of

George IV, Beldham made an unbeaten 23 with a badly damaged leg, 'bringing away his bat garlanded with the victories of forty years'.

'Take him for all for all,' said one contemporary, 'we ne'er shall look upon his like again.'

Beldham retired to Tilford, where he spent his last forty-one years, dying in his ninety-seventh year, the last survivor of the great Hambledon era. He briefly ran a public house, but judging by the accounts of those who went to pay homage, his thoughts never strayed far from his sporting past. Up to the end, on a wall in his kitchen blackened with age, hung his most precious possession, his bat.

Beldham's first-class record (from 1801): 72 matches, 2,374 runs, average 19.30.

# INTERREGNUM

1799–1826

After the untimely departure of HARRIS, bowling went into serious decline. No one remotely matched his speed or accuracy, and in any case, batsmen were coming to terms with 'length' bowling. Several attempts were made to restore the balance between bat and ball – the size of the wicket was nearly doubled – but the batsmen's domination grew unabated. In the end, many believed the only way forward was to legalize roundarm bowling, a style with which some experimented in minor matches but which aroused divergent opinions. Traditionalists dismissed it as crude 'throwing'.

Edward Budd and William Lambert, two of the best all-round cricketers, tried to gain acceptance for the new method in 1816 but it was outlawed by MCC, the guardians of the Laws, and when John Willes, its leading exponent, employed it in a match at Lord's in 1822, he was no-balled by the umpire and strode from the field, swearing he would never play again. LILLYWHITE and James Broadbridge, both of Sussex, then picked up the revolutionary torch, but MCC again blocked their path.

Eventually, in an effort to resolve the debate, it was agreed in 1827 to stage three trial matches between Sussex and England. The new bowling proved decisive in all three games and the following year MCC decreed that the bowling arm could be raised as high as the elbow. This ruling failed to satisfy most players and umpires and was regularly flouted; by 1835, it was formally accepted that the arm could in fact be raised as high as the shoulder.

During this turbulent evolutionary period, one further disrupted by the Napoleonic Wars, it was impossible to draw meaningful comparisons between bowlers. Statistically, the most successful in the important Surrey v England match was John Wells, a baker from Farnham and BELDHAM's brother-in-law. A shrewd and dependable all-round player, his fast bowling brought him 161 wickets in the fixture between 1793 and 1810, almost twice as many as the next bowler, BEAUCLERK.

Along with Budd and Lambert, Beauclerk was originally regarded as one of the most accurate bowlers, until it was discovered that he was vulnerable to the charge. Among the faster bowlers were George Osbaldeston, a country squire who loved horses even more than he loved cricket, and George Brown of Brighton, both of whom required two long-stops to cut off their errant missiles. Brown effectively settled the debate as to who was the quicker during a single-wicket match in 1818.

LORD FREDERICK BEAUCLERK (England)

Number One: 1805–25

Born: 8 May 1773; died: London, 22 April 1850. Career: 1801–25.

Lord Frederick Beauclerk was as rakish a character as cricket has known. He was a poor sportsman, who, it is alleged, attempted to bribe scorers to help his side win and refused to run his partners' runs. He frankly confessed to making £600 a year out of playing in matches for stakes – he was the finest amateur single-wicket cricketer in England – and though there was no specific crime in that, his was an age in which corruption and 'match-fixing' were rife. He also offended many with his coarse language and autocratic behaviour – this from a man who took to the cloth – but there was no doubting that for many years he was the most successful batsman in the game.

Beauclerk was not a man solely for the big occasion. He was a man for any occasion, so long as there were guineas riding on the outcome. He took heavy toll of weak bowling and fielding sides, but also comfortably and regularly outscored BELDHAM and everyone else in the 'great' matches for which detailed scores survive from 1805 onwards. That year he was top scorer eight out of the eleven times he batted; among his innings were ones of 68, 129 not out and 102 not out. Beldham's highest score in the same games was 34.

After being introduced to cricket at Cambridge University, Beauclerk set about modelling himself on Beldham. He attracted praise for his orthodox style and willingness to adopt the scientific methods of the leading professionals, but never quite curbed his aggressive instincts. He was naturally a hitter and found it hard to resist the impulse to charge down the wicket or attempt to cut the ball off middle stump. Though John Nyren, writing in *The Young Cricketer's Tutor* in 1833, acknowledged Beauclerk as 'certainly the finest batter of his day', he was convinced that Beldham remained the greatest batsman the game had seen.

Beauclerk was no respecter of reputation, however, and went into competition with Beldham just as he did with every other 'star' player. Nyren recalled an occasion on which Beauclerk and Beldham batted together at Lord's and, 'excited to a competition', both played dazzlingly. Another time, Beldham caused a storm in a three-a-side match in 1806 by bowling to Beauclerk with a ball coated in mud and sawdust, the first recorded case of 'ball-tampering'. Thwarted once by the broad bat of Tom Walker, Beauclerk threw down his hat on the pitch and roared, 'You confounded old beast!' – or words to that effect.

After Beldham was past his best, Beauclerk's closest rival was another professional, William Lambert, who was found guilty of 'match-fixing' in 1817 and banned from Lord's for life, though there were mutterings that he had been made scapegoat for a more widespread problem. Lambert was an aggressive, unorthodox batsman, who waited to receive the ball with bat held high above his shoulder before lunging to the pitch of the ball and driving it away. In Beldham's words, he hit 'what no one else could meddle with'. Others championed the cause of Edward Budd, a prodigious and unapologetic hitter. Beauclerk, though, had no time for him – 'he always wanted to win the game off a single ball' – and Beldham, in part, agreed with his verdict. 'If Budd would not hit so eagerly,' he said, 'he would be the finest player in all England.' In the last few years of Beauclerk's career, his scores were closely matched by WARD.

Although he sometimes put up money to stage matches, Beauclerk was not a popular man and history judged him accordingly. He was an influential figure at Lord's after giving up playing seriously in 1825; indeed, cantankerous and bitter, he was now a man to be feared more than ever. His death in 1850 went unrecorded in the obituary columns of *The Times*, a sure sign that this great-grandson of Charles II had fallen out of society's favour.

Beauclerk's first-class record: 99 matches, 4,555 runs, average 27.27.

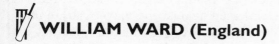

WILLIAM WARD (England)

Number One: 1825–33

Born: Islington, Middlesex, 24 July 1787; died: Westminster, London, 30 June 1849. Career: 1810–45.

Batsmen needed a champion in the turbulent period of the 1820s and they found one, in more ways than one, in William Ward, financier, politician, sportsman and autocrat. Ward wielded considerable clout both with his bat – which was one of the heaviest in history at 4lb – and within MCC. Hailing from a landowning family near Cowes, he strode the corridors at Lord's as though they belonged to him; which in a way they did, as he subsidized improvements to the old pavilion – before it burned down in a fire in 1825 – and bought the lease to the ground from Thomas Lord to safeguard its future.

During a period in which there was a growing lobby in favour of roundarm bowling, Ward led all resistance to change, denying that there was a need to restore balance between bat and ball. When it was finally decided that bowlers should be permitted to raise the height of the delivery arm, Ward saw to it that MCC decreed in 1828 that it should not stray higher than the elbow, a decision denounced by some as a 'shabby compromise'. Those who favoured the new methods muttered darkly about what they saw as Ward's selfish and short-sighted motives. He certainly had little reason to desire change, because he was one of the most prolific and aggressive batsmen in the game. Like William Lambert, he got to the pitch of the ball and hit it hard, a style that critics claimed was killing the game. Some of his scores in minor matches were huge.

Ward established his reputation in 1820 with the first double century ever recorded. His 278 for MCC against Norfolk at Lord's – which stayed the highest score on the ground for 105 years – contained a let-off before he had made 30, and was taken off a weak attack, but was such a colossal score by contemporary standards that it excited great wonder. It took him three days to compile and some of the time he was batting with BEAUCLERK, who hit an unbeaten 82. Over the next few years Ward scored no less heavily than his Lordship.

In 1825, the year of Beauclerk's last appearance, Ward scored the first ever century for the Gentlemen against the Players, an innings ended when he was struck by one of Brown's thunderbolts, but his real test came with the experimental matches between Sussex and England in 1827 to try out the roundarm method. His performances were keenly anticipated. Budd had long said that opposition to the new style stemmed from the fact that 'Mr Ward could not play it'; Beauclerk, referring to Ward's bulk (he stood 6ft 1in and weighed 14 stones), dismissed him as 'too big to play'.

Unwilling to give up his heavy bat, which had been designed to deal with underarm deliveries, Ward nevertheless top scored in both England innings in the second experimental match, at Lord's. He subsequently demonstrated that he had worked out a method of playing the new bowling that was to get him by better than anyone else in the immediate aftermath of the revolution, before his form deteriorated in 1834 as his weight did indeed become a problem. Nyren referred to him as 'one of the safest players I remember to have seen' and in 1832 Pierce Egan wrote of Ward, 'No man will deny, I am sure, when I say / That he's without rival first bat of the day.'

Ward, who learned the game at Winchester and was the last Number One batsman to be fostered by an English public school before MAY 130 years later, continued to appear for Hampshire until his late fifties. Now and again he would bludgeon one of the new tearaway speed merchants into submission, Mynn among them. He also carried on fighting – and losing – ideological battles. It was at his insistence that the Gentlemen–Players match of 1837 was played on handicap, with the Players defending four-stump wickets 3ft high and 1ft wide, making for a target twice the normal size. The game became known as 'Ward's folly', as he and his fellow amateurs were beaten by an innings.

Ward's first-class record: 130 matches, 4,022 runs, average 18.97.

Record against Number One bowlers:
v Lillywhite 1827–33: 13 matches, Ward 22 innings, 359 runs, average 17.95 (highest score 42); Lillywhite bowled him four times.

FREDERICK WILLIAM LILLYWHITE (England)

Number One: 1827–49

Born: Westhampnett, Sussex, 13 June 1792; died: Islington, Middlesex, 21 August 1854. Career: 1825–53.

Though he was only 5ft 4in, William Lillywhite stood head and shoulders above his contemporaries for years. His recorded tally of wickets was not surpassed until more than twenty years after his death, and he was justifiably known during his career as 'The Nonpareil'. When he died, a victim of the cholera epidemic that swept London in 1854, a large memorial was erected over his grave in Highgate Cemetery, paid for by public subscription. A long inscription referred to him simply as 'Lillywhite' and stated: 'Rarely has a man received more applause in his vocation . . . From an humble station he achieved a worldwide reputation.'

Lillywhite, the son of a brickyard manager, delighted in the lofty position to which he rose. He dressed flamboyantly – perhaps in an effort to compensate for his lack of inches, he always played in a tall hat – and frequently boasted of the superiority of his talents. On one occasion he claimed he could bowl a ball onto a small piece of paper, and on another declared himself more accurate than the bowling machine devised by Nicholas Felix – and then proved it by hitting a set of stumps with greater frequency. 'I bowls the best ball in England,' he said, 'and I suppose if I was to think every ball, they'd never get a run!'

Accuracy was the cornerstone of his method. He bowled at a slow-medium pace, imparted little spin and employed only a few variations in flight, but thought carefully about what he did and knew that if he put the ball in the right spot, the unevenness of the pitches would work to his advantage. Though details about his early career are scarce, it is believed that he played infrequently before he was thirty and never bowled underarm. Certainly, by the time trial matches were held in 1827 to try out the new roundarm method, Lillywhite was clearly the best exponent of a style that was to transform the nature of the game. Lillywhite remained in the vanguard of change and during the 1840s his bowling arm often ventured above the shoulder, when to do so was still, in the Laws at least, illegal.

The remarkable thing was that Lillywhite remained at the head of the field for so many years, at a time when roundarm bowling enabled a new breed of hostile fast bowlers to prosper. The best of them were certainly feared for the physical injury they could inflict – the introduction of leg-guards, or pads, and gloves soon followed their arrival – but their early methods were erratic and they were obliged to sacrifice speed for accuracy.

Lillywhite was contemptuous of their efforts and criticized their shortness of length and wayward direction: 'They can't bowl to bowl anyone out,' he said. He, meanwhile, was likened to an automaton – appropriately so, in an era Thomas Carlyle termed the Mechanical Age. 'He was indeed like a piece of machinery,' Haygarth wrote, 'and in his old age wanted only a little oiling, when he would have been as effective as ever.' Lillywhite played his last important match at the age of fifty-seven and was still bowling superbly in his sixties. That his game never deteriorated was something of which he was rightly proud.

The bowler who most closely rivalled him was Alfred Mynn, a hugely built man of Kent farming stock and one of the first to operate roundarm. He bowled at speeds not seen before. In his early years, Mynn, with an arm 'as straight as a piston', was only interested in bowling fast, but with the help of Willes, who saw in him the chance to realize the dreams denied himself, gradually acquired more sophistication, reaching his peak during the 1840s.

The speed at which Mynn bowled – the ball left his hand 'as if propelled from a Whitworth gun' – and his life-size personality captured the imagination of the public in a way no cricketer had before. His all-round talents, earning him the title of 'The Champion Cricketer', briefly enabled Gentlemen to compete on level terms with Players, but even in Mynn's heyday Lillywhite's performances in these matches more often than not outshone his own. When the Slow Bowlers took on Fast Bowlers in 1840 and 1841, Lillywhite's team emerged victorious over Mynn's both times, and as late as 1848, when a letter was published in *Bell's Life* protesting at the advanced years of many players chosen for representative teams, Mynn – who was rapidly putting on weight – Felix and PILCH were cited but Lillywhite deemed an exception: 'The gentlemen who select the elevens for the great matches seem to forget that, except in some very rare instances (Lilly, for example, who is indeed a phenomenon), age must, will, and does tell.'

Two other leading fast bowlers were Samuel Redgate and Harvey Fellows, whose careers were short but contained success against Pilch. Redgate, of Nottinghamshire, rivalled Mynn for speed in the 1830s but was less consistent, while Fellows, from Eton, was reckoned during the late 1840s to be faster than Mynn had ever been and a terror on anything but the flattest pitches. One man who took wickets in similar numbers to Lillywhite was William Hillyer, a medium-paced bowler who operated in tandem with Mynn and was described by those who frowned at the height of Lillywhite's arm as 'the best of all bowlers'. Many placed him ahead of Mynn. Lillywhite himself felt that Charles Harenc, another Kent player, who possessed clever changes of pace, was his nearest rival; in 1834 *Bell's Life* went further, saying that Harenc stood 'pre-eminent' among bowlers.

Lillywhite was no less boastful of his superiority over batsmen, though he knew that with Pilch he had a contest on his hands. Others knew it as well, and would tease Lillywhite. It was sure to bring a rise. 'I wish I had as many pounds as I have bowled Pilch,' he would snap back. In more reflective moments, he conceded: 'Have me to bowl, Box to keep wicket, and Pilch to hit, and then you'll see cricket!'

Lillywhite capitalized richly on his sporting success. He became landlord of a public house and proprietor of a cricket ground in Brighton in 1837, and when those ventures eventually failed he moved to London, where he established his own sports goods retailers, the genesis of the Lillywhite's business which thrives today. He also ran a firm that advised in the preparation and maintenance of pitches throughout the country. Some of his sons and nephews followed in his footsteps as players and took up the reins of his businesses after his death.

Lillywhite's first-class record: 245 matches, 1570 wickets, 1355 in innings for which analyses survive – average 10.89.

Record against Number One batsmen:
v Ward 1827–33: 13 matches, Ward 22 innings, 359 runs, average 17.95 (highest score 42); Lillywhite bowled him four times.
v Pilch 1834–49: 68 matches, Pilch 124 innings, 2,703 runs, average 23.92 (two centuries, highest score 117); Lillywhite was credited with his wicket 44 times.
v Parr 1849: 1 match, Parr 1 innings, 50 runs; Lillywhite dismissed him once.

FULLER PILCH (England)

Number One: 1834–49

Born: Horningtoft, Norfolk, 17 March 1804; died: Canterbury, Kent, 1 May 1870. Career: 1820–54.

Better than anyone else Fuller Pilch, 6ft tall, powerful and quick-thinking, possessed the technique and temperament to cope with the special demands of playing roundarm fast bowling on rough pitches. Mitford praised his 'unrivalled science and talents' and Haygarth observed in 1862 that 'his superiority was so great that but few [players] were jealous of him . . . Considering the fine bowling and fielding he has had to contend against, Pilch has proved himself to have been the best batsman that has ever yet appeared.'

The secret to Pilch's success was a masterly forward-defensive technique. Although many players since BELDHAM and Fennex (who claimed Pilch as a disciple) had possessed a forward defence, none deployed it with more certainty, or put it to better effect, than Pilch, 'his bat going down the wicket like the pendulum of a clock'. He was mocked for it – it was dubbed 'Pilch's poke' – but it smothered the ball before it rose and broke, and to execute the stroke against fast bowlers on uneven turf required great bravery.

The results spoke for themselves. Pilch scored ten centuries in all matches – then an unrivalled tally in a game familiar with low scores – and between 1831 and 1843 provided half the twenty instances of batsmen averaging more than 20 runs per innings in a season. His success inspired his two elder brothers to compile the first batting averages, published in a contemporary periodical, *Bell's Life*, in 1840 (rudimentary bowling averages followed three years later). In 1834, the year in which he proved beyond doubt that he was the best batsman in the game, Pilch scored 87 not out, 73 and 153 not out for Norfolk against Yorkshire; 105 not out for England against Sussex; and 60 for the Players against the Gentlemen. When Redgate dismissed him for a pair at Lord's the following year, the event was greeted with astonishment.

Pilch dealt with the bowling of LILLYWHITE better than anyone, as the bowler himself grudgingly acknowledged. 'Pilch has batted so long to Lillywhite,' Mitford wrote in 1833, 'that he may be said to be perfectly master of his balls.' But Pilch's personality could not have been more different from that of the egotistical Lillywhite. 'He was a remarkably quiet man,' William Caffyn wrote of Pilch, 'with no conversation, and never seemed happier than when behind a churchwarden pipe, all by himself'.

Though he was born in Norfolk, Pilch played a lot of early club cricket for Bury St Edmunds in Suffolk. He was identified at an early age as a batsman of unusual skill, but it took him time to shake off a reputation as a chancer. He appeared in his first important match at the age of sixteen, alongside his two brothers for Norfolk v MCC at Lord's in 1820 – the game in which WARD scored 278. His own two innings amounted to two runs, but over the course of the next ten years it became obvious that he would eventually leave Ward far behind. Pierce Egan devoted several lines to the up-and-coming star of East Anglia in the *Book of Sports* in 1832, the work in which he described Ward as 'without rival first bat of the day':

> Another "bold tailor", as fine a young man
> As e'er hit a ball and then afterwards ran,
> Is from Bury St Edmunds, and Pilch they him call,
> In a few years 'tis said he'll be better than all.
> At present his batting's a little too wild,
> Though the Nonpareil hitter he's sometimes been styled:
> So free and so fine, with the hand of a master,
> Spectators all grieve when he meets with disaster.'

Pilch transformed fortunes in 1834. That year, he won two single-wicket contests against Thomas Marsden – famed for scoring 227 against Nottingham in 1826 in his early twenties – the first in Norwich, the second in Marsden's home town of Sheffield, where the crowd numbered 20,000. This double triumph, plus his prodigious scores in other matches, made Pilch a desirable commodity, and the following year, Kent signed him as player-manager on a salary of £100. Four years later, they increased his wages to persuade him not to accept an offer to join Sussex. In return, Pilch rewarded Kent with nineteen years of loyal service, helping them become a formidably strong side capable of competing with England on equal terms.

They arguably possessed the three best batsmen in the game, for in addition to Pilch their side contained Mynn and Felix. Both were close friends, more colourful characters and more popular with the public, but the batting of neither matched Pilch's own. Mynn, making use of his tremendous strength, was a calculating hitter, the best Redgate and Hillyer said they ever encountered. With Mynn, batting was something of a gamble, but in the circumstances he was surprisingly consistent and the results were sometimes eye-catching. He scored 283 runs in four innings in 1836, and it was reckoned that during his prime he scored runs at the unprecedentedly fast rate of 30 an hour.

Felix, who not only invented the first bowling machine but also developed one of the earliest types of batting pad, was of more scientific bent. A left-hander, he was a great stylist and almost as skilled as Pilch at dealing with fast bowling. Curiously, though, he was far less successful at handling slow bowling.

Pilch maintained his position for a long time – it was often stated that he was unrivalled as a batsman for fifteen years – and did not play his last important match until the age of fifty, though he was on the wane several years before that. His decline was signalled in a very public manner during the Gentlemen–Players match of 1849 when, at the age of forty-five, he was seen to flinch at the extreme pace of Fellows. Pilch scored 24 of the 65 runs the Players mustered in the first innings, but the sight of him playing Fellows, who took ten wickets in the game, with his head half turned away caused a sensation. Almost immediately, PARR was accepted as his successor.

Pilch, who never married, had no need to return to his original trade of tailor in retirement. He remained in his adopted county and became a publican – as he had once been in Norfolk – running the Saracen's Head in Canterbury. He also took up umpiring and stood in GRACE's first representative match.

Pilch's first-class record: 229 matches, 7,147 runs, average 18.61.

Record against Number One bowlers:
v Lillywhite 1834–49: 68 matches, Pilch 124 innings, 2,703 runs, average 23.92 (two centuries, highest score 117); Lillywhite was credited with his wicket 44 times.

GEORGE PARR (England)

Number One: 1849–60

Born: Radcliffe-on-Trent, Nottinghamshire, 22 May 1826; died: Radcliffe-on-Trent, Nottinghamshire, 23 June 1891. Career: 1844–70.

George Parr was the first great batsman to emerge from the north of England and only the second major cricketer from that region after CLARKE, in one of whose trial matches at Trent Bridge he was discovered at the age of eighteen. Parr became known as the 'Lion of the North', a tribute both to his reputation as a batsman and his influence. By taking over the running of the All-England XI from Clarke and virtually controlling the professional side of the game during a delicate period of its development, Parr wielded power given to few.

It was his batting that brought him this power, and it brought it quickly. 'Parr very shortly after appearing in the cricket field became the best batsman in England, which proud position he held for several seasons,' Haygarth wrote in 1863. 'His scores will be found enormous; and his wonderful displays of science, and his success in all parts of England, have been the theme of many a tongue.'

Parr was born one of nine children into a family that was said to have farmed the land around Radcliffe-on-Trent for two hundred years. Cricket was a passion among the males, George's father, uncle and at least two of his four brothers also playing the game. Parr's showing in Clarke's trial earned him an appearance in a match between the North and MCC (with PILCH) at Lord's in 1845. Parr failed in his first game in front of the man whose position he would inherit (as Pilch had done when he first played in front of WARD), scoring just a single. But a year later, Parr made his reputation with an impressive innings of 59 in a match staged at Lord's in honour of Felix. On the strength of that performance, he was chosen to play for Players against Gentlemen at the age of twenty.

Within three years few were dissenting from the view that Parr was without peer. He made a brilliant start for the All-England XI in 1847, scoring 100, 78 not out and 64 in his first three games, each the highest score in the game and each against eighteen or more in the field; and a sequence of big scores in important matches in 1849 set him out on his own. Frederick Lillywhite's *Cricketer's Guide* for that year referred to Parr as England's 'pet' (or 'favourite') and in 1850 he amassed 1,164 runs in all matches, more than twice Pilch's aggregate. His decisive innings of 65 not out in the Gentlemen–Players fixture was 40 more than the next highest individual contribution in the match.

For the next decade, Parr effortlessly sustained his domination in the 'great' matches – Gentlemen v Players, North v South and All-England XI v United England XI. No one remotely approached his total of fifteen scores of over 40, many of which decided the games. The next best tally was five by the graceful Joseph Guy, another Nottinghamshire professional, whom Clarke described as elegant enough to perform 'before the Queen in her parlour'. Parr briefly lost form in 1854, but one contemporary report commented, 'The Surrey cracks, Caffyn and Julius Caesar, pressed him a little, but he still maintained his pride of place.' Troubled by ill health from 1858 onwards, Parr saw his output of runs plunge in 1860, the year in which CARPENTER, Hayward and Daft were reaching their peaks. Even so, he played on for another ten years.

Parr was a short man, thick set, strong and extremely courageous in dealing on uneven pitches with the dangerous fast bowling that still dominated. These characteristics frequently earned him comparison with boxers, one of whom, going by the name of 'Bendigo', once challenged him to a contest (Parr, who was then rising to prominence, declined).

A skilful and resourceful player, Parr made a significant contribution to the canon of batsmanship. Pilch's forte had been the off side; Parr demonstrated the opportunities for scoring on the leg side. The stroke that became his particular speciality was the sweep; and at Trent Bridge a tree stood on a line with this shot, into which he hit so many balls that it became known as 'Parr's tree'. When he died, one of its branches was placed on his coffin.

His skill off front and back foot pointed the way to the all-encompassing technique of GRACE. 'At the time I joined the All-England XI in 1850 there is no doubt that Parr was the most dangerous bat in England,' William Caffyn, the Surrey player, wrote in his autobiography. 'He gave one the impression that he was able to deal with all kinds of bowling on all kinds of wickets. When one has said that he played thoroughly sound cricket, one has given a general outline of the play of George Parr. He certainly played a different game to anyone who had preceded him, using his feet and going out to drive straight balls far more than anyone else. His style of defence was "low down" both in playing forward and back, and in this he presented a strange contrast to Pilch.'

Though Parr dealt capably with fast bowling, he was fortunate to find himself rarely in opposition to JACKSON, who played with him for Nottinghamshire and the Players. While both were at their height they met only once in England, in a match between Single and Married in 1858 in which Parr scored 36 and 18 without Jackson dismissing him; but they had another, less pleasant, encounter in North America a year later. After a match had finished early, the touring English players divided forces for an impromptu game, and Parr, facing Jackson, took a blow on the elbow that prevented him from taking the field again on the tour. He said though, that the only bowler he could not hit to leg was Fellows.

Parr's position in the game made him a natural choice to take over the All-England XI after Clarke's death in 1856. He captained and managed the team and was far more popular with the players than his tight-fisted predecessor had been. Parr championed their right to seek the most lucrative engagements for themselves, which led to a bitter dispute with the southern clubs when the professionals discovered they could earn more appearing for the travelling XIs than at Lord's and the Oval. A virtual boycott of London venues in the 1860s hastened the fragmentation and demise of the XIs that had brought the professionals such riches, though Parr's All-England XI was the one side that never split.

Parr was the target of much vitriolic criticism during this quarrel – which he settled with Lord's by making a farewell appearance there in his last season, but left unresolved with the Oval – and it took its toll. He was a neurotic character, who found peace in few things besides his beloved shooting and fishing. Though he led two of the first three English teams to tour overseas – the inaugural mission to North America in 1859 and one to Australasia four years later – he did so with extreme reluctance, being a bad sailor. Both trips were financially successful, but he declined to join a tour of

Australia in 1861 because he regarded the terms of £150, plus first-class travelling expenses, unsatisfactory.

Parr made a good living out of the game – he received lucrative benefits from MCC in 1858 and Nottinghamshire, belatedly, in 1878 – which must have been some compensation for the fortune his father was believed to have squandered. After retiring as a player, Parr had little further involvement in cricket but lived out a prosperous old age – in which he was a martyr to gout – with fond memories of the past, his house in Radcliffe being full of photographs and prints of his sporting past. Shortly before he died, he married his housekeeper.

Parr's first-class record: 207 matches, 6,626 runs, average 20.20.

Record against Number One bowlers:
v Lillywhite 1849: 1 match, Parr 1 innings, 50 runs; Lillywhite dismissed him once.
v Clarke 1850–53: 4 matches, Parr 8 innings, 113 runs, average 14.12 (highest score 47); Clarke took his wicket three times.
v Wisden 1853–56: 8 matches, Parr 15 innings, 316 runs, average 21.06 (highest score 55); Wisden took his wicket five times.
v Jackson 1857–60: 1 match, Parr 2 innings, 54 runs, average 27.00 (highest score 36); Jackson failed to dismiss him.

◎ WILLIAM CLARKE (England)

Number One: 1850–53

Born: Nottingham, 24 December 1798; died: Wandsworth, Surrey, 25 August 1856. Career: 1826–55.

As a player, William Clarke was an anachronism. A slow underarm bowler who first played for Nottingham as a teenager in 1816, he carried on long enough to see his methods briefly and bizarrely regain their potency. When he set out, his method, modelled on that of his tutor Lambert, was commonplace; by 1850, it was unfashionable but dangerous to those inexperienced in how to deal with it. He was thirty-seven when he played his first important match and forty-four when he played a second, but for ten years after that he rarely left centre stage. He bamboozled a generation of batsmen preoccupied with fast roundarm bowling.

Clarke's technique aroused the contempt of some contemporaries, including PILCH, and the admiration of others, among them Felix, Caffyn and Daft. Historians have described Clarke as the first great leg-break bowler, but he turned the ball only gently, most of the problems he posed coming from subtle variations of pace and flight during long, attritional spells. If batsmen wanted to score runs off him, they were obliged to take risks and hit out, which was precisely what Clarke wanted, for he read the game shrewdly and set his fields skilfully. Much slow underarm bowling was expensive, but not his; and from 1846, the year in which he joined the MCC groundstaff, to 1853, he averaged a phenomenal 340 wickets a year in all matches. Many were taken against minor opposition but he also dominated the 'great' matches, especially after LILLYWHITE all but stopped appearing in them after 1849.

Like Lillywhite, Clarke, who lost an eye early in his career, conceded that Pilch played his bowling better than anyone else, but his claim that Pilch never mastered him is misleading. Pilch rarely scored heavily against Clarke, but nor was he often out to him: between 1834 and 1849, when Pilch was at his best, Clarke dismissed him seven times in forty-six innings.

Though he guarded it fiercely, Clarke was not motivated by his reputation as a player. He was a businessman, who used the game to amass a considerable fortune, though it is believed he gambled away most of it before his death. Originally a bricklayer, he became a powerful figure in Nottingham cricket – organizing and captaining the Nottingham side and acquiring, through a second marriage, the lease of the inn that adjoined the Trent Bridge ground – before leaving for London in 1846 (probably after the death of his wife) and establishing what he ambitiously promoted as his 'All-England XI'.

As an entrepreneur, Clarke was certainly not an anachronism. He saw the opportunities presented by the growth of the railway system to sign up a clutch of leading players and take them the length and breadth of England to play exhibition matches against rudimentary but enthusiastic locals. It was an extremely successful operation and Clarke was posthumously praised for popularizing the game, though his sole motive was financial gain, and the short-term result was that the structure of the game was undermined for a quarter of a century.

Clarke was an unpopular character. He conducted the affairs of his team with the autocracy of a Napoleon and the tight-fistedness of Scrooge. He dwelt apart from his players – living on cigars and sodas for lunch and whole ducks for supper – and restricted their weekly wages to £6 while he himself took many times that; he disputed umpiring decisions and had them overruled; he was reluctant to pass on tips; and, as always, he kept on bowling himself, with no regard for his advancing years, 'always expecting', chided Haygarth, 'to get a wicket with his next over'.

He received his come-uppance when a group of players, led by WISDEN, revolted and formed their own travelling team, the United All-England XI, in 1852. Stung by this betrayal, Clarke would have nothing to do with their operation. Felix, too, mischievously gave away many of his secrets by publishing a pamphlet entitled *How to Play Clarke*.

Clarke's eclipse as a bowler by Wisden was also a humiliating affair. Wisden had rivalled him for years, often while they worked in tandem for the Players or All-England, but the turning point came in August 1853 when they bowled unchanged together through two innings for England against Kent. Wisden gave an incredible display and a clear demonstration of his superiority, taking eight wickets for a mere 36 runs while Clarke claimed seven for 106.

The matter did not end there. The following year Clarke was not invited to represent the Players and he responded by refusing to release PARR and two other leading players from a minor All-England fixture to play in the game, an act that resulted in Clarke being barred from playing for the Players again. He promptly included himself in an important match he was arranging between England and Sussex at Brighton, but did himself no favours. 'Sussex had a much better slow bowler available,' Lillywhite's *Cricketer's Guide* observed. 'A comparison between Clarke's figures and those of Wisden in this match proved that Clarke ought not to have played.'

Clarke's first-class record: 143 matches, 795 wickets, 409 in innings for which analyses survive – average 10.13.

Record against Number One batsmen:
v Parr 1850–53: 4 matches, Parr 8 innings, 113 runs, average 14.12 (highest score 47); Clarke took his wicket three times.

◎ JOHN WISDEN (England)

Number One: 1853–57

Born: Brighton, 5 September 1826; died: Westminster, London,
5 April 1884. Career: 1845–63.

Of all the famous 'fast' bowlers in history, John Wisden was probably the smallest. He possessed few physical attributes in favour of pursuing such an activity and in the end it was physique, rather than technique, that let him down. He stood just 5ft 4$\frac{1}{2}$in and, when his career began, weighed only 7st; but between 1848 and 1859 he averaged 225 wickets per season in all matches and in 1851 claimed more than 450. Little wonder, then, that he was given the nickname of 'The Little Wonder'.

In fact, though Wisden set out to bowl as fast as he could, by the time he reached his peak his pace was closer to medium-fast. By then, his action was smooth and rhythmical, and it was generally agreed no one had bowled straighter or to a steadier length at such speed – Wisden had discovered the accuracy that eluded the majority of 'wild and reckless' fast roundarmers. He, James Grundy of Nottinghamshire and Edgar Willsher of Kent (whom GRACE reckoned one of the best bowlers he ever faced) were among the first to loosely combine the control of LILLYWHITE with the speed of Mynn.

Wisden, indeed, had the advantage of playing alongside Lillywhite at Sussex in his formative years. He first appeared for the county at the age of eighteen and within five years was one of the most successful professionals in the game. There must have been much to learn from Lillywhite – another tiny man – but, in his ability to cut the ball sharply from outside the off stump at pace, Wisden developed a method which copied none.

He began to rival the haul of wickets of CLARKE in 'great' matches from 1850, the year in which, at twenty-three, he achieved his most enduring feat: bowling down all ten wickets in an innings for North (for whom he was a 'given' man) against South at Lord's, a feat never repeated at first-class level. Not until he comprehensively outbowled Clarke in a match between England and Kent at Canterbury in 1853, though, did he appear to be accepted as a consistently superior performer to the man now twice his age.

During his five years as Number One, Wisden tied down the best batsmen in the country with his relentless line of attack. Comparisons must also take account of the fact that Wisden, unlike Clarke and JACKSON, often found himself having to deal with PARR. When the South met the North at Lord's in 1855, Wisden and Clarke both took eleven wickets for their respective sides, but Wisden proved much harder to score off, even though Parr played two substantial innings for the opposition. When he died, the almanack which Wisden had founded described him as, in his day, 'a bowler unsurpassed'.

By 1858, Wisden was in decline. His fitness was on the way down and his weight on the way up, and he had started to dabble in underarm lobs the previous year, a season in which he nevertheless produced some exceptional performances. His size continued to mushroom, so that by the time he stopped playing, at the early age of thirty-six, he weighed 11st.

Wisden did not brood over his fading powers. He was too pragmatic for that and had business interests in the game that were increasingly demanding his time. He had been the central figure in the breakaway from Clarke's All-England XI in 1852 and the establishment of the rival United All-England XI – he took twelve wickets the second time the teams met in 1857, when a truce was agreed following Clarke's death – and set up an equipment business in 1855, initially in partnership with Frederick Lillywhite, which grew into a successful and long-standing enterprise. He also possessed a half-share in a ground at Leamington with Parr, with whom he took the first English touring team to North America in 1859.

In 1864, the year after his last match, he first produced *Wisden's Cricketers' Almanack*, which, by the time of his death, was acknowledged as 'the most accurate and authentic record of the game'; ever since, it has dispensed – among other things – invaluable assessments of the game's leading players. It remembered him fondly: 'A quiet, unassuming, and thoroughly upright man. A fast friend and a generous employer.'

Wisden's first-class record: 186 matches, 1109 wickets, 681 in innings for which analyses survive – average 10.38.

Record against Number One batsmen:
v Parr 1853–56: 8 matches, Parr 15 innings, 316 runs, average 21.06 (highest score 55); Wisden took his wicket five times.

◎ JOHN JACKSON (England)

Number One: 1858–66

Born: 1827 (?); died: Brounlow Hill, Liverpool, 4 November 1901.
Career: 1855–67.

For nearly ten years, John Jackson stood head and shoulders above every other bowler in the game. Haygarth described him as among the 'fastest, straightest and best bowlers ever'. *Wisden*'s obituary notice was more reserved, saying that he was 'on his day, the best fast bowler in England' – though it appears coloured by his eventual, unhappy fate. A more accurate indication of Jackson's hold over the public imagination is given by his nickname, 'The Demon'. It was typical of his ill luck that even that sobriquet did not remain his – it was soon annexed by SPOFFORTH.

Jackson was a striking figure at his peak: he stood over 6ft, weighed more than 14st and, off a short run, bowled at a speed that put the fear of God into legions of batsmen. The critics argued over his exact pace: some old-timers reckoned he was not as fast as Fellows, but E.M. Grace judged his pace as only slightly below that of the overarm fast bowlers of the 1890s.

Speed was not all there was to Jackson. He possessed a good technique, was strong, accurate and could bowl well in any conditions. One contemporary player, quoted in *Wisden*'s obituary, reckoned that Jackson had a greater command of the ball than any other bowler of extreme pace: he could break the ball either way and skilfully vary his pace and length. Less subtly, he also bowled a fast full-toss at around the top of the stumps.

Details of Jackson's early life are vague. Contemporary evidence points to him being born at Bungay, Suffolk, in 1833 and making his first appearance for Nottinghamshire at the age of twenty-one, but his death certificate suggests he was born around 1827, in which case he began his county career at twenty-seven, which is more consistent with his several previous engagements as a club professional. The most picturesque version of events portrayed him as the son of a gentleman brought to Nottinghamshire as an infant, who gained his strength from running barefoot with the hounds – a child of nature not unlike Emily Brontë's contemporary literary creation, Heathcliff.

What is known is that Jackson, like PARR, was discovered by CLARKE, playing for a local side against the All-England XI, though it was Parr who was instrumental in his being selected for North v South within a year of his Nottinghamshire debut. Jackson appeared three times in that fixture in 1857, claiming a total of 37 wickets, and between then and 1863 created frequent mayhem in contests ranging from the lowliest odds-match to the greatest fixtures in the calendar. He took 1,899 wickets in that period and only one batsman, Caffyn, took a century off Nottinghamshire when Jackson was playing. Jackson became the principal star of the All-England XI, enjoying great public acclaim and becoming the first cricketer to be featured in *Punch*, in August 1863. He went on Parr's tours to North America and Australia and was a success on both.

With the decline of WISDEN, Jackson firmly established himself as the game's leading bowler in 1858, the year in which he took nine for 27 as a 'given man' for Kent against England at Lord's. He maintained his position with little trouble for several years, before his form began to fall away in 1865. The following year, his first-class career was effectively ended by a leg injury.

Among the best of Jackson's contemporaries were two men from Cambridgeshire, George Tarrant and Billy Buttress. Tarrant was also fast and dangerous but generally rated inferior to Jackson for speed, destructiveness and reliability – GRACE described his bowling as 'all over the place like a flash of lightning'. Buttress's pace was only medium, but he genuinely broke the ball from leg. However, he had 'a failing for pints' and was never chosen for a 'great' match.

By this time, numerous bowlers were raising their delivery arms above the legal limit of shoulder height. They received the tacit support of many umpires, who believed the law was outmoded, and John Lillywhite brought the issue to a head by no-balling Willsher in an important match at the Oval in 1862. This led to MCC passing a law permitting the arm to be raised to any height, though it was about twenty years before the last roundarmer disappeared from the game.

After his injury, Jackson plied his trade in club cricket, travelling the length and breadth of Britain in the pursuit of work. When he was too old to play, he settled around Liverpool, where he briefly found employment as a groundsman and caterer but, incapable of reading or writing, he soon felt the pinch of poverty. Nottinghamshire belatedly gave him a benefit in 1874, which raised £262, but it was the last substantial sum of money he received and, having long outlived his fame, he died a pauper in the Liverpool workhouse.

Jackson's first-class record: 115 matches, 655 wickets, 650 in innings for which analyses survive – average 11.52.

Record against Number One batsmen:
v Parr 1857–60: 1 match, Parr 2 innings, 54 runs, average 27.00 (highest score 36); Jackson failed to dismiss him.
v Carpenter 1860–66: 16 matches, Carpenter 29 innings, 597 runs, average 22.96 (highest score 63 not out); Jackson took his wicket seven times.

ROBERT PEARSON CARPENTER (England)

Number One: 1860–66

Born: Cambridge, 18 November 1830; died: Cambridge, 14 July 1901. Career: 1855–76.

By 1860, with PARR on the wane, three batsmen vied for supremacy: Richard Daft, a team-mate of Parr at Nottinghamshire, and Robert Carpenter and Thomas Hayward, both of Cambridgeshire. All were northern professionals and all technically accomplished players, nimble on their feet and skilful at playing fast bowling on rough pitches, but none was destined to receive due recognition because of the stupendous player who followed quickly in their wake.

It was a subject of much debate as to which of the three was best, but Carpenter's claim seems the most persuasive. He and Hayward were regularly bracketed together as the finest batsmen in England – Daft was prepared to place them equal first – but Parr himself was adamant that Carpenter was the superior. Parr had no reason to discriminate against Hayward; on the contrary, Hayward, like Daft, was a member of Parr's All-England XI, while Carpenter's allegiances lay with the United All-England XI. Moreover, when these sides met, Carpenter had to contend with the bowling of JACKSON and Tarrant and responded with some heroic defiance. With Carpenter, Hayward, Jackson and Tarrant in the same side, Cambridgeshire were briefly among the strongest counties in the country.

Carpenter had a superb defence. He was a master of back play and renowned for the calm way he brought down his bat on vicious shooters. E.M. Grace, himself among the leading batsmen of the period, said at the time of Carpenter's death that there had never been a finer back player. *Wisden* reinforced this view in its obituary of Daft, who died in 1900, when it stated: 'It is a fair criticism to say that while Daft and Hayward were far ahead of Carpenter in point of style, Carpenter's was, perhaps, the hardest wicket to get.' He was also a fiercely aggressive batsman, willing to go down the pitch to attack, and was judged an even better player of slow bowling than of quick.

Comparisons between the three were made harder by the rift between players from north and south, which kept Parr, Hayward, Carpenter and Daft away from Lord's and the Oval for many important matches. Instead, they spent a lot of their time playing for the travelling XIs against local XVIIIs and XXIIs, matches in which Hayward, in particular, excelled. But before the disruption set in – the northerners often pulled out of matches at the eleventh hour – Carpenter and Hayward had already begun to set new standards in batsmanship.

Carpenter was a late developer – slower than Hayward, who was five years his junior – and did not appear in an important match until he was twenty-four; before then, he had played club cricket in Godmanchester, Huntingdonshire, and at Ipswich. But he then quickly established himself, and both he and Hayward were members of Parr's team to North America in 1859 and Australia four years later, when, according to *Wisden*, 'both were at the height of their fame'.

They started steadily to outscore Parr for the first time in 1860. In July of that year, each scored a century for the Players against the Gentlemen, Carpenter at the Oval – where he became the first to hit the ball out of the ground with the wickets pitched at the centre – and Hayward at Lord's. Hayward scored more runs in all matches that year but the quality of Carpenter's performances was higher, notably in his superb 39 against Jackson which saved the United All-England XI from defeat by All-England.

Carpenter scored another century against the Gentlemen at the Oval the following year and in 1862 gave his best display against Jackson and Tarrant, top scoring in each innings with 63 not out and 39 at Lord's. Though his appearances in important matches were sporadic, he scored runs as heavily as anyone and when the north–south dispute was settled in 1870 it became clear that while Hayward's game had lost its edge, Carpenter's had not. But by then, both had been supplanted by GRACE.

Carpenter and Hayward, who formed the first great middle-order batting partnership, were different in method and character. Carpenter was strong, upright and composed; Hayward short, delicately built and of a nervous disposition. Unlike Carpenter, Hayward was a forward player. Carpenter's batting could be brutal; Hayward's exhibited a gentle touch and fine timing. Hayward played his last match at the age of thirty-seven and died four years later, in 1876, two months after Carpenter's final appearance.

Daft, who was perhaps even more graceful than Hayward, did not reach his peak until after W.G. Grace's rise to prominence. When an England First XI played a Next XIV in July 1860, Daft was only chosen for the second-string side, and for several years far and away his best innings was held to be a century for North v South on a treacherous Lord's pitch in 1862. E.M. Grace, an amateur, was an unorthodox and dangerous hitter for several seasons from 1862 onwards, but inconsistent.

After retiring as a player, Carpenter umpired for many years and lived to see his son Herbert embark on a long and successful career with Essex. Herbert learned his cricket in Cambridge in the company of Hayward's nephew Thomas Walter, who became one of the best batsmen of his day.

Carpenter's first-class record: 143 matches, 5,220 runs, average 24.39.

Record against Number One bowlers:
v Jackson 1860–66: 16 matches, Carpenter 29 innings, 597 runs, average 22.96 (highest score 63 not out); Jackson took his wicket seven times.

WILLIAM GILBERT GRACE (England)

Number One: 1866–86 and 1895–96

Born: Downend, Bristol, 18 July 1848; died: Mottingham, Kent, 23 October 1915. Career: 1865–1908.

So long after his day, it has become fashionable to belittle the achievements of W.G. Grace on the basis that it is now possible to confront him as shamateur and charlatan without embarrassment. Middle class but playing as an amateur, he received substantial sums through the game to set up his medical practice, to make a second tour of Australia, and in recognition of his remarkable exploits. He demanded favours, too, from the game's officials, as F.B. Wilson so graphically described (after Grace's death) in recounting his appeal for leg-before against Grace in a game at Crystal Palace: 'He missed the ball entirely . . . and ran down the wicket shouting, "Out if I hadn't hit it, well bowled, out if I hadn't hit it". . . . the umpire's hand was up. But he put it down again and signalled a "hit".'

But the contemporary view was that Grace gave up a great deal for the good of the game. *The Times* viewed his 1895 testimonial as some sort of recompense, stating that it hoped he would not regret 'that he sacrificed, during the years of his prime, his profession to the national game, and was content to be, instead of a busy country doctor, the greatest cricketer in the world'. Whatever anyone's sentiments, it is unarguable that cricket owes Grace more than it does any other player.

His career can be divided into two phases. The first saw him in his pomp: a pioneer, revolutionizing the accepted parameters of the game, both technical and statistical, and popularizing it as a spectacle. It was a period in which his personal supremacy was so great that it was trite to say he was the best batsman of the day and one of the most successful bowlers. He was, at that time, easily the greatest cricketer there had ever been.

The second phase, which began in the early 1880s, saw him only occasionally touch such extraordinary heights again, as he did so memorably in his 'Indian summers' of 1895 and 1896, when in his late forties. But, such was the reverential regard in which he was held, it escaped the notice of many, himself included, that others were more consistent performers and superior craftsmen. To most people Grace was still 'The Champion' – a title that reflected his all-round ability at the game – and that is what he remained even after his death. As the inscription on the Grace Gates, erected in his memory at the members' entrance to Lord's in 1923, stated, he was simply 'The Great Cricketer'.

There were good reasons why the first phase closed when it did. Grace had grown older and physically bulkier. He had also qualified as a medical practitioner in 1879 and begun thinking about winding down his cricketing commitments and embracing the life of a country doctor. A complete vocational change would never have come about but it required the arrival of international competition from Australia to revive Grace's passion for a game in which he was rapidly running out of challenges.

Grace loved nothing more than a sporting challenge. He was also proud of his pre-eminent position and quick to realize – like most cricketers after him – that Test matches provided the greatest available test of character and ability. He played in the first nine home Test series against Australia and, in the end, did not retire from serious cricket until the age of fifty.

The eighth of nine children of cricket-loving parents from Downend, near Bristol, Grace was schooled in the game from his earliest days. It was a happy, highly disciplined upbringing. As a small child, he watched his father (himself a country doctor), eldest brother and uncle play for Bristol against the All-England XI in 1854 and 1855; on the latter occasion, CLARKE presented another brother, Edward (E.M.), with a bat and coaching manual, a book which ended up in the hands of the young W.G. (it fetched £4600 at auction in 1996). He played his first match at the age of nine and his first representative game at fifteen, as a 'lanky, loose-limbed youth . . . full of life and vim', scoring a spirited 32 for Bristol against an All-England attack containing Tarrant and JACKSON.

In 1864, he left the West Country for the first time to play in important matches, as a replacement at Hove and the Oval for E.M., still in Australia with PARR's team. He earned some flattering notices and by the following year, when he made his first appearances in first-class cricket, was already being talked of as one of the best all-round players in the country: before 1877, when he turned to spin with good effect, he was a capable brisk roundarm medium-pace bowler and rival to SHAW.

From here, Grace's rise was remarkably swift – eloquent testimony to his extraordinary ability, dedication and vision. He benefited from watching the successes and errors of his elder brothers, especially the best of them, E.M., who used a heavy bat and had a penchant for hitting across the line, making him the scourge of length bowlers. W.G. opted instead for a lighter bat and concentrated on playing with a straight bat and developing a strong defence. He also began to practise each year from early March.

He came into a game in which scoring levels were rising. This may have owed something to the transition towards overarm bowling, a style which batsmen found easier to sight than the more erratic roundarm method. Standards in the preparation and maintenance of pitches were also improving, so that by the early 1870s there was even talk of enlarging the size of the stumps (this did not in fact happen until the 1930s). Many, if not all, surfaces would still have been considered unfit by subsequent generations, but English bowlers found their work increasingly hard. It took SPOFFORTH and the first wave of Australians to show the way forward.

Grace established his fame in 1866, at the tender age of eighteen, with two exceptional innings at the Oval against strong bowling: an unbeaten double century v Surrey and 173 not out for Gentlemen of the South v Players of the South – after which he was first called 'champion'. *Wisden*'s obituary stated that it was in this season that Grace 'proved himself, beyond all question, the best batsman in England'.

Two years later, he scored his first century for Gentlemen v Players (a fixture he influenced even more than had Mynn, a generation earlier), an innings of 134 not out in a total of 201 which he thereafter described as 'my finest innings'. For South v North, he became the second man after Lambert to score twin centuries, and was hailed – probably for the first time – as 'the father of English cricket'. The year after that, *John Lillywhite's Cricketers' Companion* stated that he was 'generally admitted to be the most wonderful cricketer that ever held a bat'. Grace was then twenty-one years old.

From 1869 until 1880, Grace's domination with the bat was breathtaking. He topped the English averages in every year except 1875 and 1878, and during this period averaged 50 while his nearest rivals averaged barely half that. His triple centuries – 344 for Gentlemen of MCC v Kent and 318 not out for Gloucestershire v Yorkshire – within eight days in August 1876 were the first in the game's history, eclipsing WARD's 278 in 1820 as the highest innings on record. He became the first batsman to score 2,000 runs in a season in 1871 (his aggregate of 2,739 standing as the record for twenty-five years) and repeated the feat with 2,622 runs five years later. These were the sorts of total other players acquired in an entire career. 'What is to be done with him?' the *Sporting Gazette* asked in 1873. 'He is really ruining the cricket in first-class matches. He demoralises the fielders, and breaks the heart of the bowlers.'

There became two sorts of cricket: that which did not involve Grace, and that which did. That which did created tremendous interest among the public: through his exploits, Grace became the first cricketer to gain appeal with the rapidly growing urban working class. In the process, he helped county cricket establish itself across England on the back of the groundwork done by the travelling XIs (by 1895, an organized county championship was in operation). When Grace scored 79 and 116 at Trent Bridge in 1871, the factory hands of Nottingham flocked to see him, the three-day match being watched by a total of 25,000 people. There was the story, possibly apocryphal, of the notice on the gate to a county ground, which proclaimed: 'Cricket Match: Admission six pence: If W.G. Grace plays, admission one shilling.' But it was recorded as fact by the *Sporting Life* that Grace 'had to pass to his dressing-room through a living lane of excited hand-clapping people, who had, directly the last wicket fell, rushed to the pavilion enclosure like a swarm of bees to applaud and stare at the Gloucestershire gentleman'.

One of the most fundamental things Grace did was to assert the batsman's supremacy over the fast bowler, who had held sway for thirty years. Six feet tall, broad-shouldered and muscular from his early playing days onwards, Grace – the first opening batsman to be Number One – showed that it was possible to deal with bowling of high speed even on the roughest pitches. These were the duels he relished most. 'The faster they bowl, the better I like them,' he would say.

One of his finest innings came against FREEMAN, whom he rated above all others, and Tom Emmett at Lord's in 1870, when he scored 66 with the ball flying about his ribs, shoulders and head. 'Tom Emmett and I have often said it was a marvel the doctor was not either maimed or unnerved for the rest of his days, or killed outright,' Freeman said. Emmett's verdict was more blunt: 'He should be made to play with a littler bat.' Another fast bowler Grace rated highly was Jemmy Shaw, the Nottinghamshire left-armer, with whom he sparred memorably in the early 1870s.

Grace, indeed, all but drove the fast bowler out of the game in England, their places being taken by a generation of bowlers who resorted to 'off-theory' in an effort to curb his scoring. 'He killed professional fast bowling,' one former player recalled in the 1920s. 'For years they were almost afraid to bowl within his reach!'

The Australians were another matter. When they first visited Britain and beat MCC at Lord's in one day on 27 May 1878, it was immediately clear that they possessed in Spofforth a bowler superior to any England could boast. In the MCC match, Spofforth sensationally bowled Grace second ball in the second innings, which, combined with the outcome of the game, forced English and Australian cricket to reappraise their relationship, and Grace his future.

In the first fifteen years of his career, Grace altered the whole conception of batting with a technique that served him whatever the pitch, whatever the bowling, whatever the needs of his side. He unified successful methods that had previously lain in several hands, and applied thought to areas never before explored. His footwork and placement were exceptional and underpinning his game was a philosophy which stated that everything was subordinate to the task of scoring runs (he was not known for his elegance). Obvious though that may sound, it ran contrary to many accepted practices, as Grace himself spelled out in his book, *Cricket*, ghosted by Methven Brownlee.

'Some of the players I have met,' he wrote, 'possessed a beautifully free style, and gave the impression of being able to score largely; but somehow the runs never came. Some had a cramped and ungainly style, which provoked severe comments; but nevertheless the runs did come. Then there were others who kept up their wickets for hours for very small scores; while opposite them were free-hitters who made runs in a tenth part of the time. Now it will not do to say that all of them may not be described as first-class batsmen . . . It may be safely laid down that the duty of a batsman is to make runs, and that he who can make them quickly or slowly as the occasion requires belongs to the very highest class.'

Watching Grace bat was thus a revelation for those familiar with the masters of previous generations. On Grace's death, *Wisden* recounted an old cricketer, who had regarded PILCH as the last word in batting, seeing Grace bat for the first time. 'Why,' he exclaimed after a few minutes, 'this man scores continually from balls that old Fuller would have been thankful to stop.' Daft said that the keys to Grace's success were his capacities for practice and self-denial.

'He revolutionised cricket,' RANJITSINHJI wrote. 'He turned it from an accomplishment into a science; he united in his masterly self all the good points of all the good players and made utility the criterion of style . . . He turned the old one-stringed instrument into a many chorded lyre. But in addition he made his execution equal his invention.' Possibly Grace's most far-reaching achievement was to master forward and back play and draw on both with equal dexterity. 'Until his time,' H.S. Altham wrote, 'a man was either a back player like CARPENTER or a forward player like Hayward, a hitter like George Griffith or a sticker like Arthur Haygarth or Harry Jupp. But W.G. was each and all at once.'

In the first phase of his career, Grace's supremacy was such that it became accepted practice to talk of the 'next best amateur' and 'best professional' of the day. During the 1870s, while Grace was viewed as a 'freak of nature', the elegant and powerful William Yardley was among those who could lay claim to the former title, Carpenter and Daft to the latter.

As his second phase began, Grace found the standard of bowling rising, and the competition from other batsmen, too; nor did the fact that he was playing less because of medical duties help his form. But he responded to the big challenges, scoring England's first ever Test century in 1880 and taking three more hundreds off the Australians in 'side' matches four years later.

By the mid-1880s, Grace was playing more first-class cricket than ever, having arranged locums to assist his practice but his growing weight, a tendency to pick up bothersome injuries, and an increasing inability to punish bowling that was generally tighter than it had been in his early days meant that the gulf between himself and others was no longer so apparent. Indeed, in the cases of Billy Murdoch, the first great batsman produced by Australia, and the Nottinghamshire professionals SHREWSBURY and William Gunn, there was not one. Grace batted with rare freedom in scoring 170 out of 216 for two in the Oval Test of 1886, but was reprieved four times before reaching his hundred; he could not have played the masterly innings Shrewsbury produced in the Lord's Test three weeks earlier.

To some extent, Grace's influence and reputation shielded him from the harsh realities of his leanest years, though he had a remarkable capacity for coming good whenever a poor spell prompted mutterings of a terminal decline. His performances were ordinary in the extreme in the early 1890s, but proved the preliminary to a brilliant late flowering in 1895 when, at the age of forty-six, he became the first batsman to score 1,000 runs in May and the first to reach 100 hundreds in a career. He scored 2,000 runs that year and again in 1896, and with Shrewsbury not the same force after his year out of the game, and a new generation of superb young amateurs yet to prove themselves, Grace was briefly out on his own again.

He generally showed his age, though, against the fastest bowlers – RICHARDSON dismissed him cheaply time and again – but even then, he occasionally rolled back the years by bludgeoning one into submission, as he did with Kortright in a county match at Leyton in 1899: though forty-nine years of age and emerging black and blue, he scored 126 out of a total of 203. That year, Grace tacitly conceded he was no longer the player he had been by terminating his careers with Gloucestershire and England. But by then he had founded his own club, London County, which fulfilled first-class fixtures for six seasons.

Cricket made Grace one of the most famous men in the Empire. When he went to North America in 1872 he was toasted as 'the champion batsman of cricketdom' and, taking a team to Australia the following year, was feted like a king, but he permanently struggled socially to adjust to his position. His character was curiously and disappointingly underdeveloped, fossilized into that of a child besotted by games, and seemingly incapable of interest in much else. He was never astute tactically and petulant when denied his own way. He abandoned his medical practice when it finally got in the way of his sport and, forced by age to cut down on cricket, filled his days with less strenuous activities such as bowls, golf and curling.

Cricket also made him wealthier than any other British games player of his day. Although money meant a great deal to him and his brothers, he could be generous with it, and donated the receipts from a match staged for his benefit to Shaw, whose own benefit had been ruined by the weather. Though he wanted to win, he was not beyond dispensing practical advice to others.

Grace, who married the daughter of a cousin, had three sons and one daughter; two of his children sadly predeceased him. Despite his perhaps overenthusiastic efforts, none of his sons was as successful at cricket as he would have liked. He opened the batting with W.G. Grace junior for Gloucestershire against Sussex at Bristol in 1896, but the contrast was pathetic: son scored 1, father 301.

Grace's first-class record: 869 matches, 54,211 runs, average 39.45.
Test record: 22 matches, 1,098 runs, average 32.29.

Grace's Coopers & Lybrand ratings 1877–85 and 1895: 1877–79: did not play. 1880–85: 2, 2, 4, –, –, –. 1895: 1.
Leaders: 1880–81: C. Bannerman (Aus). 1882–83: G. Ulyett (Eng). 1884–85: A.G. Steel (Eng).

Record against Number One bowlers:
v Freeman 1867–71: 6 matches, Grace 12 innings, 452 runs, average 41.09 (one century, highest score 122); Freeman took his wicket four times.
v Shaw 1872–78: 41 matches, Grace 71 innings, 3,980 runs, average 61.23 (16 centuries, highest score 192 not out); Shaw took his wicket 29 times.
v Spofforth 1878–86: 24 matches, Grace 36 innings, 882 runs, average 25.20 (three centuries, highest score 116 not out); Spofforth took his wicket 15 times.
v Richardson 1895–96: 8 matches, Grace 14 innings, 342 runs, average 26.30 (one century, highest score 118); Richardson took his wicket seven times.

◎ GEORGE FREEMAN (England)

Number One: 1867–71

Born: Boroughbridge, Yorkshire, 28 July 1843; died: Sowerby, near Thirsk, Yorkshire, 18 November 1895. Career: 1865–80.

George Freeman's playing days were few – he effectively played just the five seasons from 1867 to 1871 before retiring as a professional cricketer to take up a lucrative career as an auctioneer, after which his sporting appearances were strictly limited. But there was little question that he was the finest bowler in the game for that period.

GRACE, who was not given to praising fast bowlers lightly, said that Freeman was the best fast bowler he ever faced. 'When he hit you,' he once said, 'you felt as if you had been cut with a knife or a piece of the skin had been snipped off.' *Wisden*, in its obituary of Freeman, stated: 'By general consent he was the finest fast bowler of his generation.' And there were precious few slow bowlers who could rival him either.

Freeman's reputation was not based on the quantity of wickets he took, because even at his height he did not play as much cricket as some and appeared only once for the Players against the Gentlemen, but in the five years in which he reigned supreme he played 26 county matches for Yorkshire and claimed 194 wickets at a cost of less than ten runs each. In his one match for the Players, in 1871, he took three wickets in four balls and six for 86 in all. Those 86 runs were all that came off his 64.1 four-ball overs.

In terms of quantities of wickets, others did better. James Southerton, who bowled slow off-breaks for Surrey, Sussex and Hampshire, took over 150 wickets in 1868, 1870 and 1871, but never struck such terror into the hearts of opponents as did Freeman, nor commanded their respect to the same degree. Grace was also a prolific wicket-taker and his bowling perhaps suffered by being cast in the shadow of his spectacular batting, though he had one important advantage: he did not have to bowl to himself.

Freeman quickly rose to prominence, emerging just as JACKSON and Tarrant were beyond their peaks. Standing 5ft 10$\frac{1}{2}$in, weighing 14st and delivering the ball from shoulder height, he was one of the last of the great roundarm fast bowlers. He did not deliver the ball at the highest speed but was accurate and possessed a deadly off-break that made him virtually unplayable on a pitch giving him any help.

Grace coped with this bowling immeasurably better than any of his contemporaries, but even he finished only rarely on the winning side against Freeman at his height. One occasion was when Grace scored a brilliant 122 out of a total of 173 for South v North in 1869, Freeman taking thirteen wickets in the match for the North; another, with Freeman in the early days of his semi-retirement, saw Grace make a defiant 150 out of 294 for Gloucestershire v Yorkshire in 1872. But the encounter both men recalled most vividly took place on a pitch dangerous even by Lord's lowly standards of the day, in 1870. Grace, opening the innings, survived long enough to be last man out, but was left badly bruised for his trouble.

Deadly though Freeman was on poor surfaces, he said that he preferred to bowl on the more reliable pitches at the Oval (because they enabled him to regulate his off-breaks, while rougher ground was liable to upset his calculations) and proved his point by taking ten for 43 from 69.3 overs there in a match against Surrey in 1870. Freeman toured North America with Willsher's team in 1868 and was the side's leading bowler, gathering remarkable hauls in odds-matches, including 27 wickets for 24 runs against a Philadelphia XXII.

Freeman's nearest challenger was arguably Tom Emmett, one of his Yorkshire team-mates, with whom he formed a devastating partnership. They rose to fame at about the same time, Emmett, a fast left-arm bowler, first playing for the county a year later than Freeman, in 1866. They bowled unchanged together in a match six times – routing Lancashire for 30 and 34 in 1868, when Freeman claimed twelve wickets for 23 runs – and helped Yorkshire to an outright claim of the title in 1867 and 1870, plus a share of it in 1869. 'It is quite safe to say that a more deadly pair of purely fast bowlers never played on the same side,' *Wisden* stated in 1904.

Freeman was a modest man, who held little store by his sporting fame. He had few qualms about giving up cricket to enter business, even though he could have long remained unchallenged. Having turned amateur, he declined requests for ten years to play for Gentlemen v Players, saying that his form did not justify the compliment.

'George Freeman was a man of singularly fine presence,' *Wisden* said in its obituary, 'and in the Yorkshire XI of his day was by many degrees the most striking and picturesque figure.'

Freeman's first-class record: 44 matches, 288 wickets, 284 in innings for which analyses survive – average 9.84.

Record against Number One batsmen:
v Grace 1867–71: 6 matches, Grace 12 innings, 452 runs, average 41.09 (one century, highest score 122); Freeman took his wicket four times.

◎ ALFRED SHAW (England)

Number One: 1872–78

Born: Burton Joyce, Nottinghamshire, 29 August 1842; died: Gedling, Nottinghamshire, 16 January 1907. Career: 1864–97.

Alfred Shaw took up the challenge that GRACE presented with greater success than any other bowler. Grace's aggression, and the aggression he inspired in other batsmen, forced bowlers to find greater accuracy and cunning. Shaw, known as 'the Emperor of bowlers', provided these two things.

He was a master of containment. Standing just 5ft 6½ in, operating off a short run-up with a high arm action, his command of length, flight and pace, allied to a natural slow break from the off, was more than enough to tie down most batsmen – and usually enough to contain Grace, even if it did not often get rid of him quickly. Shaw rarely bowled a long hop or full toss; indeed, he rarely sent down a bad ball at all, as his remarkable career figures suggest. He delivered some 24,700 four-ball overs, of which about two-thirds were maidens and from which only 24,579 runs were scored. He thus bowled more overs than he conceded runs.

But Shaw did not contain for containment's sake. He used it as a means of destruction against a generation of batsmen who, with a few exceptions, knew little about survival on unreliable pitches, especially those affected by rain. His rewards were often startling and during a career spanning thirty-four years he claimed over 2,000 wickets at a cost of a mere 12.12 runs each.

Shaw's success against Grace was qualified but unrivalled, and confirmed that a slow bowler had a better chance of getting him out than a fast one. During their long careers, Shaw dismissed Grace on forty-nine occasions including twenty times bowled, both figures unmatched by any other bowler; but Grace often scored heavily against him. Grace gave a fair assessment of the situation when he said: 'On a good wicket, when batting against him, I did not find it difficult to play the ball; but I had to watch him carefully, and wait patiently before I could score.' Shaw was blunter: 'I puts the ball where I pleases, and Mr Grace puts it where he pleases.' Nevertheless, Grace reflected that between 1870 and 1880, Shaw was 'perhaps the best bowler in England'.

Shaw's best season against Grace was 1875, when he dismissed him on eleven occasions, ten times for scores of 35 or less. One such occasion was for Nottinghamshire against a strong MCC side, Shaw returning the astonishing analysis of 41.2 overs, 36 maidens, 7 runs, 7 wickets, a performance that *Wisden* described as 'the most wonderful display of the mastery of the ball over the bat ever delivered by a bowler'. Grace struggled to 35 and remembered it as one of his best innings.

Shaw, the youngest of thirteen children, was sent to work at the age of ten following the death of his mother and spent five years as a farm hand before concentrating on cricket. In his early days with Nottinghamshire and on the Lord's groundstaff, he was a bowler of medium pace, hardly spinning the ball and enjoying little success. Ambitious to achieve more, he took the decision in about 1870 to drop his pace and turn the ball, thus embarking on the career as a slow bowler during which all his great feats would be achieved. His change of style virtually coincided with the retirement of FREEMAN. Shaw soon showed himself to be the most accurate bowler in the country and by 1874 had taken all ten wickets for MCC v North at Lord's. He claimed 150 wickets in the seasons of 1875, 1876 and 1878, at averages respectively of 9.34, 13.68 and 10.95.

Between 1872 and 1878, Shaw had no rival as a slow bowler – on his death in 1907, *The Times* stated that he was the leading slow bowler in history – but his supremacy was challenged by bowlers of other styles, such as Grace, bowling roundarm at a brisk medium pace, and two fast bowlers, Emmett of Yorkshire and Morley, the Nottinghamshire left-armer, with whom Shaw often wreaked havoc. Shaw required more deliveries, on average, to take his wickets than any of these three, but did so more economically – far more so, in the case of Grace. Grace's bowling, in fact, was never apparently taken as seriously as the figures suggest it should. He was very dependent on an unreliable pitch for help and in 1871, at the end of a seemingly successful season for him with the ball, the *Sporting Gazette* stated, 'Mr W.G. Grace would not earn his salt as a bowler.' Later, when he turned to slow bowling, he was notorious for giving at least one free hit an over.

Shaw bowled the first ball in what was to be recognized as the first Test match, at Melbourne in 1877 – when he was England's most successful bowler with eight wickets for 89 runs from 89.3 overs – but did not play in England that year because of bronchitis. He showed he had lost none of his skill by starting the 1878 season with match returns of ten for 55 from 72.2 overs for MCC v England, easily outshining Grace as bowler, and eleven for 55 from 94.3 overs for Nottinghamshire on a wet pitch at Trent Bridge in the first match of the Australians' tour.

Five days later, he was a member of the MCC team beaten in one day by the Australians, SPOFFORTH bowling in a manner which no Englishman could approach. Spofforth's success on that tour showed to what extent English cricket had fallen under Shaw's spell, with countless slow and slow-medium bowlers using a high arm action to give them accuracy and operating on a steady line outside off stump. Though Shaw was occasionally apt to bowl for maidens, many of his imitators were little interested in, or capable of, attack, and despite Spofforth's example, it was not until RICHARDSON emerged in the 1890s that England produced another top-class fast bowler.

Shaw's last great season was 1880, when he claimed 177 wickets at only 8.54 runs apiece, a record for a bowler taking 100 wickets in a season. After that, he rapidly lost effectiveness but continued to play for another seventeen years, latterly with Sussex. He then took up umpiring, relinquishing the role through poor health only two years before his death.

Cricket was Shaw's life and business, and a profitable business at that. He was one of the game's earliest and most adventurous entrepreneurs, initiating strikes among the players at Nottinghamshire for proper remuneration – the county was for years the most successful in the country – and touring Australia five times and North America twice as player, captain or manager.

These ventures were usually arranged in association with James Lillywhite and SHREWSBURY, with whom he established a sports goods firm. When Shaw died in 1907, he was buried in the same churchyard in Gedling as Shrewsbury – but not twenty-two yards away, as legend once had it.

Shaw's first-class record: 404 matches, 2028 wickets, 2027 in innings for which analyses survive – average 12.12. **Test record:** 7 matches, 12 wickets, average 23.75.

Shaw's Coopers & Lybrand rating 1878: –.
Leader: T. Kendall (Aus).

Record against Number One batsmen:
v Grace 1872–78: 41 matches, Grace 71 innings, 3,980 runs, average 61.23 (16 centuries, highest score 192 not out); Shaw took his wicket 29 times.

FREDERICK ROBERT SPOFFORTH (Australia)

Number One: 1878–87

Born: Balmain, New South Wales, 9 September 1853; died: Ditton Hill Lodge, Long Ditton, Surrey, England, 4 June 1926. Career: 1874–97.

Frederick Spofforth's contribution towards the development of bowling was scarcely less dramatic or far-reaching than GRACE's in batting. Just as Grace united in himself the finest skills of those who had gone before, so did Spofforth. He was also the first fast-bowling Number One to make use of the freedom to raise his delivery arm to its full height.

For this reason, Spofforth created a sensational impression on his first tour of England, in 1878. By then, aged twenty-four, sinewy of frame and standing 6ft 3in, he had developed a technique that was unlike anything seen before: a natural sprinter, he charged to the wicket off a nine-pace run-up before leaping into the air, his right arm thrust high, and launching himself into delivery and a full follow-through.

It was this awesome tide of physical effort, as much as the speed he generated, that earned Spofforth the nickname of 'The Demon'. He won the title within days of arriving in England, some feeling he earned it through his sprint to the wicket, others because of his breathtaking leap. Ivo Bligh attributed it to the latter – the 'terrifying aspect of his final bound' – but Pelham Warner felt Spofforth's Mephistophelean appearance also played a part: the hooked nose, piercing eyes and concentrated aggression. 'He looked like a Demon every inch of him,' George Giffen wrote, 'and I really believe he frightened more batsmen out than many bowlers have fairly and squarely beaten.' The stare of disparagement he cast towards opponents was famous.

Spofforth's speed became a matter of considerable debate. Some thought him the quickest the game had then seen: Grace called him 'terrifically fast' and bracketed him with RICHARDSON and Kortright. Others described him as no more than medium pace. Judging by the way the best wicketkeepers stood up to him, his speed cannot have been great by modern standards, and it is probable that he varied his pace according to the conditions, especially after his first flush of youth; this alone would account for the wide discrepancies in assessments of his speed. What is not in dispute is that Spofforth was the finest bowler of his day and thus the first cricketer outside England to claim first place as batsman or bowler.

That a foreigner could be superior in any department of the game caused offence to Englishmen, yet at the same time gave them cause for self-congratulation. Their army, navy and traders had been taking sports with them to all corners of the British Empire throughout the nineteenth century, and cricket had taken root in several quarters; but the most fertile area was Australia, where a number of English professionals had stayed behind after taking part in the pioneering tours of the 1860s.

Spofforth, the second of three children of a Yorkshire father and New Zealand mother, was born in Australia but spent some of his early years in Auckland, New Zealand, before the family settled in Sydney, where he attended Eglington College. As a bowler, he originally modelled himself on George Tarrant, whom he had seen bowl during the 1863–64 tour. Tarrant ran in off a long and lively run and bowled as fast as he could, though naturally with a roundarm action. Spofforth initially tried to do the same, but after watching Southerton and SHAW, both slow bowlers, decided to combine all three styles. He successfully experimented with the techniques of swing and break and also mastered a top-spinner.

At the age of twenty-one, he played his first match for New South Wales and aroused comment with his skilful variations; two years later, he was making his debut for Australia in what became regarded as the second Test match ever played. He had refused to play in the first, two weeks earlier, because the selectors would not give him the wicketkeeper he wanted.

He first visited England a year later and, although he commanded an impressive control of the ball, generally tried to bowl as fast as he could – to devastating effect. By 1882, however, he had moderated his pace and become arguably the most intelligent, sophisticated and deadly bowler the game had seen. So devoted was he that he would lie awake at night, puzzling over ways to get out opponents.

'Spofforth struck me as being a very remarkable man possessed of rare mental ability and of other assisting personal qualities which enabled him to bring to a successful conclusion almost anything he took in hand,' J.W. Trumble, who toured England with him in 1886, wrote in 1928. 'He started as a fast bowler and then studied medium-pace and slow bowling, his objective being a completely disguised combination of the three paces . . . His action on delivery was exactly the same for all of the three paces, and it was in his magnificent concealment of change in the pace of his bowling that he stood out from all other bowlers of all time . . . Spofforth, like Grace, was a great master in strategy and resourcefulness.

'He quickly sized up a batsman, and soon realized his strong and his weak points and rather preferred to tackle a batsman on his pet strokes than otherwise. He was never more dangerous than when luring a batsman on.' Trumble attributed Australia's pulling a Test out of the fire at Sydney in February 1885 entirely to Spofforth's use of the slower ball. England, needing only 20 with four wickets standing, lost by six runs.

What set Spofforth apart in the eyes of many English onlookers was his deadly accuracy. Like FREEMAN, but unlike many county bowlers devoted to off-theory, he aimed to hit the stumps, sometimes by means of a cleverly disguised yorker but usually with the help of sharp break from the off. More than half his 853 first-class victims were bowled, though he also made original use of fielders situated close in on the onside. In a minor match at Bendigo in 1881–82, Spofforth became the first bowler to take all twenty wickets in an eleven-a-side match – and all twenty were bowled. His precision may also explain how wicketkeepers such as Murdoch and Blackham were able to stand up to him in his early days.

In all matches on the 1878 tour, which included games in Australasia and North America, Spofforth took 763 wickets; two years later, following a similar route, he claimed another 714. On each occasion, his scalps cost him around six runs apiece. In 1882, in first-class matches alone, he took 157 wickets at 13.24 and in 1884 another 207 at 12.82, including a return of seven for three against an XI of England at Birmingham.

It had taken him only two matches to show what he was capable of in 1878. Bowling fast and straight on a 'quagmire' of a pitch at Lord's on 27 May, with Harry Boyle, a medium-pacer who was also a notch above most Englishmen, for support at the other end, Spofforth took six for four – including a hat-trick – in 23 balls in the first innings and four for 16 in 36 balls in the second. Seven of his wickets were bowled, two stumped and one caught-and-bowled, his victims including Grace for a second-ball duck ('The . . . ball knocked his leg bail thirty yards and I screamed out "Bowled",' Spofforth recalled). A strong MCC side had been dismissed for 33 and 19 and beaten in a day.

The result caused a sensation and made the reputations of the Australians in general, and Spofforth in particular, overnight. Until that point their best bowler had been reckoned to be a left-armer by the name of Frank Allan, dubbed the 'bowler of the century', a title he never remotely lived up to. 'From that day forward,' *Wisden* stated in his obituary, 'Spofforth was always regarded as a man to be feared, even by the strongest teams.'

He caused havoc among county sides during the remainder of the tour, and a few months after returning home virtually single-handedly beat England in a Test match in Melbourne, claiming thirteen for 110, including the first Test match hat-trick.

Three years later, he was the key figure in Australia's first, sensational Test win in England, at the Oval. England needed only 85 in the fourth innings to win but fell eight short thanks to Spofforth's match-winning spell of four for two from eleven overs. In all, he took seven for 44 in the innings, fourteen for 90 in the match, and at the end of the game was carried to the pavilion by his jubilant team-mates. England could no longer deny that Australia were their equal on the cricket field, and a mock obituary in the London *Sporting Times* – the inspiration for the Ashes myth – memorialized the remarkable fact.

Spofforth was a proud and fierce competitor, and true patriot. When England embarked on scoring the 85 runs they needed, he boldly declared to his team-mates: 'This thing can be done.' He was also fired up to do well by an MCC member, ignorant as to Spofforth's identity, referring to the Australians in his presence as 'niggers'. He always saw through the hypocrisy of English claims regarding cricket's supposedly morally beneficial effect.

The breadth of Spofforth's skill and his achievements inspired a generation of English and Australian bowlers. By the late 1880s, the game was dominated by highly resourceful medium-pace bowlers, masters of line and length and adept at variations in pace, flight and break.

The duels between Spofforth and Grace were on a different plane from most of the cricket then being played, though with the exception of one encounter in Australia in 1873–74 when Spofforth was still a teenager, their meetings took place when Grace's best years were behind him. It is perhaps hardly surprising, then, that Grace's overall record against Spofforth was unexceptional, though he did score three centuries against him in 1884 and a fourth – in a Test match – in 1886, when Spofforth was not fully fit.

Spofforth did not lack confidence in bowling to the great man, setting aggressive fields and trying out numerous psychological ploys. 'I never had any particular difficulty in getting him out,' he reflected. 'I clean bowled him seven times.' Grace readily accepted that Spofforth was the finest bowler in the world.

His main competition for this title came from Joey Palmer – unquestionably Australia's next-best bowler and whom some regarded as the most difficult of all on a true pitch – and Edmund Peate, of Yorkshire and England, who with A.G. Steel, a Lancastrian, vied for the position of the best slow bowler in the world. Steel's quickish leg-breaks brought him 164 wickets at nine apiece in 1878 while he was still at Cambridge, and he would have been an even more imposing figure had he played regularly; Peate, a left-armer, did better in wet seasons than dry. Spofforth needed no such extreme help from the pitch. Grace said that however good the surface and however well set he himself was, he could never be confident Spofforth would not get him out.

Spofforth's career was all but over by the end of the 1886 tour. Early on, he badly broke the third finger of his right hand while fielding; it never recovered its strength, and the amount of spin he could impart on the ball was restricted. Also, before returning to Australia, he married an English girl. He played his last Test match against England at Sydney in January 1887, when he was not even called on to bowl as TURNER and Ferris dismissed England for 45. The following year he emigrated to England, his wife having been unable to settle in Melbourne.

Spofforth, whose first career in Australia had been as a bank clerk, took up a position in his father-in-law's tea company, living in

Derby for two years before moving to Hampstead to be near the firm's head office. He eventually rose to be managing director. He continued to play cricket regularly until 1905, for Derbyshire – then a second-class county – and various club sides. He made the occasional first-class appearance and in 1896, aged forty-two, took eleven wickets against the Australians for Wembley Park. He remained in England until his death in 1926, when he was survived by his wife, two sons and two daughters. He had amassed a considerable personal fortune and left a will of £164,034.

As he spent more than half his life in England, and much of his cricketing success was achieved there, Spofforth's fame in Australia was not as great as it might have been. But in exile he remained proud of his achievements and reputation – albeit a misleading one – as the fastest bowler the world had then seen.

Spofforth's first-class record: 155 matches, 853 wickets, average 14.95. **Test record:** 18 matches, 94 wickets, average 18.41.

Spofforth's Coopers & Lybrand ratings 1878-86: –, 1, 1, 1, 1, 3, 4, 2, 1.
Other leaders: 1878: T. Kendall (Aus). 1883: W. Bates (Eng). 1884-5: G.E. Palmer (Aus).

Record against Number One batsmen:
v Grace 1878–86: 24 matches, Grace 36 innings, 882 runs, average 25.20 (four centuries, highest score 116); Spofforth took his wicket 15 times.
v Shrewsbury 1886–87: 4 matches, Shrewsbury 8 innings, 398 runs, average 66.33 (one century, highest score 164); Spofforth failed to take his wicket.

ARTHUR SHREWSBURY (England)

Number One: 1886–94

Born: New Lenton, Nottinghamshire, 11 April 1856; died: Gedling, Nottinghamshire, 19 May 1903. Career: 1875–1902.

Among GRACE's most studious and successful disciples was Arthur Shrewsbury, who wholeheartedly supported the view that the duty of a batsman was not to look elegant but to score runs. Shrewsbury's style was polished, but he aroused controversy with his single-minded concentration on back play – which involved the questionable use of pads as a second line of defence – and strokes through the leg side. These techniques were frowned upon by many coaches.

Though he could bat aggressively, Shrewsbury's game was based on a near-perfect defence, nimble footwork and endless patience: he was the first man to bat for over ten hours, in which time he scored 267 and did not give a chance, for Nottinghamshire v Middlesex at Trent Bridge in 1887. It was one of ten double centuries he made between 1882 and 1892, only three fewer than Grace managed in his long career.

Shrewsbury was sometimes written off as a man to save matches rather than win them, but Charles Fry said the impression that he scored slowly was illusory: 'He does not waste time and energy banging ball after ball into fieldsmen's hands. He waits and scores, waits and scores.' His method was to go back on to his stumps and weigh up each delivery before playing his stroke at the last moment, steering and stroking the ball through the gaps in the field with skilful flicks of the wrists. 'It was said of him that he seemed to see the ball closer up to the bat than any other player,' *Wisden* stated in its obituary. 'Excepting of course W.G. Grace, it may be questioned if we have ever produced a more remarkable batsman. On sticky wickets he was, by universal consent, without an equal in his best seasons.'

But it was not only on sticky wickets that Shrewsbury was regarded as the best batsman in England. Some experts were of the opinion that in the ten years from 1885, he was out on his own as run-scorer and technician – ahead, even, of Grace. The evidence, in fact, is overwhelming. Shrewsbury topped the first-class averages in England in 1885, 1887, 1890, 1891 and 1892 – and he did not play the 1888 season because he was in Australia managing a rugby team. He also led the averages on tours of Australia in 1886–87 and 1887–88. He was a considerable Test match cricketer, the first to score 1,000 runs, and averaged over 50 in three series against Australia – in 1884–85, 1886 and 1893, all of which were won. In the last two, the figures of 60.75 and 71.00 were the highest for either side.

Shrewsbury played three exceptional innings at his peak. The first could be taken as the point at which he supplanted Grace, an innings of 164 in the Lord's Test match of 1886, when he survived for almost seven hours on a pitch successively fiery, slow and sticky, against an Australian attack containing SPOFFORTH. One member of the opposition said that he had not thought it possible for a batsman to display such mastery in such conditions; some respected observers, including Lord Harris, deemed it the greatest innings they ever saw. Not even Grace, they said, could have played as well. Shrewsbury himself said it was the innings of his life.

The second was the 81 he made out of a total of 167 for Players v Gentlemen at Lord's in 1891, of which *Wisden* said: 'His play was far better than any other living batsman could have shown against the same bowling on the same wicket.' The third was the century he took off Australia at Lord's in 1893, against TURNER in conditions that were almost as demanding as those seven years earlier. Having been dismissed cheaply by Turner four times in twelve days at Sydney in 1887, Shrewsbury rarely failed against him again on important occasions.

Statistically his greatest year was 1887, when he averaged 78.71, then a record for an English season. Altham wrote that by then 'his supremacy defied comparison', but many contemporary sources held Grace's reputation dear and to them the fact that Shrewsbury dwarfed 'The Champion' numerically – his average was 24 points higher in 1887 – made little difference. They qualified their praise for Shrewsbury by stating he was the best 'professional' batsman, an unnecessary distinction but one that excused the need for comparison with Grace.

It was a distinction that must have riled Shrewsbury, who had fought for the rights of the downtrodden professional from the early days of his career. He led strikes by Nottinghamshire players for fees to match those commanded by the best-paid Australian and English players, action that led to him being dropped for two matches as a disciplinary measure, though it also gained the strikers rewards. Determined to capitalize on his standing in the game, Shrewsbury set up a lucrative sports goods firm with his close friend SHAW (Grace would be among those who would use their bats) and they, along with James Lillywhite, organized four ambitious tours to Australia in the 1880s, initially reaping handsome dividends.

Such influence and entrepreneurial boldness presented a striking contrast to reports of Shrewsbury as a quiet, retiring man, who invariably wore a hat to hide the baldness which afflicted him from an early age. He did things his own way in life, as with the bat. But as a cricketer, he never quite received the recognition he deserved, and Grace had every reason to remember Shrewsbury when asked, shortly before his death, who, after himself, was the greatest batsman of his time. His celebrated answer: 'Give me Arthur!'

Shrewsbury set out to model himself as much on the elegant Daft as on Grace. Though there was a family interest in cricket – Shrewsbury was the youngest of seven children who survived infancy, and all four boys played the game – it appears he did not receive formal coaching. Nevertheless, while still a teenager and an apprentice draughtsman in the lace trade, he was identified as a player of immense potential. He first played for the Colts of England at the age of seventeen, for Nottinghamshire at nineteen and for the Players at twenty.

By the age of twenty-one, Shrewsbury was one of the best professional batsmen in England. 'He played from the first', said *Wisden*, 'like one who had little left to learn, and only needed experience.' In fact, of slight build and lacking fitness, it was not until he visited Australia in 1881–82 that his health and strength improved sufficiently for him to score the runs his talent warranted.

The batsman who most closely approached Shrewsbury was not Grace but William Gunn, a fellow professional at Nottinghamshire. Gunn, an imposing 6ft 3in tall, possessed powers of self-control and defence scarcely less remarkable than Shrewsbury's own, and they shared many large stands together, including one of 398 against Sussex at Trent Bridge in 1890 that stood for eight years as the world record for any wicket. Gunn pleased the purists with his straight bat and off-side elegance, but was not quite as skilful as his colleague and nothing like as successful at Test level. An amateur, Walter Read, who headed the averages in 1889, scored heavily for Surrey but was inconsistent against the best bowling. Australia possessed an outstanding wet-wicket batsman of their own in Percy McDonnell, another 'sticker' in Alec Bannerman, and a 'dasher' in J.J. Lyons.

Shrewsbury gave up playing county cricket in 1894 to attend to his business, which had run into difficulties during the frequent absences of its two founders. He continued to play at club level – scoring many hundreds – and eventually resumed his Nottinghamshire career in June 1895. Without quite repeating his performances of old, he maintained a high standard and many thought him still capable of appearing for England. He topped the English averages for a sixth time in 1902, at the age of forty-six, and around this time, in a private match, played a highly skilful innings on a difficult pitch against BARNES.

In the winter of 1902, Shrewsbury developed an illness which, in the words of *Wisden*, 'he could not be induced to believe was curable'. He gave up his religious practice in the nets, convinced that his cricketing days were over, and at his sister's home on the evening of 19 May 1903, tragically shot himself. His death was probably more due to hypochondria than fears of impending retirement as a sportsman. His business devolved to his nephews and he left £1,000 and his personal effects to his girlfriend. He never married.

Shrewsbury's first-class record: 498 matches, 26,505 runs, average 36.65. **Test record:** 23 matches, 1,277 runs, average 35.47.

Shrewsbury's Coopers & Lybrand ratings 1886-94: 1, 1, 1, 1, 2, 2, 4, 3, 3.
Other leaders: 1890-91: W.G. Grace (Eng). 1892-94: J.J. Lyons (Aus).

Record against Number One bowlers:
v Spofforth 1886–87: 4 matches, Shrewsbury 8 innings, 398 runs, average 66.33 (one century, highest score 164); Spofforth failed to take his wicket.
v Turner 1887–93: 22 matches, Shrewsbury 37 innings, 1,217 runs, average 34.77 (two centuries, highest score 206); Turner took his wicket 17 times.
v Richardson 1893–94: they did not meet in first-class matches.

ⓒ CHARLES THOMAS BIASS TURNER (Australia)

Number One: 1887-93

Born: Bathurst, New South Wales, 16 November 1862;
died: Manly, New South Wales, 1 January 1944. Career: 1882–1910.

With SPOFFORTH a lesser bowler for his injury, the way became clear for others to claim his mantle. And if England did not possess anyone with remotely the same potential to wreak havoc, Australia did. In Spofforth's final Test match, at Sydney in January 1887, J.J. Ferris and C.T.B. Turner routed England for 45, still their lowest total, Turner taking six wickets for 15 runs on his debut. There was not always much between their figures, but the contemporary verdict came down heavily in favour of Turner.

Turner was often referred to by his initials or as 'The Terror', a nickname that, like Spofforth's, was acquired through phenomenal achievements on his first tour of England, in 1888. 'The Terror' possessed many of the variations of 'The Demon', if not the control or range of speeds – Turner usually operated at the fast side of medium. He had a good yorker and could break the ball both ways, his chief weapon being a big off-break.

The main difference was that Turner's technique was still primitive: off a long run, he delivered the ball open-chested and with a low arm. But he skidded the ball through – at 5ft 9in, he was six inches shorter than 'The Demon' – which would explain why GRACE rated Turner's sharpness off the pitch as second only to FREEMAN's. Grace felt, though, that Turner could not control the ball to anything like the same extent as could Spofforth, and sometimes cut it too much to be dangerous.

Turner, whose early opportunities with New South Wales came when Spofforth was absent, attributed his success to the strength of his massive hands and the power this gave him over the ball. He was a country boy with a country boy's strength, and cultivated his skills through long hours of practice while working for a mail-coach company in Bathurst. He sensationally shot to fame at the age of twenty by taking all ten wickets for 36 (and seventeen for 69 in the match) for XXII of Bathurst v SHAW's XI in 1881–82. Despite this exceptional performance, he waited a year to make his state debut and five to play his first Test match.

Having made his mark for Australia, though, there was no turning back. Turner claimed 29 wickets in his first three Test matches in Australia, and more than 100 in all first-class matches in 1887–88; he remains the only man to take 100 wickets in an Australian season. He thus went to England in 1888 with a great reputation and, on the soft pitches he encountered there, fully lived up to it. He destroyed several county sides in the early weeks of the tour, and in the first Test match, at Lord's, he and Ferris caused a sensation by dismissing a strong England side for 53 and 62. Turner took ten for 63 in the match and 21 wickets at 12.42 in the three-match series, which England came back to win, Turner and Ferris working virtually alone in a weak Australian side.

The attitude of English batsmen when confronted by this pair was 'one of near panic', according to Haygarth, and Turner aroused such curiosity that he was persuaded to undergo tests at the Woolwich Observatory, where his speed was measured at an unexceptional 55m.p.h. He was fortunate that this tour, and the next in 1890, took place in wet English summers, because he was virtually unplayable on rain-affected surfaces. He took 283 wickets at 11.68 in 1888 – seventeen against an XI of England at Hastings, fourteen of which were bowled and two leg-before – and 179 at 14.21 in 1890.

In drier weather on his last tour in 1893, he again finished top of the tour averages with 148 wickets at 13.63, but was less effective than of old on a damp pitch in the first Test and did little during the rest of the series, in which he was outshone by RICHARDSON. Turner was dropped by Australia in 1894–95 because of his lack of success on hard pitches.

Many of Turner's contemporaries put him in the same class as Spofforth; indeed, some were prepared to say he was the better, though others thought that Spofforth possessed the shrewder brain and wider repertoire. F.S. Jackson said Turner was the best medium-pace bowler he faced, though he only encountered Spofforth towards the end of the latter's career.

Turner got through an amazing amount of work with Ferris, with whom he formed a productive and mutually beneficial partnership. Ferris's left-arm medium pace provided a contrast to Turner's line of attack and they were able to bowl into each other's footmarks. In eight Tests against England, they took 104 wickets between them (their team-mates claimed 21) but finished on the winning side only once. Ferris claimed 84 fewer wickets than Turner on the 1888 tour and seven more in 1890, though at slightly greater cost.

The best English bowlers during Turner's time were John Briggs and Robert Peel, two left-arm spinners, and George Lohmann, another medium-pacer but slower than Turner. Despite being confronted with better batsmen, Turner's record in Ashes Tests was superior to Briggs's and similar to Peel's, though not quite as impressive as Lohmann's. The overall Test records of Briggs and Lohmann were dramatically inflated by their performances against extremely weak South African sides, in games which were only retrospectively accorded Test status.

Lohmann was the first English bowler to master the revolutionary lessons of Spofforth and was easily the most successful bowler in England between 1886 and 1892 – he took more than 150 wickets each year – before ill health interrupted and eventually terminated his career. His 293 first-class matches yielded 1,841 wickets, or 6.28 victims per game, but none of the chief witnesses ranked him ahead of Turner (whose ratio was 6.40). Indeed, Fry said that of all English medium-pacers, J.T. Hearne of Middlesex, who rose to prominence as a Test cricketer in the late 1890s, most closely rivalled Turner 'for accuracy, variety, and quick off-break'.

Like Spofforth, Turner's first employment outside sport was in banking but when he left Sydney to pursue other business in 1897, his first-class cricket career virtually ended. A benefit match between New South Wales and the Rest of Australia was staged for him in 1910 and realized £534, but that was where his luck ran out. He married three times and died virtually penniless at the age of eighty-one.

Turner's first-class record: 155 matches, 993 wickets, average 14.24. **Test record:** 17 matches, 101 wickets, average 16.53.

Turner's Coopers & Lybrand ratings 1887-92: –, 5, –, –, –, –. *Leaders:* 1887: R. Peel (Eng). 1888: J. Briggs (Eng). 1889–90: Peel and Briggs (equal). 1891–92: Briggs.

Record against Number One batsmen:
v Shrewsbury 1887–93: 22 matches, Shrewsbury 37 innings, 1,217 runs, average 34.77 (two centuries, highest score 206); Turner took his wicket 17 times.

 THOMAS RICHARDSON (England)

Number One: 1893–98

Born: Byfleet, Surrey, 11 August 1870; died: St Jean d'Arvey, France, 2 July 1912. Career: 1892–1905.

By the time the lessons of SPOFFORTH were fully absorbed, fast bowling had been transformed. Technically and physically, Tom Richardson formed the perfect conclusion to the overarm revolution:

tall and superbly built, and operating off a long run, he delivered the ball with a high right arm and smooth rotation of the body, imparting it with genuine speed and a vicious break from the off. Always aiming to bowl at the stumps, he combined pace with some of the guile shown by the artful medium-pacers of the previous decade.

Unlike Spofforth and most contemporaries, Richardson never moderated his pace. His method was so fluid that he barely needed to – he could bowl unchanged for hours without compromising his pace, length or off-break – and, by dint of his extraordinary character, did not want to; he loved bowling and was a glutton for hard work, during a period in which the volume of cricket at county and Test level mushroomed and one ball was expected to last the duration of an innings. He set a new standard in stamina and bore the batsman no ill will, sticking faithfully to a full length and never seeking to intimidate him. The upshot was predictable: by the age of twenty-eight, Richardson was burned out and losing fitness.

In the previous five years, he had reaped a remarkable harvest on the dry, hard surfaces that he favoured. Between 1893 and 1897 Richardson claimed 1,248 wickets (1,005 of them in four successive English seasons), helped England to three series victories over Australia, Surrey to two championship titles, and produced arguably the most consistently excellent fast bowling the game has seen.

Once he arrived at the method that was to serve him so well – early in his career he made a minor adjustment to his delivery arm to counter accusations that he threw his faster ball, during an era in which 'throwing' was an 'issue' – Richardson enjoyed immediate and startling success. In 1893, at the age of twenty-two and in his second season with Surrey, he took 174 wickets at 15.40 in first-class matches and, called up to replace the injured LOCKWOOD in the final Test against Australia at Old Trafford, returned match figures of ten for 156 on his first appearance for England. TURNER took only two wickets in the same game. Nor was this a one-off: in six other appearances against the touring team, Richardson claimed 47 wickets.

He produced many great performances during the next few years. With little fast-bowling support, he took 32 wickets in the five-match series in Australia in 1894–95, nine of them in a crucial display in the deciding game, which England won. His greatest county season was 1895, when he captured 290 wickets, a record for any bowler in one season until 1928 and still one for a fast bowler, and claimed ten wickets in a match on seventeen occasions. 'Whether his skill or remarkable stamina be most admired, it is probable that no bowler of anything like the same speed has ever made the ball break back so frequently,' reported *Wisden*.

The following year, on a fast, dry pitch at Lord's, Australia were sensationally routed for 53 in the opening seventy-five minutes of the series. Bowling at lightning speed, Richardson took six for 39, and in the next game at Old Trafford operated without rest for three hours ten minutes in an heroic but futile attempt to deny Australia the 125 runs they needed for victory. He took six of the seven wickets to fall, leaving him with match figures of thirteen for 244 from 110.3 five-ball overs.

Richardson was England's leading wicket-taker in all three of the full Test series he played, but in the last of them, during his second tour of Australia in 1897–98, when he was handicapped by rheumatism, the inspiration gradually evaporated and he struggled for form. He rallied in England the following season, taking more wickets than anyone bar Hearne, whose average was superior but whose strike rate was not, but when the Ashes were next at stake, in 1899, Richardson had a relatively poor season for Surrey and was not called on by England. There were mutterings about his steadily increasing weight and the impact it was having on his effectiveness.

Richardson was one of an exceptional generation of fast bowlers. Among his contemporaries were Ernest Jones, the Australian; Arthur Mold and Arthur Woodcock, professionals with Lancashire and Leicestershire respectively; and the Essex amateur Charles Kortright. Jones and Kortright were deemed by some to be faster than Richardson – Kortright for many years thereafter was a popular choice as the fastest bowler the game had seen – but none was successful for a sustained period. Jones's action came under even more scrutiny than Richardson's, and in Australia in 1897–98 he was no-balled for throwing. Kortright, who admitted he never swung the ball, said in old age (he lived to eighty-one) that Richardson was the finest fast bowler he ever saw.

Richardson's closest rival during his years at the top was Lockwood. According to Neville Cardus, Lockwood once said that compared to Richardson, 'I wasn't in the same street.' Lohmann, Lockwood's mentor, rated Richardson the best in the world on a good pitch, while Gilbert Jessop, who rated him the best without qualification, confessed: 'No bowler has ever compelled my admiration to such an extent as did Tom Richardson.'

Born in a gypsy caravan and described by Fry as 'a cheerful brown-faced Italian-looking brigand with an ivory smile', Richardson sought a modest life once his playing days came to an end. Like many a successful bowler before and after, he became a publican and, the middle-age spread expanding ever further, died of a heart-attack during a holiday in France at the age of forty-one.

When news of his death arrived, the Gentlemen v Players match at the Oval was suspended for twenty minutes as a mark of respect. The following year, *Wisden* wrote of him: 'He will live in cricket history as perhaps the greatest of all fast bowlers. Among the only men who can be placed with him are George Freeman, John Jackson and William Lockwood.'

Richardson's first-class record: 358 matches, 2,104 wickets, average 18.43. **Test record:** 14 matches, 88 wickets, average 25.22.

Richardson's Coopers & Lybrand ratings 1893-97: –, –, –, 3, 3.
Leaders: 1893-94: J. Briggs (Eng). 1895-97: G.A. Lohmann (Eng).

Record against Number One batsmen:
v Shrewsbury 1893-94: they did not meet in first-class matches.
v Grace 1895-96: 8 matches, Grace 14 innings, 342 runs, average 26.30 (one century, highest score 118); Richardson took his wicket seven times.
v Ranjitsinhji 1896-97: 3 matches, Ranjitsinhji 6 innings, 133 runs, average 22.16 (highest score 55); Richardson took his wicket twice.

RANJITSINHJI (India)

Number One: 1896–1902

Born: Sarodar, 10 September 1872; died: Jamnagar, 2 April 1933. Career: 1893–1920.

Although his methods were popularly viewed as alien, Ranjitsinhji's batting was founded on the same principles as those of SHREWS-BURY. He favoured going back and playing late, rarely missed a ball he played at and placed it superbly, often through the leg side.

The difference was that 'Ranji' possessed an extraordinary eye, a sublime sense of timing and an even wider range of strokes: as Fry said, he had three for every ball. He attempted things that, in the hands of others, would have been laced with risk but in his own displayed all the effortlessness of genius. The speed with which he executed his shots was a revelation.

If his approach was different – which it was – it was as much because of a freshness of outlook. Coming to England from India – where he learned the rudiments of the game at public school – to complete his education, he arrived at a time when a handful of batsmen, following GRACE's lead, were tentatively exploring new avenues of scoring. Ranji joined them, uninhibitedly.

He opted to make back play the basis of his game. 'Very few cricketers pay proper attention to it,' he wrote in the *Jubilee Book of Cricket*. 'It can, I believe, be made almost, if not quite, as effective for scoring purposes as forward play is. Anyone who has seen Arthur Shrewsbury, Mr [Stanley] Jackson and Mr MacLaren play an innings on a slow wicket, or indeed on any wicket, will agree.' Almost as effective as forward play for scoring purposes – and much safer in defence. In any case, it suited Ranji, with his supple wrists, nimble footwork and lightweight bat, to cut and glide off the back foot: he stood 5ft 10in and was not strong. His trademark was a stroke of his own invention, the leg glance. The only time he went forward was to drive. As Altham said, he 'orientated afresh the setting of the cricket field'.

Ranji was the first non-white sportsman to achieve international recognition, and to the general public was an object of fascination and delight. Jessop described him as 'the most brilliant figure in cricket's most brilliant age', Sydney Southerton, editor of *Wisden* when Ranji died, said he was 'the most talked-of man in cricket' during his career.

He did not gain acceptance in cricketing circles, though, without encountering prejudice and hardship. The notion of an Indian playing the game seriously was new and his methods were unorthodox, so that it took him four years at university in Cambridge to get a game in the first XI. In the meantime, he developed his batting with club sides in the town. When it was finally realized that he was actually playing in a superior vein to others, he was widely attributed with 'unnatural' powers. Unable to understand how he could nonchalantly flick fast bowlers time and again to the fine-leg boundary, or play so late with such unerring precision, many viewed him as juggler or magician, or equated his unorthodoxy with the un-Christian – although as he was a Hindu there should have been nothing sinister in that. Others saw him as a symbol of the threats inherent in Empire. After Ranji had played brilliantly in a Test match for England – with native cricket in India in its infancy, it was decided on an ad hoc basis that he should play for England – one irate MCC member protested volubly about 'a nigger showing us how to play the game of cricket'.

But to those capable of dissecting his technique, Ranji revealed himself as an artist. 'If the supreme art is to achieve the maximum result with the minimum expenditure of effort, [he], as a batsman, is in a class by himself,' A.G. Gardiner wrote. 'The typical batsman performs a series of intricate evolutions in playing the ball; [he] flicks his wrist and the ball bounds to the ropes. It is not jugglery, or magic; it is simply the perfect economy of means to an end.' Some doubted whether the game had ever been played more beautifully. According to Fry, Ranji was 'an artist with an artist's eye for the game . . . He tries to make every stroke a thing of beauty in itself.' Jessop stated simply that Ranji was 'indisputably the greatest genius the cricket world has yet produced'.

He appeared to be an exotic flower, an impression enhanced by his preference for playing in billowing silk shirts, but his methods were the result of long hours of study and practice at Cambridge, where one of his coaches was Dan Hayward, nephew of Thomas. Ranji achieved little for the university in terms of runs, but two fine innings against the Australians in 1893 ensured that he became the first Indian to win a 'blue'. Coming down in 1894 after failing to sit his Bar examinations, he was under pressure to return to India, but stayed and accepted an invitation to play for Sussex the following year. (That he had not fulfilled his residential qualification for the county escaped general notice.)

Ranji created a sensation by scoring 77 and 150 not out in his first match for the county, against MCC at Lord's, and continued to arouse intense interest throughout the rest of the 1895 season. His aggregate of 1,775 runs was then a record for a player in his first season of county cricket and he was hailed as a figure almost as popular as Grace, a remarkable thing given the attention paid to Grace during a year in which 'The Champion' scored 1,000 runs in May and reached his century of centuries.

Grace again scored over 2,000 runs in 1896, but this time Ranji well and truly put him in the shade. By scoring 2,781 runs and ten centuries he broke one of Grace's major batting records and equalled another, and gave a performance of consummate brilliance on his Test match debut against Australia at Old Trafford. He scored 62 in England's first-innings total of 231 and an unbeaten 154 in their second of 305 as he fought a lone action to leave Australia a challenging target (they were set to make 125 and won by three wickets). By that point, all but a few diehards accepted that the Indian was the best batsman in the game, if not the most dazzling there had ever been.

'No man now living has ever seen finer batting than Ranjitsinhji showed us in this match,' the *Manchester Guardian* stated. 'Grace has nothing to teach him as a batsman; and none of the men of renown of thirty years ago could have exhibited a more thorough mastery of every point in the game . . . Altogether, his innings was a masterpiece.' *The Times's* correspondent said there had never been as near-perfect an exhibition in an important match, while George Giffen, who played for Australia, reflected the following year: 'Ranji is the batting wonder of the age. His play was a revelation to us, with his marvellous cutting and his extraordinary hitting to leg. I have never seen anything to equal it.' Pelham Warner said that Jones, Hugh Trumble and Clem Hill 'were always talking of that innings'.

Ranji's average in the series was twice that of any other player on either side, and there can be little dispute that he remained the world's first batsman for the next six years. Technically he was playing a game no one, bar perhaps the emerging TRUMPER, could approach, and statistically he was also out on his own during a period in which batsmen with patience and a sound method could thrive. He fell only slightly short of 2,000 runs in 1897, and the following winter – despite England losing the Test series heavily – he enjoyed a personally outstanding tour of Australia, during which he played the greatest innings of his life in the first Test at Sydney, fighting off illness to make a brilliant 175 against an attack containing Jones and Trumble.

Stopping off on the way back in India, he missed the following English season but returned in 1899 to play a masterly defensive innings to save England from defeat in the first Test against Australia and became the first batsman ever to score 3,000 runs in a season. He passed the landmark again the next year, when he scored five double centuries and averaged 87.57. At that point, the three highest seasonal aggregates stood to his name.

Between 1899 and 1901 Ranji scored 8,692 runs in England, a tally approached by Robert Abel, Fry and Tom Hayward, another nephew of Thomas, all of whom scored over 7,500. Abel and Fry – who never toured Australia – did little in Test cricket between 1896 and 1902, Hayward much more, scoring more runs at a higher average than any other player in the Ashes Test series of 1899, when his skilful century at Old Trafford evoked memories of Shrewsbury. Though he received fewer plaudits, Hayward was a more accomplished player than the amateur Fry, who admitted to having one stroke, played off the front foot and going to 'ten different parts of the field'. Archie MacLaren played less frequently and scored less heavily in county matches, but often rose to the big occasion, especially in Australia, where the pitches suited his aggressive strokeplay.

Australia possessed a brilliant shot-maker in Joe Darling, the first man to score three centuries in one Test series, but their finest player was Hill, a precocious left-hander who, after failing in 1896, scored 1,532 runs in Ashes Tests between 1897 and 1902, more than any other player. Hill was outstanding on hard pitches – he averaged over 100 in Australia in 1900–01 – and, like Ranji and Fry, was strong on the leg side. BARNES, who greatly admired Ranji, judged Hill one of the hardest batsmen to remove.

It was the visit of the Australians in 1902 that marked Ranji's decline. That year, plagued by financial problems that almost took him into the bankruptcy courts, he cut a distracted figure and dropped out of the final month of the season. He failed in the three Tests in which he played, his inability to rise to the challenge in a pulsating finish to the fourth Test at Old Trafford costing England the Ashes and him his place in the side. He recaptured something of his form in 1903, but was now out of favour with cricket's establishment and less committed to the game. At the end of the following season, he returned to India, drawing his career as a regular player to a close at the age of thirty-two. He took to the field again in 1908, 1912 and 1920, in more relaxed, and very different, circumstances – as ruling prince of an Indian native state and society figure.

Like Shrewsbury, Ranji found critics reluctant to put him on a par with Grace at his best, though in his case this had as much to do with a lack of what Stanley Jackson called 'sympathetic interest for Indians' as reverence for Grace. 'Many critics are too apt to admire the latest performer,' protested R.H. Lyttelton in 1899, 'and some have gone so far as to couple the Indian with Grace as equal in merit. The Indian has yet to show himself to be a really great bat on wickets that favour the bowler.' In fact, Ranji played many brilliant innings on rain-affected pitches: his century against Nottinghamshire on a drying surface at Brighton in 1895 was described as 'almost the finest innings of the year'. Grace conceded that technically he was not Ranji's equal, and Bob Thoms, the long-serving umpire, said that Ranji was the greater of the two 'because he had more strokes'.

Though Ranji was in penury for most of his playing days, cricket transformed his life, materially and socially. Born in lowly circumstances in a remote village in north-west India – the first child to the second wife of an alcoholic father who neglected his family – but briefly considered as adoptive heir to a distant relation, the Jam Sahib of Nawanagar, who sent him to be educated at a princes' college, he subsequently used his fame as a sporting 'prince' to further his claim to the succession. When the Nawanagar throne conveniently fell vacant in 1907, Ranji's standing in the eyes of the British civil servants – gained almost exclusively on the cricket field – sealed his selection.

The patronizing attitude of the British establishment towards its colonies riled him as much as it did SPOFFORTH, but Ranji was essentially pro-Empire – his status as a ruling prince came to depend on it – and, like the Australian, was more content in the mother country than in his native land. In later life, Ranji liked nothing more than to spend his time shooting and fishing with the tweedy aristocracy in Scotland and Ireland. His lack of enthusiasm for giving India the encouragement of a cricketing legacy attracted strong criticism there; he smoothed his nephew Duleepsinhji's path towards a career in England, where his own impact had been greatest.

Ranji acquired great wealth during his twenty-six years as ruler – apart from palaces and countless possessions, he left £185,958 in his will – but little happiness. Torn between satisfying the expectations of native Indians and immersing himself in the European lifestyle that he preferred, he formed romantic attachments with British women but baulked at marriage.

Ranjitsinhji's first-class record: 307 matches, 24,693 runs, average 56.37. Test record: 15 matches, 989 runs, average 44.95.

Ranjitsinhji's Coopers & Lybrand ratings 1896-1901: –, –, 5, 2, 2, 2. *Leaders*: 1896–97: R. Abel (Eng). 1898: J. Darling (Aus). 1899–1901: T.W. Hayward (Eng).

Record against Number One bowlers:
v Richardson 1896–97: 3 matches, Ranjitsinhji 6 innings, 133 runs, average 22.16 (highest score 55); Richardson took his wicket twice.
v Lockwood 1898–1901: 6 matches, Ranjitsinhji 7 innings, 573 runs, average 81.85 (three centuries, highest score 197); Lockwood took his wicket once.

ⓦ WILLIAM LOCKWOOD (England)

Number One: 1898–1901

Born: Old Radford, Nottinghamshire, 25 March 1868; died: Radford, Nottinghamshire, 26 April 1932. Career: 1886–1904.

William Lockwood, a Nottinghamshire man by birth and upbringing who spent most of his career with Surrey, formed with RICHARDSON the first pair of outstanding modern fast bowlers. They played together many times for Surrey, the Players and, in one series, for England, but their great days did not coincide. Lockwood, the elder by two years, was at his best from 1892 to 1894 and again from 1898 to 1902; Richardson's best years were 1893 to 1897.

The two phases of Lockwood's career were quite distinct, as between times his career all but collapsed under the twin pressures of him turning to drink, following his failures in Australia in 1894–95, and a terrible domestic tragedy involving the death of his wife and child. He went downhill so rapidly that by 1897 he was not even in the Surrey team – but, determined to revive his flagging career, he spent the winter regaining fitness and returned the next year to play as well, if not better, than before. Now into his thirties, he proved himself, when fit, England's most dangerous bowler, and retained the potential to destroy opponents for the next three years.

Though of smaller stature, Lockwood, like Richardson, made full use of his superb physique, delivering the ball off a long, bounding run with a powerful whip of the body and high arm action. Neville Cardus described them as 'surely the two most beautiful fast bowlers ever seen in action at the same time'. Lockwood, too, commanded a sharp break-back, but his special strengths were the pace he got off the pitch, a natural inward swerve and his slower ball. Having started at Surrey earlier than Richardson, he benefited more from the tuition of Lohmann, who taught him the art of disguise.

Lockwood's talent was more mercurial than his partner's: he could not match him for speed, stamina or temperament, but on his day touched greater heights. 'Lockwood [stood] for a genius which, if in its very nature less consistent, reached at times a pitch almost demoniac,' Altham wrote. 'At his best there was an indefinable something of vitality and devilry about him.' Fry stated in retirement that Lockwood was 'without qualification the best fast bowler I ever played with or against . . . All the leading batsmen who played against Lockwood and Richardson and the other great fast bowlers of the time were agreed that Lockwood was the most difficult.' Lockwood himself said that Richardson was the superior performer, but Fry was supported in his opinion by Murdoch and RANJITSINHJI, who said that, however well set he was, Lockwood was capable of producing an unplayable ball.

Lockwood took over 150 wickets in 1898. So did Richardson, but Lockwood claimed his victims more rapidly, at a more economical cost, and generally made the more telling contributions. When they dismissed Yorkshire twice in one day at the Oval, Lockwood took eleven wickets to Richardson's seven. Over the next three years, Lockwood was not among the most consistently successful bowlers but tended to take wickets in the games that mattered: in 1899 he helped Surrey win the championship and bowled superbly on a true Oval pitch to take seven for 71 in the first innings of the fifth Test against Australia, after various injuries prevented him playing in the first four. He also regularly shone for the Players at Lord's. When he and George Hirst reduced the Gentlemen from 203 for one to 245 all out in 1901, with Lockwood taking five of the nine wickets, *Wisden* said: 'As to the superlative quality of their bowling, there could not be two opinions.'

Lockwood achieved more in important matches during this period than either the young Wilfred Rhodes, with his miserly orthodox left-arm spin, or Hirst, fast left-arm. While these two claimed great numbers of wickets in county games, especially inside Yorkshire on the sorts of bowlers' pitch Lockwood rarely saw at the Oval, they remained unproven at higher levels. Lohmann and Peel had played their last Tests in 1896 and Briggs his in 1899, in a career prematurely halted by mental illness.

Australia's leading bowlers were Jones, Trumble and Monty Noble. Jones, match-winner in the only Test to be decided in England in 1899, could be quick and hostile – he was overly fond of the short-pitched ball – but had little to fall back on when conditions were unhelpful. Trumble and Noble were far more disciples of SPOF-FORTH than either TURNER or Jones, medium-pacers with a wide range of variations who built up impressive records during long Test careers. However, they were not especially effective at this time – though when he toured New Zealand with the Melbourne club in 1900, Trumble was billed as 'the greatest bowler in the world'.

Noble generally acted as support for the other two, but was the more significant historical figure, being among the first genuine exponents of 'swerve'. A few players in earlier times had possessed the knack of swinging the ball, but it was not until the turn of the century that a broader mastery was achieved. Noble could swerve the ball and still retain control of his length, and his trick of swinging the ball away and then applying his stock off-cutter was one he passed on to BARNES in Australia in 1901–02.

Lockwood was not chosen for that tour, because of doubts about his stamina and MacLaren taking a gamble on Barnes. In fact, Lockwood bowled magnificently against Australia the following summer, taking eleven wickets at Old Trafford and playing an important part in England's victory at the Oval, but in another two years he had indeed had enough and gone into retirement.

He fell on hard times in later life. Returning to his native Radford, he continued to attend big matches but presented a dishevelled and sorry-looking figure, and was eventually confined to a wheelchair by arthritis.

Lockwood's first-class record: 362 matches, 1,376 wickets, average 18.34. **Test record:** 12 matches, 43 wickets, average 20.55.

Lockwood's Coopers & Lybrand ratings 1898–1901: –, –, –, 3.
Leaders: 1898: R. Peel (Eng). 1899–1901: E. Jones (Aus).

Record against Number One batsmen:
v Ranjitsinhji 1898–1901: 6 matches, Ranjitsinhji 7 innings, 573 runs, average 81.85 (three centuries, highest score 197); Lockwood took his wicket once.

SYDNEY FRANCIS BARNES (England)

Number One: 1901–19

Born: Smethwick, Staffordshire, 19 April 1873; died: Chadsmoor, Staffordshire, 26 December 1967. Career: 1894–1930.

No bowler has inspired such unanimity of feeling among his contemporaries as Sydney Barnes. Almost all the leading players of his day averred that he was not only the finest bowler of the time but the best they had ever seen. Among his army of supporters were MacLaren, Hill, Noble, Rhodes, Warner, J.T. Tyldesley, Charles Macartney, HOBBS, Woolley and Herbert Strudwick, but in stark contrast to TRUMPER, Barnes was not a popular idol. He was seen too little, and was too reserved a character, to inspire national tributes.

Barnes's career was so stupendous that a few extraordinary facts will suffice to illustrate it. He played professionally from the age of twenty-one to sixty-seven and in those forty-six years claimed, in all competitive matches, 6,229 wickets at 8.33. He took all ten wickets in an innings twelve times. In 27 matches for England he claimed 189 wickets at an average (16.43) and strike rate (a wicket every 41.65 balls) unmatched by any twentieth-century bowler with 100 Test wickets to his name. His 49 wickets against South Africa in 1913–14 – in only four matches and on matting – remains the record for a Test series; his 34 against Australia in 1911–12 sealed England's then greatest victory away from home and was an Ashes record for thirteen years; and his match figures of seventeen for 159 at Johannesburg in December 1913 stood as the Test record until 1956.

It is a simple matter, also, to outline his methods, so comprehensive were they. Barnes, like SPOFFORTH, produced a synthesis of the best attributes of his predecessors. He adapted his style according to the pitch he was bowling on – and performed superbly on any surface – but the pace he most commonly operated at was brisk-medium, bounding in off a short run. He was a tall man (he stood 6ft 1in) and made the most of his height. 'As my arm came up to the top I hooked – yes, hooked – the ball from the sky and whipped it down the pitch,' he said. He extracted bounce and claimed he never bowled a ball without spinning it; and his long, powerful fingers enabled him to impart spin – sharp enough to tear pieces out of soft turf – without any tell-tale break of the wrist.

From behind this near-impregnable disguise, Barnes unveiled almost every type of ball imaginable (except the googly, which he claimed not to need): leg-breaks, off-breaks, inswingers, outswingers and top-spinners, though he maintained that the key factor was the speed of the ball off the pitch. He bowled an immaculate length, varied his flight and bowled to his field as perhaps no one had previously: like CLARKE, he bowled not at the stumps but to the batsman's weaknesses. 'I never bowled at the wickets: I bowled at the stroke,' he once said. 'I intended the batsman to make a stroke, then I tried to beat it. I tried to make the batsman move. The time a batsman makes mistakes is when he has to move his feet.'

An arch-perfectionist and driven by a carefully nurtured dislike of batsmen, Barnes never stopped experimenting and it took him several years to perfect his most famous delivery, what Cardus christened 'the Barnes ball', a fastish, late-inswinging leg-cutter that pitched on leg stump before hitting off. This was the mirror-image of the ball Noble had taught him, the outswinging off-cutter, of which he was also master. When Macartney watched Barnes from the non-striker's end dismiss Trumper with it at Sydney in 1907, he said, 'It was the sort of ball a man might see if he was dreaming or drunk.'

Yet Barnes's career was not one of untrammelled success. On the contrary, it scarcely followed conventional lines and was fraught with disputes and misunderstandings. For a start, he took part in little county cricket, the staple diet of most professional players in England. Barnes, whose father dabbled in cricket and worked for the same Staffordshire firm for sixty-three years, wanted financial security and believed the best way to get it was to play league cricket at the weekends and work during the week in a job he would keep the year round.

Barnes noted the dissatisfaction of many professionals with the terms of their employment with counties and country, and had seen what had happened to some of them, who 'after fleeting years as famous cricketers, feted and fussed, dropped out, returned to the mine or factory, or, at best, took a fourth-rate beerhouse, trading as best they could upon their faded glories'. In saying this Barnes may have been thinking of his hero RICHARDSON, who inspired in him an early if short-lived desire to bowl at high speed, and a love – which he retained – of bowling, bowling, bowling.

Barnes played two seasons of county cricket, for Lancashire in 1902 and 1903, chiefly because it was a condition of his going on his first tour of Australia in 1901–02, under the captaincy of MacLaren, who also led Lancashire. Despite injury problems and distracting disagreements with the club's committee, which was clearly wary of this proud, taciturn and independently minded character, he took 226 wickets at 19.41 – being the first bowler in the country to 100 wickets in 1903 – but terms could not be agreed for 1904 and Barnes returned to the leagues and signed for Staffordshire, a minor county. Lancashire renewed their overtures several times without success.

As he remained in work as an active cricketer perhaps longer than anyone else, and then worked for Staffordshire county council until shortly before his death at ninety-four, it can hardly be said that Barnes chose the wrong career path, but it created problems with those in the upper echelons of the cricket world. The amateurs who ran the game, and whose ethos was to play, when asked, whenever one could, could not fathom why Barnes did not share their idealism, and they had little opportunity to get to know a player they rarely saw. Nor was Barnes the type to court favour; indeed, there were times, in first-class cricket but never in the leagues, when he looked wilfully unproductive. Fry, his England captain in 1912 and the only man to publicly declare himself not a wholehearted admirer, complained: 'Barnes rarely said anything . . . He was not by nature an enthusiast.'

But Barnes knew he was a great bowler, and resented it when others did not appear to share his view or chose clearly inferior players ahead of him; this was perhaps the cause of those days when, in the words of Altham, 'his temperament got the better of him, with disastrous results'. Certainly he never forgot the slights or found it easy to trust people, though team-mates testified that they did not find him 'difficult'. Asked who was the best captain he played under, Barnes replied: 'Me. When I have been bowling, I have been captain.'

The upshot was that Barnes was rarely an automatic choice for England, or other representative sides. His Test career would not have got off the ground when it did but for MacLaren taking a wild gamble and inviting him to join his tour of Australia in 1901–02. Barnes, having first played club cricket at fifteen and claiming only three hours' tuition in his life, was then twenty-eight and had played seven highly productive seasons in the Lancashire League. He showed off his repertoire to MacLaren in the nets and, asked to play for Lancashire in their last match of 1901, took six Leicestershire wickets for 70. It was enough to convince MacLaren, but an ignorant world was perplexed. The newspapers asked: 'Who is this man Barnes?'

Barnes showed them within a matter of weeks. The first Test match he played in, at Sydney in 1901, was also the first he had seen and, not knowing what the occasion meant, he was unaffected by nerves. His first victim was Trumper, whom he caught off his own bowling with the second ball he sent down to him, and his opening spell, spread over two days, lasted 32 overs, by which time Australia were 152 for eight. He finished with five for 65 and England won by an innings.

In the second Test at Melbourne he again bowled superbly, with MacLaren, whose attack was not strong, even more reluctant to take him off. Barnes took thirteen wickets but Australia, having the better of the conditions, won. After the game, MacLaren presented him with the ball and told him he had bowled as well as Richardson. When Barnes broke down with a knee injury early in the next match and England went on to lose the series, some judged his absence to have decided the fate of the Ashes. In two matches, he had outbowled Noble, Trumble and Jones and shown himself to be head and shoulders above the rest of his own attack, some of England's best bowlers being at home (LOCKWOOD was not chosen and Yorkshire refused to release Hirst and Rhodes). The Australians were in no doubt: they felt Barnes was the finest hard-wicket bowler ever sent to their shores.

However, lines of communication were primitive and when England met Australia at home a few months later, Barnes, incapacitated initially by his knee trouble, was regularly overlooked by the selectors. By taking unilateral action on the morning of the game, MacLaren got Barnes into the side at Sheffield, where he took seven wickets for 99, but the other selectors took umbrage at this decision and immediately dropped their most dangerous bowler.

Warner, later one of Barnes's greatest admirers, then left him out of the next side to tour Australia in 1903–04, in the misguided notion – one propagated by *Wisden* – that Barnes could not bowl an off-break. Shortly after the team was announced, Barnes and Warner met in a county match at Lord's and Barnes bowled him up the hill with a perfect off-break. In truth, Barnes broke the ball both ways from his early league days but preferred the leg-break; he started to swing the ball in Australia in 1901–02. He did not play in any of the Tests against Australia in 1905, though Fry wrote in his autobiography that Barnes was then the best bowler in England; nor in any against South Africa in 1907; nor in the first two Tests against Australia in 1909, omissions which Macartney described as 'astonishing', though Barnes's health may have been a factor as he had caught whooping cough from his son. Barnes had toured Australia eighteen months earlier and bowled magnificently in a weak side. Warner described him then as 'the great bowler of the tour'; Noble described him simply as the world's finest bowler.

It was Barnes's brilliant success in a winning cause in Australia in 1911–12 that belatedly changed things. Now aged thirty-eight, he constantly troubled his opponents with inswinging leg-breaks and bowled one of the greatest spells in history on the first morning of the second Test, on a plumb pitch at Melbourne. Having surprisingly been denied the new ball in the first match, he began now by removing Warren Bardsley, Hill, Charles Kelleway and Warwick Armstrong for one run in five overs, and at lunch, when Australia were 32 for four, Barnes's figures read: 9–6–3–4.

He had had a fever for two days before the match and by the end of his spell could barely see the other end of the pitch. Warner wrote: 'The present generation of Australian cricketers admitted that they had seen no finer bowling and the older men were equally enthusiastic . . . It was certainly one of the greatest feats, if not the very greatest, ever accomplished in a Test match and no Spofforth, or Palmer, or Richardson, or Lockwood, Lohmann or TURNER could possibly have surpassed it.' At about this time he also wrote of Barnes: 'He is, on all wickets, the finest bowler in the world today – that, at all events, is the opinion of the Australians.'

Barnes played in all six Tests at home to Australia and South Africa in 1912 and was enticed to tour South Africa in 1913–14, a trip he had turned down eight years earlier. This time he was promised financial assistance if his wife and family joined him, though the terms of the arrangement came under dispute and Barnes stood down from the fifth Test, despite the prospect of claiming a fiftieth wicket in the series. *Wisden* described his form in 1912 as 'conclusive evidence that he is, at the present time, the best bowler in the world'. In fifteen Tests between December 1911 and February 1914, in one of which he did not bowl, Barnes claimed 122 wickets and was near-unplayable. South Africans described him as the finest bowler they had seen.

As it happened, because of the First World War, Barnes did not play Test cricket again, but throughout the war years he, along with many other leading cricketers, played league cricket, and he remained the most respected bowler in the game. Fender remembered playing in a charity match at Bradford in 1918 involving first-class players. Barnes completed a spell of 12–3–24–4, but deserved better figures and Fender confessed: 'None of us knew what on earth to do against him.' But when first-class cricket resumed in 1919, Barnes, at forty-six, made it clear he had retired from representative matches, a decision he reinforced by declining an invitation to join MCC's first post-war tour to Australia in 1920–21.

He did not resume his career with Staffordshire until 1924 but played league cricket continuously up to 1940 and his form did not betray his age until he was in his sixtieth year. As late as 1928, members of the West Indian touring side said that they faced no better bowler than Barnes, who, playing for Wales, took twelve wickets against them.

Between 1901 and 1919, no bowler matched Barnes's statistical achievements at Test level, his temperament for the big occasion, or his ability to bowl as well on good pitches as on bad, abroad and at home. Once Trumble had played his last Test in March 1904, the best Australians were Frank Laver, John Saunders and Albert Cotter, who had their days but were erratic. Walter Brearley was perhaps the best out-and-out fast bowler in England, but he was at least as temperamental as Barnes was supposed to be and his performances lacked consistency. Schofield Haigh, the Yorkshire fast-medium bowler who topped the national averages five times in eight years, needed pitches to be in his favour. Hirst – reaping greater rewards since cutting his pace and concentrating on swinging the ball – and Rhodes were superior to both, but their records in representative matches were unexceptional, barring two good series for Rhodes against Australia in 1902 and 1903–04. Rhodes rarely bowled after 1910, in order to concentrate on his batting.

England's next-best bowler after Barnes was probably the artful Colin Blythe, like SMALL and Felix a violinist and like Rhodes a slow left-arm spinner. He took 100 Test wickets at 18.63 in nineteen matches, but felt the strain of international cricket and did not play for England again after 1910, when he was at his peak. RANJITSINHJI and Jessop were among those who rated him ahead of Rhodes.

Even greater claims were made for the best in the first wave of googly bowlers. Googly bowling, arguably the most important advance in bowling since the overarm revolution forty years earlier, was developed by an English fast bowler, B.J.T. Bosanquet, who, weary of battling away on flat pitches, turned his mind to producing an audaciously disguised delivery: an off-break delivered with a leg-break action. He may not have been the first to toy with the googly, but did it skilfully enough to enjoy brief glory up to Test level and it was quickly taken up, with more enthusiasm and greater prospects of success, among South Africans and Australians.

Among the best of these was Ernest Vogler, a South African and a master of disguise, who took 119 wickets at 15.62 in England in 1907, fifteen of them at 19.66 in three Tests, prompting R.E. Foster, the England captain, to state that Vogler was 'perhaps the best bowler in the world' at that time, though Aubrey Faulkner, the second-best googly bowler in South Africa, ranked Vogler behind Barnes. Two years later, Vogler took 36 wickets in five home Tests against England, but is rumoured to have taken to drink, and achieved little thereafter.

Barnes liked to dictate terms to batsmen but admitted he found it hard against Trumper. By reading him from the hand and using superb footwork, Herbie Taylor of South Africa had an excellent record against Barnes, but the best batsman Barnes said he bowled to was Hobbs, whom he only encountered in league cricket.

Barnes's first-class record: 133 matches, 719 wickets, average 17.09. **Test record:** 27 matches, 189 wickets, average 16.43.

Barnes's Coopers & Lybrand ratings 1902–14: –, –, – ,– ,– ,–, 3, 2, 3, –, 1, 1, 1.

Other leaders: 1902–04: H. Trumble (Aus). 1905–06: W. Rhodes (Eng). 1907 and 1909–11: C. Blythe (Eng). 1908: J.V. Saunders (Aus).

Record against Number One batsmen:
v Trumper 1902–12: 14 matches, Trumper 25 innings, 812 runs, average 33.83 (two centuries, highest score 166); Barnes took his wicket seven times.
v Hobbs 1912–18: they did not meet in first-class matches.

VICTOR THOMAS TRUMPER (Australia)

Number One: 1902–12

Born: Darlinghurst, New South Wales, 2 November 1877; died: Darlinghurst, 28 June 1915. Career: 1894–1914.

Perhaps more than any other Number One batsman bar Barry RICHARDS, Victor Trumper could not be measured by the number of runs he scored. If arithmetic were the sole criterion, he would not have towered above the other batsmen of his day as he did; indeed, others might have ranked ahead of him. But his contemporaries were not in doubt: most held Trumper to be not only the best batsman of his time but, at his untimely death in 1915, the best then produced by Australia, ahead of Charles Bannerman, Murdoch, Noble, Bardsley, Hill and Macartney. Macartney's best days actually came later, but he, like some of the others, freely admitted that he was unfit even to be compared to Trumper. Many who also saw BRADMAN swore that Trumper was the more accomplished batsman, even though Bradman was by far the heavier run-scorer.

It was the manner in which he batted that set Trumper apart. His genius was, Altham once wrote, 'essentially qualitative rather than quantitative, revealed in terms of spontaneous art rather than in any acquired technique'.

For all but the last few years of his career, defence played little part in Trumper's game. He did not believe there was a ball bowled that could not be scored off – Fry said he had three strokes for every ball – and thus committed himself to the most unorthodox and audacious strokes. An opening batsman, he was aggressive from the

The All England XI of 1847 arguably contained the best batsman and bowler of the day in Fuller Pilch (*second from right*) and William Lillywhite (*fourth from right*). They were soon supplanted by, respectively, George Parr (*second from left*) and William Clarke (*seventh from left*). Illustration from a drawing by Nicholas Felix. (M.C.C.)

One of the most enthralling sights in cricket is to see the top players pit their wits against each other. Fuller Pilch faces William Lillywhite in W. H. Mason's engraving of a match between Sussex and Kent at Brighton. (M.C.C.)

Brian Lara was, in the opinion of *Wisden*, 'beyond dispute,
the greatest batsman in the world' in 1994. (*Allsport*)

Shane Warne established a hold over the minds of opponents in a way few bowlers in history have matched. (*Allsport*)

first ball, not bothering to play himself in. 'Spoil a bowler's length,' he would say, 'and you've got him.' BARNES said he found it harder dictating terms to Trumper than to any other batsman; Noble said there was no shot of which Trumper was not the master. There appeared no limits to his cricketing imagination.

Like RANJITSINHJI, Trumper possessed a superb eye, a quick pair of feet, moved with the ease of a natural athlete and played the ball late – so late, in fact, that bowlers would start to appeal for leg-before only to see Trumper's bat connect at the last fraction of a second. Unlike Ranjitsinhji, he scorned gloves, believing they impaired his touch, and used a heavy bat – one his steely wrists effortlessly whipped into life, before they lost some of their strength late in his career and he was obliged to moderate his methods.

'He dealt with the good-length balls in the way that an ordinary forcing first-class batsman deals with half-volleys and long hops,' wrote Colonel Philip Trevor, MCC's manager in Australia in 1907–08. 'Our steadiest professional bowlers, indeed, have said that they would rather bowl to Ranji than bowl to Trumper. They knew, they said, more exactly the extent of evil that could happen to them when they bowled to him than when they bowled to Trumper.' Trumper scored his runs faster than Ranjitsinhji – at 56 an hour, as against 50 – and any other leading batsman except Jessop, who was a calculated hitter.

On good pitches, Trumper tore attacks to shreds: witness his innings of 335 in 165 minutes for Paddington v Redfern in Sydney in 1902–03; his 185 not out for Australia v England at Sydney in 1903–04, his century coming in 94 minutes and Arthur Lilley, the England wicketkeeper, describing it as the best innings he saw; and his 293 in 180 minutes for the Australians against Canterbury at Christchurch in 1913–14, praised as the greatest display of batting then seen in New Zealand. Generally speaking, though, Trumper preferred a challenge, to the point that he was actually reckoned to be more dangerous when facing a strong attack on a rain-affected pitch.

He produced many brilliant innings in such conditions, several times during the wet English summer of 1902, which saw him at his audacious best. That year he scored 2,570 runs at an average of 48.49, with eleven centuries, and in the fourth Test at Old Trafford, the game which marked Ranjitsinhji's fall from favour, Trumper confounded all attempts to keep him quiet on the first morning by scoring a century before lunch, an innings that helped decide match and series. Eighteen months later, on what Warner, the England captain, described as a 'real beast' of a pitch at Melbourne, Trumper scored 74 out of an Australia total of 122, in an assault so savage that Hirst and Rhodes quickly resorted to off-theory to contain him.

In fact, although Trumper was not renowned for his consistency, he scored more heavily than the vast majority of his contemporaries. Between 1902 and the point in 1911–12 at which he was supplanted by HOBBS – after Trumper had made the last of his eight centuries for Australia in the first Test at Sydney, Hobbs reeled off hundreds in the next three matches – Trumper scored 2,522 Test runs at 45.03, an average only narrowly behind those of Bardsley, Hobbs and the ungainly but effective South African Faulkner, all of whom had only recently emerged on the international scene. Hill's tally of 1,945 runs was the next highest, but he averaged 38.90. Trumper's record in grade cricket in the Sydney suburbs, among the people with whom he felt the closest affinity and sought to please most, better reflected his dominance. In nineteen seasons, he scored 8,946 runs at 69.34.

Over the course of three successive Test series against England – in 1905, 1907–08 and 1909 – Trumper's record was only modest but he still played dazzlingly, especially in making a century at Sydney in 1907–08, and his record was again superior to most. Only Hill boasted a higher average, and that by a small amount. Few English batsmen played Test cricket regularly at this time, the vagaries of selection policy being as much to blame as their own frequent unavailability to tour. Jackson and Fry did well with the bat in 1905 but never visited Australia; the talented and highly individual George Gunn shone in Australia in 1907–08 but was not originally chosen for the tour and played in only six other Tests up to 1912. J.T. Tyldesley, whose appearances were more frequent, was a superb wet-wicket player whom MacLaren thought could, on his day, play as breathtakingly as Trumper, but he averaged 30 in his England career.

Trumper may have been unorthodox but his methods were founded upon sound first principles. While others struggled to come to terms with the new googly bowling, he adapted quickly – after being bowled by the first ball Bosanquet ever sent down to him. The peak came when he struck a magnificent 214 not out in 242 minutes against South Africa's googly attack at Adelaide in 1910–11. Among those who struggled against this innovative style were Ranjitsinhji (temporarily) and Tom Hayward (permanently). Hayward, whose aggregate of 3,518 runs in 1906 stood as the record for an English season until 1947, possessed in other respects the soundest technique and was the most imperturbable English professional of his generation, but he did not have an answer to these new-fangled twirlers. He was stumped in three successive Test innings against Vogler and Faulkner.

There were extenuating circumstances for Trumper's occasional troughs, for his health was poor and he was not always physically equal to the demands of top-class cricket. 'Unfortunately, owing to the fact that he did not enjoy the best of health, Trumper had many bad days,' Darling, one of his Test captains, wrote in his memoirs, 'but when fit and well there was only one cricketer in it as champion of the world, and that was Trumper.' Trumper's wife wrote ruefully after his death: 'He started sport too young.'

He was also far more interested in the success of his side than personal glory, and totally selfless. An intensely private person and self-effacing to an extreme, he enjoyed cricket but not its attendant glories. He disliked the adulation of the crowds, far preferred the company of his family to admirers and did not drink or smoke. He seemed to live intently for other people, so numerous were his acts of kindness to friends and strangers. Many found his personality baffling. 'His nature was just as hard to describe as his cricket, because one cannot recall in one's acquaintance with men a nature like his,' Frank Iredale, a team-mate, wrote. 'He looked upon his cricket more as a duty than a sport.' He was poorly organized and often took the field in crumpled shirts and baggy trousers.

Trumper's form was so sketchy in his early days that his career might have been short-lived but for the support and belief of some influential people. His first mentor was his father, a migrant from London who settled in the Paddington suburb of Sydney, an area then surrounded by slums. Trumper first took a serious interest in the game at Crown Street Superior Public School (actually not a public school at all), and when his father realized that the eldest of his eight children possessed a special talent for the game, he encouraged him in every way he could. Each day before work, he played with him in a local park – some of the many hours of practice his son put in during his schooldays.

It was Noble, himself a former pupil at Crown Street, who persuaded Trumper to join the Paddington club in 1896, in the first significant step of his career. The following season, at the age of twenty, Trumper averaged 204.20 for the club and played against the touring MCC side; he was out for 5 and 0 but Ranjitsinhji saw enough to predict a great future for him. Noble and Charles Bannerman both coached the brilliant but unorthodox youngster before realizing that it was a futile exercise. 'Victor was a law unto himself,' Noble conceded.

Trumper's idiosyncratic style counted against him and he was not originally chosen for Australia's tour of England in 1899, but a superb innings of 75 in a late trial match won him inclusion, on reduced financial terms, at the eleventh hour. He failed in the first Test, but scored a sparkling century in the second at Lord's and was put on an equal footing with the other players. He scored 300 not out against Sussex, then the highest innings by an Australian in England, and won the lasting admiration of Noble, who said at the end of the tour that Trumper would become a greater batsman than Ranjitsinhji. Trumper remained an integral part of the Australian team until he became embroiled in a financial dispute with the Australian board in 1912 and he, along with several other players, did not tour England that year. As it turned out, he did not play for Australia again.

Trumper's reticence, honesty and inclination for living from day to day gave him little head for the business enterprises he undertook towards the end of his life – fortunately bolstered by a benefit fund that brought him almost £3,000. At one time and another, he worked in a sports store, a shirt and tie shop, as a teacher, government employee and secretary to the Australian Rugby Football League.

Trumper won the affection of all classes in Australia and his successes against England helped fuel the country's young flames of nationalism. When he died at the age of thirty-seven – from Bright's disease, shortly after contracting scarlet fever, in a private hospital near to the place where he was born – twenty thousand people lined the Sydney streets, forming a three and a half-mile procession behind his funeral cortege. The pall-bearers included TURNER, Noble, Bardsley and Macartney.

Trumper's first-class record: 255 matches, 16,939 runs, average 44.57. **Test record:** 48 matches, 3, 163 runs, average 39.04.

Trumper's Coopers & Lybrand ratings 1902–11: –, –, 1, 4, 2, 2, 1, 3, 5, 3.
Other leaders: 1902–03: C. Hill (Aus). 1905–07: F.S. Jackson (Eng). 1909: V.S. Ransford (Aus). 1910–11: J.B. Hobbs (Eng).

Record against Number One bowlers:
v Barnes 1902–12: 14 matches, Trumper 25 innings, 812 runs, average 33.83 (two centuries, highest score 166); Barnes took his wicket seven times.

JOHN BERRY HOBBS (England)

Number One: 1912–28

Born: Cambridge, 16 December 1882; died: Hove, Sussex, 21 December 1963. Career: 1905–34.

Jack Hobbs – who learned the art of batting in the same town-and-gown Cambridge environment as CARPENTER, Thomas Hayward and his nephew, and RANJITSINHJI – was known by all who played with him as 'The Master'. To them it was inconceivable that there could be a more complete player, and one, MacLaren, even wrote a book about him called *The Perfect Batsman*. When Hobbs retired from Test cricket in 1930, the Australians delayed the match to give him three cheers, the first time this had been done for any player.

One of the few critics to qualify their praise for him was Noble, who wrote in 1925, arguably Hobbs's greatest year: 'My admiration for him is very great. I would like to be able to bracket him with Victor TRUMPER, not as a record breaker, but as a batsman, but it would not be honest to do so.'

Hobbs's modest social background and humility – which he retained after his knighthood in 1953 for services to the game, the first professional sportsman to be so honoured – made him an accessible figure to the public, who held him in the same high regard as did the players. He always dealt courteously with the public, and when it was decided on his retirement to build gates in his memory at the Oval, enough money was raised also to construct a wall right round the ground where Hobbs revealed so much of his glory. He was equally popular in Australia, where a crowd of

60,000, then a world record, packed the Sydney Cricket Ground during a Test in 1928 after a local newspaper arranged a birthday fund for him.

No other batsman's technique has been so highly praised. If the supreme tests of a batsman's skill are facing a genuinely fast bowler on a lively pitch and a top-class spinner on a 'sticky' one, then Hobbs was truly a consummate performer. He was never known to be seriously discomfited by any fast bowler, and certainly never acknowledged that one was too fast for him. In retirement he nominated Neville Knox, a Surrey colleague, as the best he saw. He thought GREGORY not as fast as his galloping run-up suggested, and had the record to back up his case.

Hobbs gave some of the most accomplished performances ever seen on 'sticky' wickets. Once, in playing an innings of 134 in a county match at Leicester in 1920, he scored more than the entire opposition mustered in two innings; and for England against Australia at the Oval in 1926 and Melbourne in 1929, by sharing partnerships of 172 and 105 with Herbert Sutcliffe when the ball was spitting nastily, helped turn likely defeats into famous victories, in the first instance to regain the Ashes after fourteen years. Many of his peers, including Percy Fender, said he was a better player than BRADMAN later became for this reason alone, though Bradman actually made little effort to come to terms with rain-affected pitches.

No less important to Hobbs's reputation was his role in breaking the power of the googly. Like Trumper, he used his speed of thought and footwork to deal with the battery of South African googly bowlers, led by Vogler and Faulkner, and give hard-pressed teammates a lead. He played well against them in two non-representative matches in 1907 – he did not make his Test debut until he was in Australia a few months later – and was in a class of his own when he met them again on their favoured matting in South Africa in 1909–10: in five Tests, Hobbs averaged 67.37, double the figure of the next-best player on his side, and gave the first indications that he was blossoming into a great player. In Australia a year later, Herbert Hordern, another googly bowler, took Hobbs's wicket five times, but said that he did not once deceive him.

When Test cricket resumed in 1920 after the First World War, Hobbs enjoyed a great rivalry with Arthur Mailey, the Australian leg-spinner. Each claimed the upper hand, Mailey – supported by his wicketkeeper Bert Oldfield – arguing that Hobbs could not pick his googly. Though this may have been initially the case, Hobbs amassed a great number of runs against Mailey. He regarded googly bowling as the greatest challenge he faced.

Hobbs never played in a first-class match against BARNES, the bowler he regarded as the best he saw, but they met occasionally in the Bradford League during the war, when Hobbs played for Idle and Barnes for Saltaire. Hobbs passed this test as well. In a Priestley Cup match at Idle in 1917, he treated Barnes with near contempt, advancing down the pitch time and again to drive him. 'He had no weaknesses,' Barnes admitted.

The bare bones of Hobbs's career tell their own tale. With his powers unimpaired until he was into his fifties, he accumulated more runs (61,760) and more centuries (199) in first-class cricket than anyone in the history of the game and more runs (3,636) and more centuries (12) against Australia than any other England player. His greatest season was 1925, when he scored sixteen centuries (which remained a record until 1947), including an unbeaten 266 for Players v Gentlemen (the record for the fixture) and, amid unprecedented media attention that caused his form to falter in a way no bowler ever managed, equalled and then eclipsed GRACE's then-accepted tally of 126 first-class centuries. Hobbs's Test record was superb: he was the first batsman to score 5,000 runs and rarely failed in his 61 appearances.

As Grace had done, Hobbs produced a superb synthesis of the best available techniques. Watchful and quick on his feet, he was always in the right position, going forward or back, always right behind the ball, and his play had about it immense calm, grace and clarity of purpose. Whatever the conditions, he looked good.

Remarkably, Hobbs acquired his superb judgement not through any kind of academic study of other players in the way that, say, Ranjitsinhji did (when Hobbs scored his hundredth hundred in 1923, Ranjitsinhji sent him a gift inscribed, 'From a humble student of the game'). Hobbs was the eldest of twelve children of a groundsman and umpire at Fenner's and Jesus College, and experienced what he himself described as a 'lowly upbringing'. He was no student. He absorbed the game by watching matches at Fenner's and on Parker's Piece – where he saw Tom Hayward, his idol, and Ranjitsinhji play – and undertaking primitive ones of his own with college servants. He also invented solitary games involving the use of a single stump – as a bat – and a tennis ball.

Though encouraged by his father, who did not live to see him prosper, Hobbs, who stood 5ft 9½in, received no formal coaching and the only player he even loosely modelled himself on was Hayward. Throughout his life, it was said, Hobbs played bowling by 'feel' rather than by logical thought processes. When first faced with googly bowling, he played it off the pitch before realizing that he 'felt something different' when the googly came out of the bowler's hand. Thus, he seemed to play the game by a sixth sense. The result was that he perhaps looked more natural than any other batsman who ever lived.

This may explain why, by 'feeling' his way against bowling, Hobbs got better and better, at least in mathematical terms. Having not played in an organized match until he was twelve, he did not score a century until he was eighteen. On the recommendation of Hayward, to whose attention Hobbs's ability was drawn, he was given a trial by Surrey and, shortly after, a contract. In his first match for the county, with Grace captaining the opposition, Hobbs scored 88, and on his championship debut he made 137 before lunch against Essex, who had been offered the chance to look at him but declined. He scored 1,317 runs in his first season. 'I thought I knew it all then,' he recalled. 'Later I found out I did not. Opening with Tom Hayward, I learned what balls to leave alone and what to go for. I learned the scoring strokes to improve and those to drop.'

Hobbs himself said he never played better than before the First World War. He was slimmer, stronger, more agile and fitter – he always took care over his fitness and did not show his age until 1930 – and better able to attack the bowling. In those days, he delighted in scoring freely and stealing quick singles, which was the basis of his first-wicket partnerships with Rhodes, Andrew Sandham and Sutcliffe. When he first caught sight of Hobbs, Warner wrote: 'I have just seen a young batsman, and he plays just like a good amateur.' When Hobbs took apart a strong Australia attack on a difficult pitch at Edgbaston in his first home Test, in 1909, Fry, his partner at the time, said later that it was the only innings he saw from the other end that compared with watching Ranjitsinhji at his best.

Before the war, Hobbs was a front-foot aggressor; afterwards, he scored more of his runs off the back foot. The five-year hiatus had taken its toll on him physically, added to which he was unwell with appendicitis in 1921 and did not regain his stamina for two years. Also, batsmen generally were being given less freedom and Hobbs, like everyone else, was obliged to cut out certain strokes and use his pads as a second line of defence. Less audacious, he inspired even greater confidence than before and, astonishingly, scored over 35,000 runs and 132 centuries after the war and after the age of thirty-six.

He always looked back wistfully on his early period. 'You could play cheeky shots and make 50 or 60 and feel life was worth living,' he said on his seventieth birthday. 'Then came the exasperation when they started counting your hundreds, publishing averages, and it was all figures. They think too much of figures these days.' Hobbs never cared for statistics and even after the war he would, if circumstances allowed, play for fun before throwing his wicket away in a bout of extravagant strokes, often after reaching his hundred.

Hobbs first laid a convincing claim to be regarded as the world's best batsman on the tour of Australia in 1911–12, during which he scored centuries in the second, third and fourth Tests and amassed 662 runs in all, then a record for an Ashes series. After scoring a century in the first match, Trumper, by contrast, did little in what transpired to be his last Test series. *Wisden* stated that on this tour Hobbs revealed himself as 'potentially the most resourceful batsman in the world on plumb wickets', while the triangular tournament with Australia and South Africa in the wet English summer a few months later 'proved him now beyond question the most accomplished performer on bad ones'.

For most of the rest of his career, there was little question that Hobbs was the best batsman. In 1908, *Wisden* deemed him the third-best professional batsman in England behind Hayward and J.T. Tyldesley, and the following year Hobbs outshone Hayward in the Surrey side for the first time. It was the tour of South Africa in 1909–10 that saw him firmly established as England's best, and after that, his position only ever came under threat fleetingly before he was finally and emphatically dethroned by HAMMOND in Australia in 1928–29. Among Englishmen, the precocious J.W. Hearne showed immense potential before the war, but subsequently failed to live up to it at the highest level; Patsy Hendren, a prolific and durable scorer for Middlesex, did not often do himself justice against Australia; while Philip Mead, Hampshire's equally reliable left-hander, was an adhesive but unenterprising player whose ponderous movements restricted his opportunities at Test level.

Second in line was undoubtedly the cool, methodical Sutcliffe, Hobbs's trusted opening partner for England, whose average of 66.85 in Ashes matches is the second-highest among batsmen with 1,000 runs, 23 points behind Bradman's and 12 ahead of Hobbs's. In his first series against Australia, in 1924–25, Sutcliffe outscored Hobbs, but Hobbs returned home and reaffirmed his position with a record-breaking season in England. Sutcliffe, who began his days as a stylist, later made the most of his abilities with powers of defence and concentration rarely, if ever, seen before (Bradman said Sutcliffe had the best temperament of any cricketer he saw). But Sutcliffe himself conceded that he did not possess the gifts of Hobbs, Hammond or HUTTON. Frank Woolley, who remained incomparably elegant throughout his long career, commanded many admirers but his record for England was surprisingly modest. He only twice averaged over 50 in a series, both times at home to South Africa.

No Australian or South African seriously threatened Hobbs's pre-eminence, although Macartney – another denizen of the Sydney region, who practised on the backyard pitch belonging to Trumper – and Taylor, of South Africa, one intent on demoralizing opponents, the other a superb technician, at times played brilliantly in their contrasting ways. Macartney, who was as much a law to himself as was Trumper, would have achieved more in Tests had he not suffered a nervous breakdown in 1924, forcing him to miss a year's cricket. Bill Ponsford set new standards of scoring on the true pitches and in the timeless conditions of state cricket in Australia – twice breaking the world record with innings of 429 and 437 – but rarely reproduced this form at Test level, being much less happy when the ball was doing something.

Without determination and pugnacity, Hobbs would never have risen to the heights he did, nor been such a priceless player on the big occasion. If anything inspired him, it was the desire that he – and later his wife and four children – should escape the poverty he knew as a child. 'I thought cricket was a chance of making money,' he once said. Make money he did, investing the proceeds of two benefit matches and a testimonial into the sports goods shop he opened in Fleet Street in 1919 and building it into a substantial business, so that towards the end he no longer needed to play for a living. He was duly grateful for the prosperity the game brought him.

Hobbs's first-class record: 834 matches, 61,760 runs, average 50.66. Test record: 61 matches, 5,410 runs, average 56.94.

Hobbs's Coopers & Lybrand ratings 1912–28: 1912–14: 1, 1, 1. 1921–28: 1, 1, –, 1, 1, 1, 1, 2.
Other leaders: 1923: H.W. Taylor (SA). 1928: H. Sutcliffe (Eng).

Record against Number One bowlers:
v Barnes 1912–18: they did not meet in first-class matches.
v Gregory 1919–24: 10 matches, Hobbs 19 innings, 1,109 runs, average 69.31 (four centuries, highest score 205 not out); Gregory took his wicket six times.
v Tate 1925–28: 4 matches, Hobbs 6 innings, 150 runs, average 30.00 (highest score 49 not out); Tate took his wicket once.

ⓌJACK MORRISON GREGORY (Australia)

Number One: 1919–24

Born: North Sydney, New South Wales, 14 August, 1895; died: Bega, New South Wales, 7 August 1973. Career: 1919–28.

Jack Gregory was not the most technically accomplished bowler in the years immediately after the First World War – Ted McDonald, his comrade-in-destruction for Australia, was superior in that respect – but he was certainly the most influential. Gregory loomed large in the popular imagination and his athletic fielding and belligerent left-handed batting were but a small part of the effect.

Gregory and McDonald generated unusual speed, but Gregory also exuded a raw energy and when he had a new ball in his hand there was a whiff of cordite in the air. Operating together, they created a sense of combined menace not previously matched by a pair of top-class fast bowlers. While McDonald glided over the turf and let the ball slip with a graceful and rhythmic action, Gregory, 6ft 3½ in and massively proportioned, charged in at full gallop for twenty yards before launching into a giant leap that covered three yards prior to him releasing the ball with a full, high sweep of the arm. On pitching, the ball seemed to explode from the ground.

McDonald's bowling was graceful, restrained, accurate and dependable, Gregory's unpredictable in quality and direction, which only added to the apprehension of the unfortunate batsman, who was torn between expecting a ball pitched short and rising awkwardly into his ribs and one of fuller length breaking back from outside off stump. There was just no knowing.

Gregory – the third member of his family to play Test cricket – thus succeeded where Ernest Jones had failed thirty years earlier. Jones used the short-pitched ball to try to intimidate a generation who would not be cowed; Gregory found himself dealing with opponents, many of whom were deficient technically and mentally, HOBBS and Woolley being notable exceptions. Gregory, wedded to the outdoors by cricket and farming, possessed a rare gusto for life and epitomized, in Cardus's words, 'young manhood in excelsis'; much of England's younger generation, like Australia's, had been lost in the war, and it seemed that those who remained had no appetite for the onslaught from this decommissioned artilleryman.

Gregory was discovered in unusual circumstances, not in his native Sydney, where he played lower-grade cricket, but in England at the end of the war by the organizers of the Australian Imperial Forces XI that toured the country in 1919. They were put on to him by Warner, Gregory having been billeted at Lord's. Gregory, aged twenty-three, was a great success for the AIF, scoring 942 runs and taking 131 wickets at 18.19. As a bowler he lacked control but unsettled many batsmen with his great speed. 'He intimidated batsmen to an extent not seen in this country since Knox was at his deadliest in 1906,' *Wisden* said. In the first season of cricket since the armistice, and with BARNES in retirement, there was not a more potent bowler.

The AIF team visited South Africa on their way home and Gregory was the leading wicket-taker with 47 victims at 13.04, including seventeen in two representative matches. On reaching Australia, he immediately caught the public imagination with some dazzling all-round performances, form he carried into the Tests with England a year later in 1920–21, when McDonald, of Victoria, was brought in to share the new ball with him for the third match.

Australia won all five matches against England in what was the first post-war Test series, Gregory contributing 23 wickets, 442 runs and fifteen catches, but there was a belief in Britain that the outcome was due to poor play by the touring team. That misguided view was shattered when Australia toured England a few months later: Australia won the first Test match in two days and the second and third in two and a half days apiece, so that the series was settled with two matches remaining. In those three games, Gregory and McDonald played the decisive part and it was of Gregory rather than McDonald, who took 27 wickets to his partner's 19 in the series as a whole, that *Wisden* said: 'To him, more than anyone else, is due Australia's unapproachable record of eight Test match victories in succession . . . [he is] the greatest match-winning force among the cricketers now before the public.'

Gregory and McDonald not only took 270 wickets at 16 each between them on the tour, they injured numerous batsmen and left those who resisted for any length of time black and blue, by-products of their speed rather than malicious intent. During the first Test at Trent Bridge, Gregory felled Ernest Tyldesley with a terrible blow on the jaw, the batsman, feared for dead at one point by the crowd, being helped from the field by a doctor; in the second, at Lord's, he struck Woolley just below the right kidney. HAMMOND played one of his earliest matches for Gloucestershire against the Australians in 1921 and Gregory, who bowled him with a ball he never saw, scared him so badly that it took several years to repair his confidence. 'Never so long as cricket is played will Gregory's bowling be forgotten,' Hammond wrote. Robert Lynd likened it to bomb-throwing.

Later that year, Gregory maintained his dominance in three Tests in South Africa – he again outbowled McDonald – and carried it into the home series against England in 1924–25, where he was completely overshadowed by TATE. Hampered by a damaged toe, Gregory took 22 wickets in the series but they came expensively and he failed until the last match to separate Hobbs and Sutcliffe quickly. He was never a force at international level again and broke down with a recurrence of an old knee problem attempting a come-back in the Brisbane Test of 1928–29, a mundane end to a glamorous career.

There were differing opinions as to Gregory's speed. Hendren reckoned him the fastest bowler he faced in a career that ran from 1907 to 1938; Sutcliffe judged him faster than McDonald; but Hobbs said he was not as quick as his charging run-up and predatory leap suggested.

The next-best bowler after Gregory and McDonald was another Australian, Mailey. Helped in his early career by Hugh Trumble, Mailey was a big spinner of the ball and easily the best leg-break and googly bowler of the early 1920s. He took 36 wickets in the first post-war series in Australia, then an Australian record against England and reward for his patience and persistence, but he was costly – it was said he bowled one full toss an over – and given a free rein only because of the inroads made by the new-ball bowlers. England's bowling resources were thin. There were those who were forces at county level, such as Rhodes, who topped the English averages in the five seasons after the war, and Alec Kennedy, of Hampshire, but they were either little use in Tests or not selected. The most talented bowler was Cecil Parkin, who purveyed a mixture of right-arm spin: ten Tests yielded him 32 wickets and one victory before some ill-advised comments ended his career.

In later life, Gregory lived in seclusion on the south coast of New South Wales, fishing and playing bowls and married to his third wife, a former Miss Australia.

Gregory's first-class record: 129 matches, 504 wickets, average 20.99. **Test record:** 24 matches, 85 wickets, average 31.15.

Gregory's Coopers & Lybrand ratings 1921–24: 2, 1, 1, 1. *Other leader*: 1921: A.A. Mailey (Aus).

Record against Number One batsmen:
v Hobbs 1919–24: 10 matches, Hobbs 19 innings, 1,109 runs, average 69.31 (four centuries, highest score 205 not out); Gregory took his wicket six times.

◎ MAURICE WILLIAM TATE (England)

Number One: 1924–30

Born: Brighton, Sussex, 30 May 1895; died: Wadhurst, Sussex, 18 May 1956. Career: 1912–37.

Maurice Tate's emergence in the mid-1920s did not come a moment too soon for English cricket, which had not possessed an accurate, penetrative bowler of medium pace or above since BARNES played his last Test in 1914, and was licking its wounds after its maulings by Australia. Comparisons between the two were frequent and not confined to their historical proximity: many of the leading batsmen of his day regarded Tate as the most dangerous bowler they played against, and well-qualified judges deemed him not far short of Barnes for control, perseverance and sustained fury. Barnes was one of Tate's admirers. 'Like me,' he said, 'he tries to get a wicket every ball, and is surprised if he doesn't.'

Perhaps the main difference was that Tate lacked Barnes's worldliness. Barnes took care to look after his own career, knowing that no one else would; Tate did not, and was taken aback when England and Sussex eventually dispensed with his services, although he was forty-two when the county released him in 1937. Having never thought of much except bowling, he had no provision for an alternative career and resorted to the option that so aroused Barnes's contempt, taking over the licences of a succession of Sussex inns.

Tate lacked Barnes's shrewd analytical brain but was credited as the first bowler to take full advantage of the seam. He also swung the ball deceptively late, gaining his movement through a turn of the body so pronounced that he had to wear a corset to safeguard himself from injury, and by 'cutting' the ball with a flick of the wrist and a drag of his long fingers. His stock delivery was one that swung away from the right-hander, but he commanded an inswinger and could also break the ball either way. Like Barnes, he could produce that deadliest of combinations, swing one way with break the other, and, like Barnes, troubled even the best batsmen on good surfaces, partly because of the 'nip' his bowling had off the pitch – especially in Australia, where the slips stood back further for Tate than for many genuine fast bowlers. It made playing back a hazardous business. As late as 1965, Ian Peebles, an England teammate, claimed there had never been a better seam bowler.

Tate played in an era in which bowlers had to be resourceful if they wanted to be successful, as pitches were increasingly overprepared. Many resorted in frustration to defensive tactics. Leg-theory – essentially a containment strategy – came into vogue and TURNER published a book entitled *The Quest for Bowlers*, in which he bemoaned the problems facing spinners operating on bland surfaces.

At first Tate closely followed the methods of his father Fred, who enjoyed a long and successful career as a slow-medium off-break bowler with Sussex. Although a coach himself, his father gave him no tuition or advice and Tate was discovered by the county's coach and offered a job on the groundstaff at the age of fifteen. The club's action may have been one of kindness, for Tate did little in his handful of appearances for the county before the war, and afterwards only slowly established himself as a capable batsman and adequate bowler.

It was not until 1922 that he began to concentrate on making general use of what had previously been an occasional quicker ball. Encouraged by his county captain Arthur Gilligan, who was as short of strike bowling as England, Tate reaped immediate rewards and from the following year his rise was meteoric. In 1923, he shone in two Test trials and completed the first of three successive season doubles of 200 wickets and 1,000 runs – a feat performed on only three other occasions in history – and was hailed by *Wisden* as 'by general consent the best bowler in England'.

Operating off an eight-yard run and rocking back in a smooth delivery, Tate wrecked the innings of countless county sides, especially on green pitches at Hove freshened by a morning sea haze. In the space of eleven days in June 1924, he and Gilligan dismissed Surrey for 41, Middlesex for 53 and South Africa – at Edgbaston, in Tate's first Test – for 30, the lowest total recorded in a Test in England. Tate took a wicket with his first ball and finished with four for six on a pitch offering little assistance. The innings occupied only forty-eight minutes.

South Africa were not a strong side, but Tate bowled consistently well to take 27 wickets at 15.70 in the series and was sent to Australia in the hope that he would be the equal of GREGORY. Tate outbowled him completely, despite suffering, like Gregory, from a badly damaged toe. He took 38 Test wickets at 23.18, a record for a visiting player in Australia. Time and again he broke through the batting with his first assault, breaches that his teammates were often unable to capitalize on. Big, powerful and seemingly tireless, Tate bowled twice as many overs in that series as anyone else on the England side.

He returned to England, in Altham's words, 'universally acclaimed as the greatest bowler in the world'. Tate himself reckoned that his first spell of the series at Sydney – nineteen overs which failed to yield a wicket – was the best he ever bowled. It was a feature of his bowling that he frequently missed the outside edge of the bat or off stump by a whisker; testimony, perhaps, to his relentlessly attacking line.

All too often he did not receive the rewards he was due in the years that followed, but even if the figures did not support the fact, he was invariably England's best bowler. He played a central part in the Ashes being regained in 1926 and although his seventeen wickets cost 41 on his next visit to Australia in 1928–29, he conceded well under two runs per over and most of his wickets were important ones. Jack White, England's slow left-armer, was equally persevering and returned the better overall figures, but Tate, supported by Harold Larwood, prevented Australia from getting off to a good start until the series was won. He no longer breathed the fire of four years earlier, but he was the bowler who worried the opposition, as he was when South Africa toured England a few months later.

Few others of the best contemporary bowlers were at their peaks while Tate reigned supreme. Gregory had faded, GRIMMETT was not yet the bowler he became, and nor, quite, was Larwood. McDonald had left Australia and Test cricket to play for Lancashire – whom he helped, in the course of eight seasons, to four championship titles, thus proving how much more durable and versatile he was than Gregory.

Charles Parker was the finest left-arm spinner but rarely appeared in big games, the England selectors consistently overlooking his huge hauls of wickets in county matches between 1920 and 1935. He played for England once in 1921, taking two for 32 from 28 overs, but never again – partly, it was said, because he had grabbed a selector by the lapels. 'Tich' Freeman, England's leading leg-break bowler, claimed even more wickets than Parker and received more opportunities at Test level, but batsmen of pedigree, with footwork and courage, were capable of taking his bowling by the scruff of the neck. Warner, though, said that Freeman 'stood out as the best bowler in England between 1922 and 1929'.

BRADMAN hastened the end of Tate's Test career, as he did those of many others. Tate had enjoyed success against him in Australia in 1928–29 and at the end of the tour was alleged to have remarked to the young Australian: 'You'll have to keep that bat a bit straighter when you come to England, or you won't have much luck there.' Tate, not only a tireless cricketer but tirelessly good-natured, disarmed many people with his friendly if frank air, but not Bradman, who took the remark as a slight, and when they met again in England in 1930 launched what HAMMOND described as a 'personal vendetta' against Tate.

Tate bowled Bradman in the first innings of the first Test with a superb break-back during a spell of three for eight that was instrumental in England gaining their only win of the summer, but that was the last success he enjoyed. Bradman farmed his bowling unceremoniously during his second-innings century and treated him ruthlessly during his double centuries at Lord's and the Oval and his triple century at Headingley. Tate claimed he missed the off stump 'by a coat of varnish' with the first ball he bowled to Bradman at Headingley, but there appears to be no evidence to support the claim.

Tate played a full part in South Africa in 1930–31, but was chosen by England only twice more at home and did not play in the Tests in Australia in 1932–33. Heavy-handed in the way they terminated Tate's playing contract, Sussex subsequently made amends by naming the main gates at Hove after him.

Tate's first-class record: 679 matches, 2,784 wickets, average 18.16.
Test record: 39 matches, 155 wickets, average 26.16.

Tate's Coopers & Lybrand ratings 1925–29: 1, 1, 1, 1, 2.
Other leader: 1929: A.P. Freeman (Eng). Tate was also top in 1930.

Record against Number One batsmen:
v Hobbs 1925–28: 4 matches, Hobbs six innings, 150 runs, average 30.00 (highest score 49 not out); Tate took his wicket once.
v Hammond 1929–30: 2 matches, Hammond 4 innings, 39 runs, average 9.75 (highest score 30); Tate took his wicket once.

WALTER REGINALD HAMMOND (England)

Number One: 1928–30

Born: Dover, Kent, 19 June 1903; died: Durban, South Africa, 1 July 1965. Career: 1920–51.

Walter Hammond established himself on England's tour of Australia in 1928–29 as beyond question the best batsman in the world. At the age of twenty-five, he not only set many records – the main one his 905 runs in the Test series – but played in a manner that showed him as a worthy successor to HOBBS, whose unwavering judgement and concentration he almost matched.

Hobbs remained a member of the England side, his powers barely diminished, but in this series Hammond willingly took on the responsibility for the batting that had rested for so long with 'The Master'. As before, the Tests in Australia were played to a finish, and Hammond displayed an austerity not apparent in the state matches or the county cricket he had played until then. He scored four centuries and the innings of 251, 200, 119 and 177 not out occupied a total of twenty-six hours.

Great things had been predicted for Hammond ever since he was granted a trial by Gloucestershire at the age of seventeen without having had any formal coaching. His record at school in Cirencester – where he scored 365 not out in a house match – persuaded the county club to cultivate him, even when he did little in three first-team matches in 1920. In his first season as a professional, he was coached by John Tunnicliffe and George Dennett, two of the best players never to appear for England, but failed again in two matches against the Australians. His only consolation was a close-hand view of his idol Macartney, whose ruthless strokeplay he would emulate.

Hammond's class was not in question, but there were to be further setbacks. He was obliged to spend two years fulfilling a residential qualification for Gloucestershire once Kent, eager to acquire for themselves such a talented player born within their county boundaries, challenged his right to play for them; and on his first tour of the Caribbean in 1925–26, he became dangerously unwell with what is now understood to have been syphilis or another sexually transmitted disease. The nature of his illness was a well-kept secret during his year-long absence, but Warner, his mentor, said that Hammond had been 'in the valley of the shadow of death'.

Between these interruptions, Hammond gave glimpses of his wide-ranging talents. He exhibited a mastery not seen at Bristol since GRACE, demonstrating that he could play on a sticky wicket by scoring 174 out of 282 against Middlesex in 1924, and showing he could handle top-class fast bowling by taking an unbeaten 250 off a Lancashire attack that contained McDonald at Old Trafford a year later. On his return in 1927, he began by scoring 1,000 runs before the end of May, which included another daring assault on McDonald at Old Trafford: Hammond scored 187 in three hours and repeatedly drove and hooked the Australian, once onto the pavilion roof. Cardus wrote: 'The possibilities of this boy Hammond are beyond the scope of estimation; I tremble to think of the grandeur he will spread over our cricket fields when he has arrived at maturity.'

Warner, writing twenty years later about Hammond inheriting Hobbs's mantle, estimated that Hobbs's reign as the world's best batsman ended in 1927, but in his early experiences of Test cricket, in South Africa in 1927–28 and at home to West Indies the following summer, Hammond failed to show the discipline that would be so apparent in Australia. One of the hallmarks of his play at its finest was the rigorousness with which he eschewed risky strokes, a policy that, after his experiences against Learie Constantine and 'Manny' Martindale in 1933, led him to abandon the hook shot and sometimes rein in his favourite, incomparable cover drive, which frequently left opponents stringing out fielders on the off side in a vain attempt to stem the flow of boundaries.

So, by 1929, Hammond was cricket's undisputed star, not only a wonderful batsman but a prehensile slip fielder and capable fast-medium bowler. He was every inch of his 6ft a superb athlete, used to dominating games by ability and sheer physical presence. When he married in April of that year, the streets were thronged with well-wishers: he was the man the public wanted to see. In batting terms he was out on his own, ahead of Sutcliffe and Woolley, the gifted but flawed Duleepsinhji, RANJITSINHJI's nephew, the prolific and immovable Bill Woodfull and Ponsford. In the English averages of 1929, only one person bettered Hammond's 2,456 runs at 64.63 and that, as it happened, was Hobbs (2,263 at 66.55); everyone else lagged more than eight points behind. The world was at his feet and Hammond might reasonably have expected it to stay that way for years to come. In many ages other than that of BRADMAN, it would have done.

Within eighteen months, Hammond's world had been fractured by this young, diminutive Australian who, as twelfth man, had so admired Hammond's double century at Sydney, describing it as 'probably the best [batting] I'd seen up to that time'. In England in 1930, Bradman all but erased from people's memories that innings and all Hammond's other achievements in Australia, and from then until Hammond announced his retirement at the end of his last, ill-judged tour of Australia in 1946–47, Bradman cast a shadow over almost everything Hammond did on the cricket field.

Bradman offended Hammond not least through his striking physical dissimilarity. Hammond, who often commented in his writings on the physique of other players, described first setting eyes on Bradman in his autobiography, *Cricket My Destiny*. Here was a 'slim, shortish boy with a grim, nervous face, whom I had never seen before, and whose name was unfamiliar to me. He looked about nineteen, and not very formidable.' But Bradman had an even larger appetite for massive scores than Hammond himself, and proved an even bigger draw-card.

While Bradman amassed 974 runs in the 1930 Test series, Hammond made less than one-third of that number. He struggled against GRIMMETT, who exposed his relative weakness on the leg side, a trait that denied him parity with Hobbs in the eyes of some. He scored four centuries on the tour of Australasia in 1932–33 – including a dazzling innings of 336 not out against New Zealand that pointedly eclipsed Bradman's world-record Test score of 334 – but otherwise, in 38 Test matches up to 1935, made only three other hundreds. He maintained that he was weighed down by the demands of being the cornerstone of England's batting; more pertinent was that he keenly felt that he had to do better than Bradman. Yet in terms of runs scored in the 26 Tests in which they both batted from 1930 onwards, Hammond did so only four times.

Bradman's presence gnawed at Hammond's increasingly fragile persona, and some who knew him well said that his attitude towards the Australian bordered on paranoia. 'Bloody Bradman!' he was often heard to mutter during 1930. There was never much affection between the two men, who were both by nature reserved, and their relationship was cool in the extreme when they led their respective countries in 1946–47. Hammond was angered that Bradman refused to walk when apparently caught in the slips early in the first Test of the series, at a time when Bradman's return to the game hung in the balance, and the Australian captain's rehabilitation was another blow to Hammond, whose own play revealed hitherto unseen flaws, expediting his retirement. Two years later it was Bradman, not Hammond, who became the second cricketer after Hobbs to be knighted for services to the game.

Bradman's avalanche of runs almost silenced debate as to their relative merits, but a few people argued in favour of Hammond.

Most were Gloucestershire or England colleagues, or Australians with axes to grind with Bradman. They pointed approvingly to the colour of Hammond's play and compared it to the functionalism of Bradman's. Two of Hammond's performances in Australia in 1936–37 stood out: an unbeaten 231 at Sydney and a wondrous 32 on a 'sticky dog' at Melbourne (Hammond's own choice of best innings). His near-flawless 240 against Australia at Lord's in 1938 also won him many admirers. But, following Grimmett's example, the Australians generally reckoned they could tie up Hammond on leg stump, in particular O'REILLY, who caused Hammond more trouble than anyone and dismissed him ten times in Tests. At worst, the tactic slowed his scoring. His 231 occupied eight hours.

Hammond, who acknowledged Bradman's abilities but said that he would rather watch Ranjitsinhji or TRUMPER, bore the traits of a 'disgruntled genius', and this was not only Bradman's doing. Hammond was by nature distant and moody, and achieved little popularity with his team-mates, with whom he rarely shared the benefit of his wisdom. Cricket, it was said, was Hammond's only means of self-realization. The only child of an army officer, his upbringing was solitary and nomadic, much of his life up to the age of eleven being spent in China and Malta. On returning to England, he was sent away to boarding school and four years later his father was killed in action.

Also, like other English professional cricketers of the time, Hammond sought to better himself socially as well as financially, but these aspirations were never quite realized. Using his fame as a sportsman, he started working as a car salesman in 1933 and within four years became director of a motor company, making him financially independent of the game and enabling him to take the controversial decision to turn amateur and thus captain England. But the transition was not that simple; as Bob Wyatt said: 'As a captain he was a bit out of his depth socially.'

After he retired, Hammond turned his back on the game and emigrated to South Africa, the home of his second wife (he was divorced from the first). But the Durban car company he was involved with collapsed in 1959 and he returned to cricket as sports administrator at Natal University, where he helped in the development of several future Test players, including Barry RICHARDS.

He died leaving no money or provision for his family. Three months later, friends in England established a memorial fund, which realized £3,500. Bradman sent a cable which was reprinted on the posters. It read: 'During his era Wally was undoubtedly England's greatest cricketer.'

Hammond's first-class record: 634 matches, 50,551 runs, average 56.10. **Test record:** 85 matches, 7,249 runs, average 58.45.

Hammond's Coopers & Lybrand rating 1928–30: 1.

Record against Number One bowlers:
v Tate 1929–30: 2 matches, Hammond 4 innings, 39 runs, average 9.75 (highest score 30); Tate took his wicket once.

Ⓒ CLARENCE VICTOR GRIMMETT (Australia)

Number One: 1930–32

Born: Dunedin, New Zealand, 25 December 1891; died: Adelaide, Australia, 2 May 1980. Career: 1912–41.

Clarrie Grimmett was the first googly merchant to become indisputably the world's Number One bowler. He was also the first slow leg-break bowler since CLARKE to hold such a pre-eminent position and had, like Clarke, a nose for detecting an opponent's weakness. Grimmett demonstrated what Mailey could not, that a googly bowler need not be expensive. Variety and invention were essential to any type of bowler on the over-prepared surfaces of the day, and Grimmett, who had both, was economical and a match-winner; even so, such was the mistrust of his art, it took many years for success to come his way.

Grimmett – who, as a man, was short, spare of frame, and often bowled in a cap to hide his baldness – did not initially help himself by wanting to be a fast bowler during his schooldays, before a few wise words from a master persuaded him otherwise. He made his first-class debut in his native New Zealand at the age of twenty, and it was not until 1925, when he was thirty-three, that he made his first appearance in Test cricket for Australia. He had emigrated there in 1914 to improve his cricket and further his career as a sign-writer, but three years at club level in Sydney and six in Melbourne brought him little joy, before South Australia spotted him and took him to Adelaide, where work was fixed up for him that would not interfere with his cricket.

He was an immediate success for his new state and, having bowled well against the MCC touring team, was chosen for the final Test against England at Sydney in 1924–25 as support for the overworked Mailey. In the event, Mailey was given only five overs as Grimmett captured eleven wickets, helped only towards the end by rain enlivening the pitch. Noble described it as 'the finest exhibition of slow bowling seen in Australia for many years'.

Grimmett was now launched on a brilliant career that saw him claim more first-class wickets than any bowler never to play county cricket, more Sheffield Shield wickets than anyone else (513), and become the first to capture 200 wickets in Tests – phenomenal achievements for one whose proper career started so late. In the process, he raised the status of leg-break and googly bowling to new heights, though he used sparingly his easily discernible googly – a delivery first shown to him by Mailey during Australia's tour of New Zealand in 1913–14 – relying instead on the ball that broke away from the right-hander's bat.

Grimmett did nothing spectacular in the Tests in England in 1926, but benefited from the experience and returned four years later to play a decisive part in Australia regaining the Ashes. By then, he was capable of turning the ball more on softer turf and flighting it better in the damp air. He took ten wickets in the first Test at Trent Bridge – in which TATE bowled his last incisive spell of the summer – and eight at Lord's, where his vice-like bowling was instrumental in England failing to escape with a draw.

HAMMOND wrote in his autobiography that within Grimmett delivering a few overs at Trent Bridge it was obvious that he had improved out of all recognition, adding that he was now, perhaps, 'the most formidable bowler in the world'. Grimmett was the first to expose Hammond's weakness on leg stump and the ascendancy he established over him – he dismissed him for five scores of under 40 in the first three Tests – was crucial to Australia regaining the Ashes. Hammond recalled: 'So long as Clarrie Grimmett was bowling, you had the nightmarish feeling somebody was after you,' adding that he found him a 'real horror . . . we all did.'

Grimmett took 29 wickets in the series and was acclaimed a master bowler, the best on either side. Australia were short of quality bowlers at this time and – thanks to BRADMAN – Tate,

England's best, was on the way out. At the end of the tour, one member of the touring team, Vic Richardson, declared: 'We could have played any team without Bradman, but we could not have played the blind school without Clarrie Grimmett.'

Grimmett's supremacy was amply confirmed over the next two years in Australia. He took over 70 wickets in a domestic season for the third and fourth times and was the leading wicket-taker in the series against West Indies in 1930–31 (33 at 17.96) and South Africa in 1931–32 (33 at 16.87). Herbert Ironmonger, a left-arm spinner who was eight years Grimmett's senior, took 31 wickets at 9.67 against South Africa, aided by a spectacular performance on a rain-affected pitch at Melbourne on which Grimmett was not called on to bowl, but the leg-spinner was the bowler the touring team feared most. 'To the batting of Bradman and the bowling of Grimmett can be assigned the real explanation for the failure of the South Africans . . . [they] established a pronounced "inferiority complex" among the visitors,' *Wisden* said. 'When facing Grimmett the South African batsmen showed an impatience to jump in and hit that almost invariably led to their undoing.'

Grimmett's methods were based on relentless, unspectacular control. While Mailey gambled on extravagant turn, Grimmett used a roundarm action to fire the ball in low, driving the batsman back and trying to get a top-spinner through to pads or stumps. So hard was he to attack, so unpredictable were his variations in flight, pace, line and length, that he was known as 'Scarlet', after the elusive Scarlet Pimpernel. To Grimmett, bowling was an intellectual challenge. O'REILLY described him as the 'most consistently active cricket thinker I ever met' and even late in his career Grimmett was working on a 'wrong wrong 'un', a delivery which looked like a googly but broke from leg.

It was during the series against South Africa in 1931–32 that Grimmett began his famous partnership with O'Reilly, whose leg-breaks and googlies were of a completely different hue. It lasted four years and fifteen Tests, yielded 169 wickets, and O'Reilly himself described it as 'one of cricket's greatest success stories of the twentieth century'. But the association was based on rivalry as well as friendship, and when O'Reilly emerged as a great bowler against England in 1932–33, Grimmett struggled for form and was dropped from the fourth and fifth Tests.

After that, Grimmett was generally reckoned to be the junior partner in the relationship. He returned against England in 1934, when the two of them claimed 53 of the 71 wickets taken by Australian bowlers in the series, and in South Africa eighteen months later their combined haul was 71 out of 98, with Grimmett taking the lion's share of 44, still a record for an Australian in a Test series.

Controversially, Grimmett was never chosen to play for his country again. The official reason was that he was too old – he was nearly forty-five when the series against England began in 1936–37 – but he worked hard at his fitness and some thought he was bowling as well as ever. When he was omitted from the party to tour England in 1938, Ponsford described it as 'sheer lunacy'.

Grimmett and O'Reilly both held Bradman responsible, Grimmett's replacement Frank Ward being a former club-mate of the new Australia captain. Bradman, it seemed, wanted Grimmett to concentrate on retaining control of his leg-break rather than evolving a second, better-disguised, googly. Grimmett duly bowled Bradman with a perfect leg-break in November 1937, but the match was his own testimonial and Bradman's dismissal before lunch took money off the Saturday gate. On Grimmett's death, O'Reilly accused Bradman of losing faith in 'the best spin bowler the world has seen'. As captain of South Australia, Bradman subsequently renewed his support for Grimmett, who took 73 wickets in the 1939–40 season.

Although he was married to a Melbourne girl for forty years, Grimmett was spiritually wedded to cricket. At his home near Adelaide, he had a cricket pitch in his garden and action photographs decorating the hall. He began coaching in the mid-1920s and was still at it well into his seventies. He bowled in the nets at the South Africans on their 1963–64 tour and claimed he could turn the ball more than anyone then in Australia. 'Social life meant little to "Grum",' O'Reilly said. 'Not until late in his career did he discover that it was not a bad idea to relax between matches.'

Grimmett's first-class record: 248 matches, 1,424 wickets, average 22.28. **Test record:** 37 matches, 216 wickets, average 24.21.

Grimmett's Coopers & Lybrand ratings 1930–32: 3, 1, 2.
Other leaders: 1930: M.W. Tate (Eng). 1932: H. Ironmonger (Aus). Grimmett was also top in 1936.

Record against Number One batsmen:
v Hammond 1930: 2 matches, Hammond 4 innings, 82 runs, average 20.50 (highest score 38); Grimmett took his wicket four times.
v Bradman 1930–32: 2 matches, Bradman 3 innings, 281 runs, average 93.66 (one century, highest score 258); Grimmett did not take his wicket.

DONALD GEORGE BRADMAN (Australia)

Number One: 1930–49

Born: Cootamundra, New South Wales, 27 August 1908. Career: 1927–49.

Anyone else with pretensions to be the world's Number One batsman should not have lived in the time of Don Bradman. The Australian's overbearing presence not only spoiled life for HAMMOND, but also for George Headley, who would otherwise have been spared the indignity of being labelled 'the black Bradman'; for the technically brilliant and cool-thinking Vijay Merchant, India's first great Test batsman; and for HUTTON and Denis Compton, both of whom, in their different ways, would have been strong contenders for the title directly before and after the Second World War. Their attitudes to being denied the honour may have varied, but anyone who gained an insight into the price Bradman paid for his pre-eminence would no longer have envied him.

As it was, Bradman had convinced everyone in the cricket world that he had no equal among contemporaries by the time he was one month short of his twenty-second birthday, when, on 11 July 1930, he scored 309 runs on the first day of a Test against England at Headingley, 'a revelation of genius,' one biographer, Charles Williams, declared, 'equal to any in the more traditional performing arts'.

Until then, there had been doubters. They were unimpressed by Bradman's then world-record score of 452 not out for New South Wales in Sydney seven months earlier – big innings in Australia were commonplace – and questioned whether his crossbat methods and general lack of 'style' would translate to English conditions.

Though the hometown press in Sydney put this precocious youth on a par with GRACE as early as March 1929, Woolley, Fender and TATE made public their reservations and several experts predicted that others, such as the graceful Archie Jackson, whose life was cut ruthlessly short by tuberculosis, would fare better in England. In fact, the world watched wide-eyed as Bradman scored 1,000 runs before the end of May and a double century in the second Test at Lord's that he himself described as his least flawed innings. But it was Bradman's first-day performance in the next Test at Headingley – where he was eventually out for 334 – that ended the argument.

Indeed, talk swiftly moved on to whether Bradman was the greatest batsman the world had seen, a debate that continued for the rest of his career, as he piled up century upon century, record upon record. In the short term, he opened up new horizons. If he could score 300 in a day, what else might he achieve? 'Will he,' Warner asked in his introduction to *Don Bradman's Book*, published late in 1930 after the Australian had taken his aggregate in the Test series with England to a record 974, 'one day play an innings of 600 or 700?'

Bradman was not simply the best batsman in the team, he was – like Grace in his early days – a team in himself. The day after his 309, *The Times* ran a leading article entitled 'England v Bradman'; six years later, Woodfull said he thought Bradman was the equivalent of two batsmen; and by the 1950s, when Australia were struggling to come to terms with life without him, the rate of exchange had risen: in the view of Hutton, Bradman had been worth three other players. 'He has upset the balance of the game as it has never been upset before by the genius of a single player,' wrote A.G. Gardiner in 1938. 'I think Don was too good; he spoilt the game,' said HOBBS in 1952. 'He got too many runs.'

But if his opponents paid a heavy price, so did Bradman. Scaling such precarious heights was a lonely and stressful business. He was one of the first sportsmen whose career was tracked by newsfilm and radio, and one of the first to take an unlisted telephone number. He only reluctantly accepted a knighthood in 1949, and his son John, a university lecturer, actually changed his surname to 'Bradsen' in 1972 to escape the endless pressure of possessing such a celebrated father. On a train journey from Sydney to Perth in 1932, the clamour for a glimpse of Don proved so great at one station that windows were smashed and doors wrenched off before the train pulled out. 'Poor old Don,' O'REILLY once said. 'We watched it more in sorrow for him than anger . . . He was never able to do anything, go anywhere.'

Bradman's phenomenal success also created jealousies among team-mates, who watched from close quarters as he was showered with financial gifts and public acclaim. On the night of 11 July 1930, Bradman was given £1,000 by an appreciative Australian businessman; rather than take his colleagues out to dinner, as they suggested, Bradman – who had always been reserved – spent the evening in his hotel room, writing his diary and letters. At the end of that tour, he travelled across Australia separately from them – at the instigation of his employer, a sports equipment manufacturer – and was feted all the way.

This disaffection was strongest among a group of players – Jack Fingleton, GRIMMETT, Stan McCabe, Ernest McCormick and O'Reilly – all of Irish origin, all Roman Catholic and mostly of a different political persuasion to Bradman, who was a Protestant and essentially a patriot and monarchist. He was, too, virtually teetotal and a non-smoker. This group suspected it was discriminated against by Bradman, although it was strongly represented in the Australia team for most of his career. Rumours of a rift marred his first series as captain in 1936–37; it was a rift that not only existed but was never healed. Alan Fairfax voiced the concerns: 'The boys in the Australian team feel that they are not getting a fair break from the crowd. Bradman, Bradman, all is Bradman . . .' When he was out second ball in his last Test innings, four runs short of assuring himself of a Test average of 100, O'Reilly and Fingleton, in the Oval press box, could not conceal their delight.

And, of course, Bradman was so good that he prompted the most dangerous form of leg-theory devised: Bodyline, fast bowling directed on the line of the batsman's body with a ring of close leg-side fielders, plus one or two on the boundary. Inspired by his clear dislike of the short-pitched delivery when the ball was 'flying' at the Oval in 1930, the strategy achieved its aim in Australia in 1932–33, Bradman's average, previously in excess of 100 in Test cricket, being kept below 60 (still more than all but one player – Eddie Paynter – on either side) and England winning the series 4–1. With a bowler of pace and accuracy such as England possessed in Larwood, it placed the batsman in obvious physical danger and was immediately condemned and soon outlawed, but for one series it was carried out with ruthless determination by Douglas Jardine, the England captain, who instructed his players to refer to Bradman as 'the little bastard'.

Bradman, who moved to Sydney from the New South Wales country as a youngster ignorant of the harsher ways of the world and ill prepared for stardom, became bitter that not everyone could enjoy the success and good fortune of others, and wary of people's motives. To protect himself from criticism – which he never took well – he exhibited a dourness and ruthlessness that was alien to his younger self. His move in 1934 from Sydney to Adelaide, where he joined a stockbroking firm willing to train him and give him time off to play, was partly done to escape acrimonious relationships within the New South Wales cricket world.

The Bodyline affair unsettled him for many months; some say the mental scars never healed. The risk of injury, the underlying personal malice and the damage Bodyline did to diplomatic relations between Australia and Britain seriously undermined his health and contributed to his one spell of lost form, early in the 1934 tour of England (he recovered to score 304 and 244 in the last two Tests). He was afflicted with headaches, impaired vision and appendicitis, which jeopardized his life and forced him out of cricket for a year. And he would suffer recurring ill health, of a nature not always fully explained.

The pressures were all the greater because, when he emerged in the late 1920s, Australian nationalism was on the rise, the Depression was biting and sport – the national cricket team in particular – was the chief vehicle of popular self-realization. The public desperately wanted a hero, and Bradman, the fifth child of a wool trader and carpenter, whose grandfather had emigrated from Suffolk to escape agricultural recession, suited them perfectly. Throughout his career he drew huge audiences to any Test, Sheffield Shield or grade match in which he played, and many of them would leave the ground the instant he was out. When a school inspector visited the New South Wales outback in 1936 and asked a class who was the greatest man alive, every child but one gave the answer: 'Don Bradman.'

For many years Bradman was known as 'the Bowral boy' – a reflection of his youth and size. When he first played for Australia in 1928–29, and in his second match became the then youngest maker of a Test century, eight years after making his first hundred

of any sort, he still looked like a boy. It was an impression reinforced by his faltering running between the wickets and his lack of
inches. When O'Reilly had first encountered him, three years earlier
in a match between Bowral and Wingello, Bradman's shortness was
the first thing he noticed. 'What struck me most about him was the
difficulty he seemed to be having in taking normal steps to the
wicket,' O'Reilly recalled. 'His pads seemed to reach right up to his
navel.' But they did not stop him scoring 234 – or two triple-
centuries during that 1925–26 season, when he was given a net at
the Sydney Cricket Ground and signed to play grade cricket for St
George, the first rung of the ladder leading to the national side. As
Hammond discovered, the lack of stature was misleading. Even in
his mature years, Bradman remained 'the little feller'.

But he never allowed any of these disadvantages to impair his
progress, if one discounts the hectic brilliance in which he indulged
directly after Bodyline. Indeed, as the years went by, and aided
by the unstinting support of his wife Jessie, he became ever more
determined to stay at the top. His comeback after the war, having
not held a bat for five years and following an illness which
led to depression, was an almost superhuman act of will-power.
'His whole career demonstrates his merciless will to win,' said
Hammond. 'Not many of us, I think, have the ruthless capacity of a
Bradman to perfect such a power as he did.'

Bradman was motivated partly by a desire to give himself and his
family financial security in the wake of the Depression. When he
was offered work outside cricket, he always considered it carefully,
and was fortunate to be offered jobs that enabled him to continue
playing. After his active cricketing days were over, he worked ably
as an administrator and journalist but gratefully sought the
anonymity of a provincial businessman, retiring from his stockbroking firm – once financial security had been achieved – at the
early age of forty-five, to play golf and lead the life of a normal
family man. There were special demands. His first son had died
shortly after birth, before the war; his second son, John, was
afflicted with polio as a teenager, and his daughter, Shirley, with
cerebral palsy.

Although Bradman's run-scoring touched new heights, there were
many aspects to his game similar to those of his predecessors. Like
Hobbs, the rapidity of his thought and footwork – he had small feet
– meant he was invariably in the right position to play a stroke. His

placement and timing were also superb, but that, too, could have been said of several players dating back to Grace. Nor was Bradman the first to create an aura of invincibility, from the unconcerned stillness of his stance to the impish grin that occasionally spread over the otherwise grim set of his face. The solitariness of sport as a child, and the game he devised with cricket stump and golf ball at around the age of ten mirrored the behaviour of the young Hobbs.

There were some crucial differences, however. Bradman not only always got into position to play a stroke, he usually had in mind an aggressive one. This was the key to his fast scoring, which was essential if a win was to be obtained in time-limit matches in England, even Tests extended to four days from the time of his first visit. He also used an unorthodox grip, as though holding a baseball bat (which was why he offended the purists by not lifting up the bat straight), the result being that when he played his favoured cuts or hooks, he rolled his tremendously strong wrists and kept the ball on the ground. The grip made off-driving especially difficult.

Several critics actually thought him technically inferior to one or two contemporaries. His unwillingness to modify his approach on sticky wickets attracted particular opprobrium – though in Australia such surfaces tended to be unplayable – and led to claims that, on all types of pitch, there had been more complete batsmen, such as TRUMPER and Hobbs (though the latter admitted that had wanted Bradman to master a sticky wicket, he could have done so). Bradman was also criticized for not being as elegant as the likes of Trumper, Woolley, Jackson or Hammond, whose praises were regularly sung by the group of disaffected Irish Catholics. In 1978, Fingleton wrote a biography of Trumper in which the main theme was the case for him being considered better than Bradman. Bradman claimed he was unconcerned. 'Style as style I never studied,' he said. 'My batting was dictated by the need of the moment.'

What singled out Bradman was a mind as sharp and analytical as any cricket has seen. He never stopped dissecting the game – six years into his first-class career he took, and passed, an umpiring examination – and his inquiries persuaded him there were no barriers to what could be achieved and no reason to show mercy towards an opponent. Changes in the Laws that affected other batsmen – the stumps were increased in size in 1931 and the leg-before rule broadened in 1937, to the consternation of some

back-foot players such as Sutcliffe – had no discernible effect on
Bradman. His batting was likened to a machine, but it was only his
mind that operated with the efficiency of a computer; his batting
was creatively tailored to the particular match. 'Cool logic was his
great secret,' Hutton said. Confronted with Bodyline, Bradman
devised a method of stepping back to leg to make room to play the
ball through the off side, and it worked well. 'You know, we nearly
didn't do it,' Jardine said many years later. 'The little man was
bloody good.'

Bradman himself said that it was his power of concentration that
set him apart from others who were potentially as good, and set
him apart it certainly did. Of the ten Test series in which he played
from 1930 onwards, his average was the highest for either side in
five of them and second-highest in four; he lay as low as third only
in his last series, against England in 1948, when he averaged 72.57
to Arthur Morris's 87.00 and Sid Barnes's 82.25. The only player to
exceed his average more than once was Ponsford, both times by
insignificant margins. Bradman also topped the national averages in
each of the four years he visited England.

Before the Second World War, Headley, a back-foot player who
was also small and nimble on his feet, came closest to matching
Bradman's figures, averaging 66.71 and scoring ten centuries in
nineteen Tests. The first great black West Indian batsman, Headley
was almost entirely self-taught and grew up in cricketing isolation
in Jamaica, well away from the southern Caribbean islands where
most of the best early players came from, among them George
Challenor, whose career had run parallel to Hobbs's. Headley was
about to leave for the United States to pursue dentistry when he first
made his mark as a cricketer at the age of eighteen: he stayed, but
his opportunities were limited. Had West Indies cricket been more
advanced – he often held his side's batting together – he would have
had a better chance to stake his claim. In the three years after the
war, Bradman's nearest rivals were Morris, who averaged 74.10 in
fourteen Tests, and Compton, 67.51 from nineteen Tests, which
embraced a spell of eight centuries in eleven matches; Bradman
averaged 105.72 from fifteen.

Despite the coolness of their personal relationship, Bradman and
O'Reilly had a deep mutual respect for each other's abilities. After
Bradman moved to South Australia, they shared some terrific duels
and O'Reilly, unlike Fingleton and Grimmett, conceded that

Bradman was the greatest batsman not only of his own era but of any other. After the Second World War, BEDSER – working on the advice of O'Reilly – had Bradman caught at backward short-leg in three successive Test innings in 1948, but even though Bradman admitted he was not then quite the player he once was, he soon came up with an answer, by eliminating the leg glance.

To some, Bradman's supremacy remained baffling. His father George, who took him to Sydney in 1921 to watch Macartney in a Test, could provide few clues. 'I would describe his batting as practically a freak,' he said. 'There is no other term which adequately describes it.'

Bradman's first-class record: 234 matches, 28,067 runs, average 95.14. **Test record:** 52 matches, 6,996 runs, average 99.94.

Bradman's Coopers & Lybrand ratings 1930–48: 1930–39: 2, 1, 1, 1, 1, 1, 2, 1, 1, 1; 1946–48: 1, 1, 1.
Other leaders: 1930: H. Sutcliffe (Eng). 1936: G.A. Headley (WI).

Record against Number One bowlers:
v Grimmett 1930–32: 2 matches, Bradman 3 innings, 281 runs, average 93.66 (one century, highest score 258); Grimmett did not take his wicket.
v O'Reilly 1932–46: 10 matches, Bradman 17 innings, 1,194 runs, average 91.84 (four centuries, highest score 251 not out); O'Reilly took his wicket six times.
v Lindwall 1946–49: 1 match, Bradman 2 innings, 133 runs, average 66.50 (one century, highest score 123); Lindwall did not take his wicket.

◎ WILLIAM JOSEPH O'REILLY (Australia)

Number One: 1932–46

Born: White Cliffs, New South Wales, 20 December 1905; died: Sydney, 6 October 1992. Career: 1927–46.

For most of his Test career – which spanned the years from 1932 to 1946, with an interruption for the Second World War – Bill O'Reilly was the world's best bowler. Among his most outspoken admirers

were two of his Australian captains, Vic Richardson and
BRADMAN, both of whom not only handled him in the field but
batted against his unique blend of leg-spinners, top-spinners and
googlies delivered with a fiery eye and fierce lick.

Each went further. Richardson, writing in his autobiography in
1967, thought him the best bowler he had seen; on O'Reilly's death,
Bradman said he was the best he had faced or seen. As for O'Reilly
himself, he seemed to care less about his reputation than keeping
warm his animosity towards all batsmen. He was a bowler down to
his bootstraps.

Comparisons were often drawn between O'Reilly and BARNES,
partly because O'Reilly challenged the assumption that Barnes was
the greatest bowler the game had seen. But they had much else in
common besides being phenomenal exponents of their craft. Both
were tall, O'Reilly standing 6ft 1in, an inch more than Barnes; both
deployed the leg-break to devastating effect and commanded practically every known ball (Maurice Leyland said that the first over he
faced from O'Reilly contained eight different deliveries, each posing
a test); and both were uncompromising spirits and competitive to
an extreme. Not for nothing was O'Reilly known as 'Tiger'.
'Hitting Bill O'Reilly for four was like disturbing a hive of bees,'
Bradman once said.

Richardson had seen Barnes's great performance at Melbourne in
1911 and placed O'Reilly ahead of him; Bradman never saw Barnes
but gave O'Reilly the nod anyway, partly because O'Reilly had the
googly in his armoury – though there was another reason. 'I never
saw Barnes, so I could not speak of how he bowled the leg-spinner,'
Bradman told Cardus. 'I only know that O'Reilly bowls it as well as
I can imagine anybody bowling it. It couldn't possibly be nastier.'
Herbie Taylor batted against both, though before O'Reilly was at
his best, and placed Barnes first; in the late 1960s, he wrote that
O'Reilly was the greatest leg-break and googly bowler in history.
Wisden went further in its obituary: O'Reilly was 'probably the
greatest spin bowler the game has ever produced'.

O'Reilly was slower than Barnes in pace, but for a spinner he was
quick – near medium pace, which added considerably to the
batsman's difficulties. Indeed, by temperament and physique
O'Reilly was ideally suited to fast bowling. He was tall, well co-
ordinated and strong, possessing stamina, long arms and big hands.
His height was a key factor in his success, for it enabled him to

extract bounce from pitches that offered him little assistance; HAMMOND wrote late in his career that he had never faced a slow bowler who made the ball jump more. O'Reilly also had a fast bowler's temper, which flared at the first irritation – a sign, it was supposed, of his Irish roots – and his repertoire included a surprise faster ball. Unlike Mailey and GRIMMETT, the googly was his stock ball; the leg-break he rolled rather than spun, because had he spun it at his pace, it would have turned too much.

O'Reilly's great strength was that he acted as chief destroyer and principal defensive weapon. His control and accuracy kept the batsman in check, while his variations, which were the product of a searching intelligence, lured them into errors. His pace made it especially difficult for batsmen to get to the pitch of the ball. Charles Barnett was asked by Gubby Allen to 'chase' O'Reilly during England's tour of 1936–37 and found it impossible; Bradman attempted something similar in the dying stages of a Sheffield Shield match three years later, with only limited success. When Grimmett – more subdued but no less persistent, and demanding completely different responses – was operating at the other end, there was no respite for the unfortunate batsmen.

Unlike Grimmett, O'Reilly was identified as an outstanding prospect at an early age, though by the late 1920s googly bowling was held in higher regard than ever before. He learned the game playing with his brothers in the family garden – he was the fourth of seven children – but at school, athletics took precedence (the hop-skip-jump is said to have contributed to the rhythm of his run-up, which was a rampage of flailing arms and legs). Having moved from the country to Sydney in 1924 to follow his father into teaching, he was thrust into the New South Wales practice squad on the evidence of one match for North Sydney, which proved to be the start of a career in grade cricket that saw him capture 962 wickets at 9.44. He made his first-class debut in 1927–28, but after qualifying as a teacher was sent to work in rural schools for three years, and his opportunities to play Sheffield Shield cricket disappeared.

Returning to Sydney in time for the 1931–32 season, O'Reilly began it fighting to command a place in the New South Wales team – he was dropped for one match, but Reg Bettington, an admirer, found a pretext for standing down so that O'Reilly could play – but finished up a member of the Test side in the series against South

Africa and being entrusted with 82 overs on his debut. They cost only 155 runs and Australia never thought of dropping him.

O'Reilly attributed his meteoric rise to his ability to marshal his talents. He always practised hard, and during his enforced three-year absence developed his googly. He had never received much coaching and consistently ignored advice from those who sought to modify his technique, happy to stick to his chest-on delivery, his unspun leg-breaks and his peculiar grip (thus alienating Mailey). Experience also taught him to reject the received wisdom that a leg-spinner should bowl to a leg trap, and he changed his line to attack the stumps. Bettington, who occasionally captained him at New South Wales, liked to turn heads in these early days by pointing out O'Reilly as 'the greatest bowler in the world'. Very soon he was.

England's tour of Australia in 1932–33 was consumed by the dispute over Bodyline but – little noticed though it was – it was during this season that O'Reilly blossomed into the great bowler he had promised to be. It was arguably the finest season of his career. Even before he bowled Australia to their one victory in Melbourne, his performances in the Sheffield Shield demonstrated that he had few rivals in Australia, Grimmett perhaps the only one. At Melbourne he claimed ten for 129 from 59 overs, taking advantage of a wearing pitch on the fourth day to undermine England's attempts to score 208. Though Grimmett played, he was hardly used. After the game, Warner, joint manager of the MCC team, acclaimed O'Reilly as 'a really great bowler'.

For the rest of the series, O'Reilly was the mainstay of Australia's attack and, in all, bowled almost as many overs as any two bowlers from each side put together. His 27 wickets cost 26.81, a performance that only Larwood, for England, could better: his 33 wickets cost 19.51, statistically a more impressive effort and, of course, influential in deciding the destiny of the Ashes. In this series, Larwood, with his fast, balanced run-up, long arms and strong shoulders, combined speed with accuracy to a degree not matched for generations – and certainly not again by himself. He needed conditions to suit him, which they did to perfection in Australia; on over-prepared pitches in England in 1930 he was expensive and ineffective, as he might have been again four years later had he not by then been forced out of the game. The Bodyline tour saw his only outstanding Test series and he was assisted by a strategy, though not of his own invention, soon to be outlawed.

O'Reilly played four further full Test series and in each one claimed more than twenty victims. In all but one – the tour of South Africa in 1935–36, when the pitches were more to the liking of Grimmett – he was Australia's leading wicket-taker and sported the lowest average of the regular bowlers. He was an outstanding success on his first tour of England in 1934, county players who encountered him as he ran through sides before the first Test hailing him as the best they had seen. Supported by Grimmett, he won the first Test for Australia with ten minutes to spare by taking seven for 54 on a wearing surface. 'Grimmett and O'Reilly overshadowed all else,' Fender wrote. 'I do not think that I have ever seen finer bowling, especially when it is remembered that they were slow bowlers and not on a wet wicket.'

O'Reilly was a master at bowling on unhelpful pitches. On a lifeless pitch at Old Trafford later in the 1934 series, he took the wickets of Cyril Walters, Bob Wyatt and Hammond in the space of four balls; and in three of the four Tests played on his second tour of England in 1938 – when he was left inconsolable at the loss, on and off the pitch, of Grimmett – he bowled magnificently in heartbreaking conditions, nowhere more so than at the Oval, where England batted over fifteen hours and topped 900 but O'Reilly's figures (three for 178 from 85 overs) remained respectable. When the chance came to bowl on something offering assistance – as it did at Headingley that year – he choked England to death in producing probably the most complete performance of his career. He took ten for 122 and Australia's five-wicket victory ensured they retained the Ashes.

As that tour finished, O'Reilly was being described as among the greatest of all bowlers. Of contemporaries, probably his closest rival was Grimmett, but during their four-year partnership O'Reilly was generally considered superior, a view shared by Grimmett himself (O'Reilly sometimes gave the palm to Grimmett). England's most consistently successful bowler was Hedley Verity, Rhodes's successor at Yorkshire and certainly the best left-arm spinner. He was persistent and parsimonious, and deadly on rain-affected pitches in particular – he took fourteen wickets on the last day of the Lord's Test in 1934 – and county matches in general. He took Bradman's wicket more times in Tests than any other bowler – eight. He was much less successful, though, in Australia.

England also possessed the leading off-spinner, Tom Goddard of

Gloucestershire, whose misfortune it was to play at a time when this type of bowling was out of fashion; he was nearly thirty-five when the leg-before rule was experimentally broadened in 1935, and nearly fifty when off-spinners returned to favour in Test cricket. His record in eight matches for England was reasonable and he took more wickets than any other bowler of his type in history.

Players from the younger cricketing countries were also starting to make their mark. West Indies possessed two outstanding fast bowlers in Martindale and Constantine, as did India with Amar Singh and Mohammad Nissar. Amar Singh was described by Hammond as 'as dangerous an opening bowler as I have ever seen'. New Zealand boasted the strongly built Jack Cowie, who made only nine Test appearances. 'Had he been an Australian,' *Wisden* commented in 1938, 'he might have been termed a wonder of the age.'

O'Reilly benefited from the stability that came to him when he married in 1933 and, a year later, acquired a job at Sydney Grammar School which did not interfere with his cricket. He had earlier threatened to retire from his previous job because of family pressures. Six years later he became secretary to a tile manufacturing company and might have continued to play for several years after the Second World War had his left knee not given way. Unfit for the series against England in 1946–47, he retired having one year earlier played his last Test, taking eight cheap wickets as New Zealand – in totalling 42 and 54 – just managed to creep past O'Reilly's age in both innings. He subsequently wrote as a cricket columnist for the Sydney *Morning Herald* until 1988, giving vent to his always forthright opinions.

Few batsmen mastered O'Reilly. He had difficulty with Leyland, whose left-handedness placed him at an advantage and who scored four centuries in five Tests against O'Reilly; and two Australians, 'Jack' Badcock and Lindsay Hassett, seemed to have O'Reilly's measure in state matches, Hassett treating him with near contempt at times. But a measure of O'Reilly's stature was that he gave Hammond more trouble than any other bowler, dismissing him seven times for 26 or less in Tests.

O'Reilly's greatest duels were reserved for Bradman. Their first meeting occurred when both were teenagers in December 1925, when O'Reilly's family lived in Wingello and Bradman's in Bowral – towns fifteen miles apart in the New South Wales outback – and they opposed each other in a match played on successive Saturdays at alternate venues. 'He didn't have it all his own way, let me tell you,' O'Reilly remembered. 'Well, not for the first few overs, anyway.' On the first day, in Bowral, Bradman scored 234 not out, but the next week O'Reilly bowled him round his legs first ball.

Playing much of their cricket alongside each other for New South Wales and Australia, they did not meet in a first-class match until October 1936, when the Australian team that had won in South Africa several months earlier without the unwell Bradman played a team captained by him in Sydney. The match was played in a festival atmosphere and Bradman scored a double century, but O'Reilly was kept from bowling at him so that the crowd could see him bat.

They subsequently experienced fiercer encounters when New South Wales met South Australia, for whom Bradman now played. Perhaps the best came at Adelaide in December 1937. O'Reilly bowled wonderfully and took fourteen wickets – including nine for 41 in the first innings – to dismiss South Australia for 225 and 191, but of those Bradman made 91 and 62 before O'Reilly removed him both times and New South Wales won by only 33 runs. 'When Bradman batted there was no relaxing,' Johnnie Moyes wrote. 'Every ball was charged with hostility, filled with venom and calculated to destroy . . . Sometimes the batsman prevailed; sometimes the bowler won the duel . . . It was a battle for mastery, one champion against another.'

O'Reilly's first-class record: 135 matches, 774 wickets, average 16.60. **Test record:** 27 matches, 144 wickets, average 22.59.

O'Reilly's Coopers & Lybrand ratings 1933–46: 1933–39: –, 2, 1, 2, 1, 1, 1; 1946: 1.
Other leaders: 1933: H. Ironmonger (Aus). 1934: H. Verity (Eng). 1936: C.V. Grimmett (Aus).

Record against Number One batsmen:
v Bradman 1932–46: 10 matches, Bradman 17 innings, 1,194 runs, average 91.84 (four centuries, highest score 251 not out); O'Reilly took his wicket six times.

Ⓒ RAYMOND RUSSELL LINDWALL (Australia)

Number One: 1946–50 and 1954–56

Born: Mascot, New South Wales, 3 October 1921; died: Brisbane, Queensland, 23 June 1996. Career: 1941–62.

Ray Lindwall was one of cricket's most natural athletes. He possessed a superb physique and, though he is chiefly remembered as a great fast bowler, excelled at several sports, including rugby league, athletics, swimming and golf. He was also an accomplished batsman, scoring his first century at twelve, the same age as did BRADMAN.

Though he was physically gifted, bowling cost Lindwall pain and effort, and he worked religiously at keeping himself in peak condition. The extent to which he succeeded – despite contracting malaria and hepatitis – is borne out by the facts that he not only became the first genuine fast bowler to take 100 Test wickets but went on past 200 as well. Time and again he defied predictions that he was finished. Indeed, by earning a recall at the remarkable age for a fast bowler of thirty-seven, he overtook GRIMMETT as Australia's leading wicket-taker. As the fastest bowler at the dawn of the nuclear age, he was christened by the press 'Atomic Ray'.

Lindwall possessed the consistency of performance and fitness that eluded so many fast bowlers before him. These included GREGORY, to whom he was compared because of the shock and fear their speed and bouncers generated as cricketing hostilities were hesitatingly renewed after a world war; and Larwood, whose Test career ended prematurely because of recriminations over Bodyline. Cardus preferred to liken Lindwall to McDonald: 'the most hostile and artistic fast bowlers I have ever seen'. Richie Benaud wrote in 1977 that Lindwall was technically the best fast bowler he had seen.

Lindwall's youthful enthusiasm for fast bowling was kindled by the sight of Larwood bowling in Sydney in 1932–33, and his smooth, purposeful run-up and delivery had a passing resemblance to those of his idol. He was not as quick as Larwood – though his terrific speed was easily enough to leave several English batsmen nursing injuries on the 1948 tour, including Compton, who top-edged a ball into his forehead during the Old Trafford Test – but more consistently fast and accurate, and more sophisticated. He could get something out of an unhelpful pitch.

Lindwall had all the chief variations, prize among them a glorious late outswinger, the product of a low arm action that also made the ball skid disconcertingly. His bouncer was devilish, coming with the same action as his slower ball, and he was a master tactician, always demanding that the batsman play a shot: of his first-class victims, 60 per cent were bowled and leg-before. 'He was an artist in a trade which all too frequently relies on brute force,' Trevor Bailey recalled near the end of his own career. 'I have never encountered a genuine fast bowler who moved the ball in the air as much, and as late, as Lindwall . . . He was the most devastating exploiter of the new ball.'

Lindwall's class was apparent from an early age, and but for the Second World War, in which he served in the Army Signals, he would have played for Australia before the age of twenty-four. He received the best help in his early days. Born in a Sydney suburb as the youngest of five children of Swedish and Irish grandparents, Lindwall's upbringing was full of hardship and misfortune. His mother died when he was seven and his father when he was seventeen. But sport was one solace and here he had the advantage of living in the same neighbourhood as O'REILLY, who was his first captain at the St George club and helped him hone his technique by the revolutionary means of photographic analysis. Then, on his first tour of England in 1948, Lindwall played under Bradman, who took care not to overwork him and steered him away from controversy over the 'drag' of his back foot by altering his run-up. Lindwall was not alone in using 'drag' – which enabled the bowler to release the ball further down the pitch – but his speed made the matter contentious.

When O'Reilly's knee injury ruled him out of the series against England in 1946–47, the identity of his successor was not immediately apparent – but it was by the end of England's tour. The previous season, Lindwall had taken 33 wickets in seven matches for New South Wales and been rewarded with a tour place to New Zealand, where he made his debut for Australia in a match not accorded Test status until three years later. He was an automatic selection at home to England and although chicken-pox restricted his role in the first Test and ruled him out of the second, he claimed the wicket of HUTTON early in the third. In the fourth he took three wickets in four balls to round off England's first innings, and in the fifth claimed seven for 63 on a perfect Sydney pitch. He generated such speed that he knocked the bat from Compton's hand.

He continued to make early breakthroughs against India a year later, when he took seven for 38 in the Test at Adelaide, and again during the early weeks of the 1948 tour of England, prompting TATE to hail him as already Larwood's equal. Assisted by the availability of the new ball every 55 overs, Lindwall was a constant menace to England and ended the series with 27 wickets at 19.62; on the whole tour he claimed 86 at 15.69. The highlight was his six for 20 in 99 balls at the Oval as England were skittled for 52 all out – their lowest total at home. The pitch was sodden but the conditions humid. Australia's formidable attack helped them go through the tour unbeaten, but *Wisden* identified Lindwall's speed as the 'biggest single weapon' on either side. It also said he 'must be placed permanently in the gallery of great fast bowlers'.

He maintained his position as the most feared bowler in the world for the next two years. The South Africans were in trepidation at the prospect of his arrival in 1949–50 and prepared by practising against baseball pitchers, though in the event, hampered by groin trouble, Lindwall never touched top speed. Even so, only Keith Miller, Lindwall's new-ball partner, approached him for effectiveness.

Miller, more upright in delivery and capable of making the ball lift disconcertingly, rarely sustained his performances as Lindwall did, nor did he possess as much subtlety. Bill Johnston, who acted as first change, was an efficient left-arm seamer but never emerged from their shadow. No other country was remotely as well endowed with match-winning bowlers – which explains Australia winning 26 of their 36 Tests after the war. England's best bowlers were Doug Wright, a potentially devastating but often expensive leg-spinner, and BEDSER, who appeared weighed down by his heavy workload until he comprehensively outbowled – and supplanted – Lindwall in Australia in 1950–51.

Lindwall remained an outstanding bowler during Bedser's pomp. He wreaked havoc at home on West Indies in 1951–52 and South Africa a year later, and bowled superbly in England in 1953 – Compton said the bowling of Lindwall and Miller at Lord's was the fastest he faced. Lindwall's pace diminished slightly, but he more than compensated for this by further developing his skills.

When Bedser fell away during England's tour of Australia in 1954–55, Lindwall was still as dangerous a bowler as any bar the briefly brilliant Frank Tyson, though Ian Johnson was criticized for using him as a stock bowler. Lindwall's fourteen wickets in the four Tests he played in that series – he missed one through injury – included Hutton twice and MAY four times. On Australia's triumphant tour of West Indies that followed, he and Miller formed a deadly spearhead for the last time, taking twenty wickets apiece and bowling with speed and intelligence. It was the first time the West Indians had encountered them since their torrid experiences in Australia. 'Ray was not appreciably slower although our pitches were not so grassy,' Everton Weekes said. 'Ray and Keith bowled as fast. Unbelievable. Sure, they were four years older than when at their peak; but they were fast.' A few months later, and now playing for Queensland, Lindwall remained among the leading wicket-takers in the Sheffield Shield. His final tour of England in 1956 was spoiled by injuries and sluggardly pitches, but he gave an outstanding exhibition of stamina in the Lord's Test.

Tyson, who was also inspired by Larwood, rose swiftly on the back of his gift for bowling remarkably quickly and made his England debut in 1954 only weeks before departing for the winter tour of Australia. After a disastrous performance in the first Test there, he reduced his run-up and, finding a captivating rhythm as a result, caused a sensation with his speed and accuracy. In four Tests he took 27 wickets and generated such pace that batsmen were still bringing down their bats as stumps were sent flying.

Many who saw Tyson in Australia, and occasionally elsewhere, said that they never saw faster bowling. He destroyed South Africa with a spell of five for five in seven overs at Trent Bridge in 1955, in one of only two Tests he played that summer because of injury, but could do little with the ball on the lifeless Northampton square and his career quickly foundered. As with Larwood, Tyson's peak barely extended beyond one triumphant tour.

Many contemporaries believed Lindwall to be the greatest of all fast bowlers. TRUEMAN described him in 1983 as 'the greatest fast bowler that's ever lived – a quick bowler with the accuracy of a medium-pacer'. Compton agreed. Hutton, significantly, rated Lindwall the best bowler he faced, although he was also troubled by the unpredictability of Miller; attempting to keep Lindwall at bay when the latter was armed with helpful conditions and a new ball was not a fair contest, Hutton felt. 'Whatever defence I had, it was useless at these moments,' he wrote. Hutton averaged almost 60 in 33 Test innings in opposition to Lindwall, who dismissed him seven times.

Lindwall and Miller attracted opprobrium for what was regarded as their intimidatory use of bouncers (or 'bumpers' as they were then known). Hutton was their main target, but Evelton Weekes also faced a sustained barrage on a grassy pitch at Sydney in 1951–52 that was condemned by most observers, including O'Reilly, who criticized the umpires for not stepping in. The West Indians maintained Weekes received twenty-five bouncers in forty balls.

The bouncer was invariably an issue during Lindwall's heyday – his unexpected and unexplained omission from the last Test in South Africa in 1949–50 was rumoured to be part of a 'peace pact' between Hassett and Dudley Nourse – and roused the ire of crowds, reviving memories of Bodyline. Lindwall was sometimes known as 'killer'; his tactics and attitude towards opponents on the field certainly revealed the killer instinct of an otherwise generous and good-natured man, and, by making the bouncer an accepted part of a bowler's armoury, set the tone for the future. Neither he nor Miller, though, targeted tail-end batsmen; that tactic came much later.

Lindwall, who gave up a job in an engineer's office in Sydney in 1949 because he could not get enough time off to concentrate on cricket, made little money out of the game. He later worked for a wine distributor, and in retirement, when he maintained his involvement in the sport through coaching, journalism and selection, opened a flower shop with his wife. A testimonial for him was organized by friends in 1993. He died on what would have been Hutton's eightieth birthday.

Lindwall's first-class record: 228 matches, 794 wickets, average 21.35. **Test record:** 61 matches, 228 wickets, average 23.03.

Lindwall's Coopers & Lybrand ratings 1947–50: 4, 1, 1, 1. 1955: 1
Other leader: 1947: J.A. Cowie (NZ). Lindwall was also top in 1953 and 1954.

Record against Number One batsmen:
v Bradman 1946–49: 1 match, Bradman 2 innings, 133 runs, average 66.50 (one century, highest score 123); Lindwall did not take his wicket.

v Hutton 1949–50 and 1954–55: 3 matches, Hutton 5 innings, 118 runs, average 23.60 (highest score 42); Lindwall took his wicket once.

v May 1955–56: they did not oppose each other in first-class matches.

LEONARD HUTTON (England)

Number One: 1949–55

Born: Fulneck, Pudsey, Yorkshire, 23 June 1916; died: Kingston-upon-Thames, Surrey, 6 September 1990. Career: 1934–60.

When BRADMAN's final match ended on 8 March 1949, who was there to take up his mantle? No one with such unconfoundable credentials; but with the newer Test countries now also producing top-quality players, there was a broader range of candidates than ever before.

Within a strong team, Australia had nurtured two accomplished left-handers, Morris and the twenty-year-old Neil Harvey (the first of numerous exceptional youngsters to be dubbed 'the new Bradman'), and a fine right-hander, Hassett. All three had taken toll of thin India and England attacks, Harvey with quick footwork and blistering strokeplay. West Indies boasted Headley's inheritors, the three Ws – Weekes, Frank Worrell and Clyde Walcott – who also made runs against England and India and were all under twenty-five years of age.

South Africa's captain was the short, powerfully built Nourse, thirty-eight years old and nearing the end of an illustrious career; before the war, he played the highest Test innings against an attack containing GRIMMETT and O'REILLY: 231 in five hours at Johannesburg in 1935–36. India had Vijay Hazare, Merchant's great rival, who built large scores with a sound defence and unruffled mind; and New Zealand boasted Bert Sutcliffe and Martin Donnelly, two accomplished left-handers approaching their peaks, though Donnelly would be soon lost to business. England possessed the raffish Middlesex pair Compton and Bill Edrich, who had ensured themselves of lasting fame with their record-breaking deeds in 1947, but also the pragmatic and more dependable Len Hutton. He was thirty-two, as was Edrich; Compton was thirty.

All these players, except Nourse, promised much, but Hutton had achieved most in the more demanding spheres of action since first playing for Yorkshire at the age of seventeen and England at twenty-one. And the day after Bradman's last first-class match, England completed a winning Test series in South Africa in which Hutton outshone every other batsman, both in terms of runs scored and refinement of technique. He would do so on several more occasions in the following six years, amply demonstrating his superiority over all comers at home and overseas.

During this period, there were a handful of real tests for a batsman. One was dealing with the bouncers of LINDWALL and Miller; another, dealing with Sonny Ramadhin and Alf Valentine, the West Indies' spin wizards; a third, coping with the best English bowlers in typical 'English' conditions.

Arguably, only Hutton passed all three. Morris and Harvey came poor seconds to him in subsequent Ashes series, Morris often failing to survive the new ball: he became known as BEDSER's 'bunny'. Harvey, a big-match player and Australia's best batsman from Bradman's retirement until his own in 1963, failed against West Indies in 1951–52 and, although his record against Lindwall and Miller in Sheffield Shield cricket was good, relied to a great extent on his phenomenal eye, often playing across the line and against the spin. As he aged his form declined sharply, as some had predicted it would: Freddie Brown described him as the worst great player he ever saw. Hassett began life as a strokemaker but never quite fulfilled his potential after the Second World War, disappointing even his admirers with his lack of adventure in Tests.

Weekes, Worrell and Walcott scored heavily in England in 1950, in unusually favourable conditions, but fared less well seven years later when the challenge was greater; they all failed in varying degrees against Lindwall and Miller in Australia. The powerfully built Walcott was a formidable hitter on Caribbean pitches, as ten centuries in twelve Tests there between 1953 and 1955 confirmed. 'Back in his own islands,' said *Wisden* at this time, 'Walcott proceeded to perform such remarkable feats that he challenged Hutton for the title of the world's best batsman.' But against all bowling, the quick-footed Weekes was the more complete player, possessing application, aggression and the vital killer instinct. Bradman said Weekes was the best West Indian batsman he had seen – better than Headley – and Bedser and Benaud thought him the most dangerous of the three. But despite feeding off each other's support, Weekes, Walcott and Worrell, who was influenced by Challenor and the most elegantly correct of the trio, failed to match the average of Hutton, who was so less well aided, in the Caribbean in 1953–54.

Edrich was so embarrassed by Ramadhin and Valentine in 1950 that it marked the beginning of the end of his Test career, while Compton's powers were greatly diminished after 1949 by a knee injury, which restricted him to one Test against Ramadhin and Valentine at their best. Compton possessed a superb defence, but while cricket was a hard-headed business to Hutton, it was only ever a game to Compton. He was inclined to gamble on pleasing himself and the crowd, going down the pitch to fast bowlers and taking risks to locate the gaps in the field. His trademark was the sweep, admittedly a stroke which he made relatively safe. He took four terrific Test hundreds off Lindwall and Miller in the 1940s, during which he gave free rein to his idiosyncratic genius, but never another against Australia. His contribution in the series of 1950–51 was nonexistent.

Hutton established himself as England's leading batsman during the first post-war tour of Australia in 1946–47, a fact explicitly acknowledged by HAMMOND, and Lindwall and Miller, who tried without success to unnerve him with more bouncers than they reserved for the rest of the England side put together.

It was a ferocious assault and, although Hutton coped superbly, it was resumed in England in 1948. When the battle raged fiercest at Lord's, Hutton occasionally flicked at rising balls and the selectors were prompted to drop him – much to the astonishment of the Australians – in the belief that his nerve was finally broken. He returned after just one game and in twelve subsequent Tests against Lindwall and Miller made more than 1,200 runs. In 1950–51, he averaged 88.83, over 50 more than the next player on either side; in 1953, his average of 55.37 was the only one in excess of 40. Reflecting on the first of these series, *Wisden* said of Hutton that he 'worthily earned the description of the finest present-day batsman in the world'.

Unlike his colleagues, Hutton also managed to fathom Ramadhin and Valentine in 1950, though too late to save the series; the 202 with which he carried his bat in the final Test was a magnificent fighting innings. Three years later, on his first tour as England captain and in the most demanding circumstances, he was instrumental in his side recovering from two matches down in the Caribbean to draw the series, scoring 169 in Georgetown and 205 in Kingston. The two innings occupied sixteen hours in sweltering heat and contained barely a false stroke.

Hutton proved himself a master of English conditions time and again. Perhaps his greatest home season was after his return from South Africa in 1949. He scored 3,429 runs, many of them with great style. It was the fourth-highest aggregate recorded in England, behind those of Compton and Edrich in 1947 (3,816 and 3,539 respectively) and Hayward in 1906 (3,518). Thinking of the uncovered pitches that they, unlike modern players, were required to play on, Compton described Hutton on his death in 1990 as 'the greatest opening batsman I have ever seen'. Hutton was also brilliant on sticky wickets, as he demonstrated at Brisbane in 1950–51, the time when O'Reilly described him as the 'finished player'.

Colin Cowdrey thought that in terms of method, Hutton was the most complete batsman he ever set eyes on: 'He was an artist, seeking and achieving technical perfection.' The verdict of *Wisden* was that Hutton was one of the two most accomplished professional batsmen produced by England. The other was HOBBS, with Hammond and Compton next in line.

Hutton shared Bradman's terrific mental resolve and apparent physical frailty. 'There was a delicacy about the way he played,' his son Richard, who also played for England, recalled. 'His strokes were due to timing rather than power. He was never robust and certainly not strong for the rigours of six-days-a-week cricket. One could think of many finer physical specimens.'

Hutton needed to be mentally tough, because England relied on him to an unhealthy degree after the war. This created a burden, as did his position as England's first professional captain this century: his appointment in 1953 was not universally approved, nor was his sometimes dour and defensive leadership style. Doubtless Hutton would have preferred, like Hobbs, to have had nothing to worry about except his batting. But he got results, regaining the Ashes in 1953 after a nineteen-year wait and masterminding their retention in Australia eighteen months later.

But the effort took its toll on his personal form and left him exhausted. Within eighteen months he announced his retirement from the England captaincy, from Test cricket, and finally, at the age of thirty-nine, from all forms of regular cricket. He had long been troubled by back pain, through standing countless hours in an unnatural position at the crease.

Hutton learned from watching Bradman. As a youthful member of the Headingley crowd he watched him score 334 in 1930, and later identified the secret of the Australian's success as his 'cool logic'. But credit for Hutton's own resolution and unshakeable self-confidence must also go to Herbert Sutcliffe, his mentor. 'I had known Herbert as long as I had known my parents and my brothers,' Hutton said. 'He led me through my early days of doubts and indecision to the promised land.'

But just as Bradman was mentally scarred by Bodyline, so too was Hutton by Lindwall and Miller. Hutton had had a bad early experience against fast bowling, being put in hospital by a blow on the head in South Africa in 1938–39. Asked why he did not hook Lindwall and Miller, he once said: 'I once got to the halfway stage, but out of the corner of my eye I could see the local hospital. So I cut it out.' In this respect he had more trouble with Miller; at least with Lindwall he had a fair idea where the ball was coming from. He much preferred facing spin bowling, although there was a theory that he had a minor weakness against off-spin. But Lindwall and Miller convinced him of the primacy of pace, and as captain he deployed fast bowlers whenever he could.

Hutton's passion for the game, and his orthodox technique, were instilled in him by Sutcliffe and his own cricket-loving family. Hutton believed that his ability came through his mother's side, though his father and brothers were good league cricketers. Fulneck contained a Moravian settlement, which ran the school and a chapel, and may have been responsible for imbuing him with his highly developed sense of responsibility. Hutton practised assidu-ously throughout his career, and by the time he was fourteen years old and playing for Pudsey St Lawrence's first XI, George Hirst, now a coach, said there was nothing more he could teach him. At that same time, Sutcliffe said Hutton was good enough to play in most county sides and predicted he would play for his country.

It was Hutton's own 'cool logic' that told him to curb his attacking instincts after the war. He did this in England's interests and it involved considerable personal sacrifice – something that his tutelage within the Yorkshire team also prepared him for. Before the war he had become a glorious strokemaker and uncritical admirer of Hammond. His cover drive was reckoned to be second only to the England captain's, and Hutton took his county colleagues aback with his seventies and eighties before lunch. In the last Test at Lord's before the war, he repeatedly drove Martindale over his head, scoring the last 96 of his 196 at better than a run a minute. He himself thought that he was then at his peak.

It was ironic, therefore, that Hutton should spend 13 hours 17 minutes scoring 364 in a timeless Test at the Oval in 1938, eclipsing the innings he had watched Bradman compile eight years earlier. It was a prodigious feat of self-control for anyone, let alone someone aged twenty-two: O'Reilly thought it the greatest innings played against him and 'for sheer concentration and dedication' unparalleled in his experience.

But in Tests after the war, Hutton only rarely escaped his self-imposed imprisonment. He did so gloriously at Sydney in 1946, when his 37 in 24 minutes against Lindwall and Miller in full cry reminded locals of TRUMPER at his finest, and at Adelaide seven weeks later lifted his restriction on hooking bouncers to potent effect. His innings of 145 at Lord's in 1953 was also laced with regal strokes. Though his strokeplay rarely lacked fluency or grace, he tended to keep his score moving by working the ball around. He played the bowling from the crease, which limited his options, especially against spin. 'He only gambled on certainties,' wrote Bailey.

Those who remembered his purple days were surprised at what they later saw and accused him of unjustified caution and setting a bad example, though another consideration to Hutton was the damage he did to his left arm in an army gymnasium during the war, when a bad break left it two inches shorter. It forced him to revise his strokeplay. 'His class was way, way above all but a tiny few in any era,' Compton wrote in 1980, 'but to me it was all the more puzzling that he remained suspicious and defensive and allowed all types of bowlers to dictate to him on good wickets, when he should have been the boss . . . As the years went by and I watched him plod against inferior attacks, I could not fathom why.' Had he made full use of his strokes, Compton argued, Hutton could have retired as 'undisputed champion' of all time.

Hutton was stung by the criticism he received at a time when he was engaged in saving Tests for England, and it may have contributed to his taciturnity – though he was by nature a sensitive, private person. His gentleness and modesty, on top of his great achievements, earned him genuine public affection and a knight-hood in 1956, but he gained small financial reward from the game as a player and created little wealth out of subsequent careers in journalism and engineering.

'I am not sure he considered himself as the world's number one,' Richard Hutton said. 'He was more conscious of his duty to those who came to watch him play and expected him to score a hundred. It was after reaching his hundred that he often started to really play and enjoy himself. England's frailty was an important factor in the way he played and he was also conscious of his reputation with the public as the holder of the world record score. He himself was not driven strongly by personal ambition.'

Hutton's first-class record: 513 matches, 40,140 runs, average 55.51. **Test record:** 79 matches, 6,971 runs, average 56.67.

Hutton's Coopers & Lybrand ratings 1949–54: 4, 3, 1, 1, 1, 1.
Other leaders: 1949: G.A. Headley (WI). 1950: A.R. Morris (Aus).

Record against Number One bowlers:
v Lindwall 1949–50 and 1954–55: 3 matches, Hutton 5 innings, 118 runs, average 23.60 (highest score 42); Lindwall took his wicket once.
v Bedser 1950–54: 5 matches, Hutton 10 innings, 646 runs, average 64.60 (four centuries, highest score 151); Bedser took his wicket four times.

⦿ ALEC VICTOR BEDSER (England)

Number One: 1950–54

Born: Reading, Berkshire, 4 July 1918. Career: 1939–60.

In the English summer of 1950, Alec Bedser looked past his best. He had carried the England attack for four years, ever since estab-lishing himself in the first post-war season of 1946 as the best fast-medium swing bowler in the country by taking 22 wickets in two Tests against India. Now he appeared to be paying the price for his punishing workload, labouring in the Tests against West Indies. He was thirty-two years old.

Yet, six months later, he was near-indisputably the finest bowler in the world. In the winter of 1950–51, Bedser toured Australia with England and found conditions unexpectedly to his liking in the Tests. He also found, in Freddie Brown, a captain prepared to nurse him for the big occasion: Bedser was to be England's strike weapon rather than simply a stock bowler. Not many bowlers could have made the change successfully, but Bedser worked tirelessly on honing his skills and possessed a superbly economical action that was capable of withstanding many more years of hard work.

Revelling in his attacking role, Bedser claimed 30 wickets at 16.06, ten of them in an heroic performance in the final Test at Melbourne, where England won their first Ashes Test for thirteen years. The Australians found him at times almost unplayable, Ron Archer saying that he had not known bowling could be so good. Although the home side won the series 4–1, it was widely agreed that England possessed the best batsman, bowler and wicketkeeper. *Wisden*'s verdict was that 'HUTTON and Bedser must be acclaimed the champions of the rubber'. LINDWALL's impact was relatively small and Australia's bowling averages were topped by Jack Iverson, a 'mystery' spin bowler whom England's best batsmen took most of the series to work out.

Bedser's success was no fluke, as he demonstrated over the next three home series. Against South Africa in 1951 he claimed another 30 wickets at 17.23; against India in 1952, 20 at 13.95; and when the Ashes were regained in 1953 he beat TATE's record by taking 39 wickets in a series against Australia, at 17.48. Bedser was the biggest single factor in England's win and his performance in the first match at Trent Bridge, where he took fourteen for 99, was described by many as one of the greatest exhibitions of bowling ever seen. Bedser himself rated it the best of his career.

He was an equally influential figure in Surrey's seven successive championships between 1952 and 1958: in each of the first six years he took more than 80 wickets at costs of less than 19. In 1952, *Wisden* remarked that 'at times he looked better than ever'.

Few bore even remote comparison. Bedser himself reckoned he was at his peak between 1950 and 1954, as did Bailey, one of seventeen players to share the new ball with him for England. During that period, Bailey wrote, 'the quality of his bowling on all types of pitches and under varying conditions was as near to perfection as any I have encountered'. In fact, English pitches were generally being prepared to help bowlers, a response to the tedium of high-scoring matches on doped surfaces.

Bedser thus remained the central figure in England's attack. Brian Statham and TRUEMAN, who frightened the Indians to death with his pace in 1952, were still at the promising stage and Bob Appleyard, an accurate off-break and swing bowler of fast-medium pace who was near-unplayable on a wet pitch, shone briefly in 1954 and 1955. LAKER and Tony Lock had their moments, but their best days lay in the future, as did those of Hugh Tayfield, who stood head and shoulders above South Africa's other bowlers. For Australia, Miller was menacing but bowled as the mood took him, and Lindwall, though a consummate operator, could not match Bedser's sustained excellence. Ramadhin and Valentine did not enjoy consistent success at Test level; off-spin was making itself felt again, but faster bowling was still master. Vinoo Mankad, who enjoyed productive home Test series against England and the newcomers Pakistan, was briefly the best orthodox left-arm spinner.

Bedser was nothing like as quick as Statham and Trueman, or Lindwall and Miller. He liked his wicketkeeper to stand up to him when he took the new ball – though, 6ft 3in and massively built, he could make the ball kick sharply off the pitch from a ten-pace run-up. But the real threat came from his ability to swing the ball late – usually into the right-handed batsman, though his action suggested the contrary – and break it from leg. On good pitches he would rely on swing and on bad ones employ the leg-cutter. Both were the stuff of batsmen's nightmares.

Bedser could produce the unplayable ball to the best batsmen whatever the condition of the pitch, and several credited him with bowling them the best ball they ever faced. They included BRADMAN, who nominated the delivery which bowled him for 0 in Adelaide in 1947. Bedser subsequently dismissed him in five successive Test innings – for scores of 63, 138, 0, 38 and 89 – and Bradman conceded that in certain conditions, Bedser was the most difficult bowler he ever faced. In fact, three of these dismissals were completed in the same way: working on an idea put to him by O'REILLY, Bedser each time had Bradman caught at backward short-leg to balls dipping in late from the off. But all he had done was reveal a minor chink in the armour of an ageing master.

Far more significant was Bedser's hold over Morris – whom he dismissed eighteen times in twenty-one Tests – and Hassett. This was central to England regaining the Ashes, as was the way he tamed an otherwise rampant Harvey. 'Like most left-handers, both were susceptible if one could make the ball go back into them off the pitch,' Bedser wrote of Morris and Harvey.

Many contemporaries rated Bedser as one of the greatest bowlers of all time. He was most frequently compared to BARNES and Tate, two other English fast-medium bowlers, renowned for their accuracy. In style he was more like Tate, using seam, swing and nip off the pitch to deceive opponents. Like Tate, too, he had stamina and used it to carry a weak post-war England attack. But temperamentally he was more akin to Barnes, with whom he shared a devotion to thrift and the work ethic. He was also skilled at bowling to his field.

Above all, after much practice, he gained command of the 'Barnes ball', the quick inswinging leg-break. This was the ball that stunned Bradman at Adelaide in 1947, that left Graeme Hole gaping in disbelief at Trent Bridge in 1953, and drew the admiration of Hassett: 'I must be a fair bat,' he said of one of his dismissals that year. 'I tried to play three shots at one ball and almost made contact the third time it moved.' MAY, who only faced Bedser rarely, said he was the best bowler of his type he encountered. Barnes himself said: 'Bedser came nearest to me in bowling a leg-break like mine. You can make a batsman, but you can't ever make a bowler.'

Bedser also shared Barnes's shrewdness. He took care to moderate his workload, opting out of tours of the Caribbean in 1947–48 and 1953–54 and – along with several others – the tour of India in 1951–52. These decisions, plus not starting his England career until he was twenty-seven years of age because of the war, prevented him becoming the first bowler to take 300 Test wickets, though he overhauled GRIMMETT and retired as the leading Test wicket-taker in history. Bedser thought deeply about his bowling but also about the wider game. He was an able deputy to May at Surrey in 1957, when the county won the sixth of their straight titles, and after he stopped playing in 1960 enjoyed a long career as an England selector, chairing the panel for twelve years and managing teams abroad.

Having been brought up in a family of straitened circumstances, Bedser had a constitutional dislike of frittering away anything (when he was first chosen for England, he thought back to his childhood, 'of my father – bless him – scraping together enough cash to offer us either a couple of days at the seaside or a bat'). Economy and hard work were two of his key principles. As they served him well, he single-mindedly adhered to them – sometimes, during his selectorial career, too rigidly when he came across bowlers who did not share his way of doing things. His outlook was similar to that of Hutton, under whose captaincy he worked so well.

He and his elder twin brother Eric, who as an off-spinner was also a member of Surrey's all-conquering team, worked in a solicitors' office from the ages of fourteen while putting in long hours of practice at cricket, a game which had no history in their family. Having grown up in Woking, they joined Surrey as teenagers in 1938 and the war and Royal Air Force only temporarily separated them from the club. By careful husbandry and investing the proceeds of their Surrey benefits, the twins established an office equipment company that was hugely profitable within years of their retirements.

Bedser's England career came to an abrupt and painful end. He went to Australia in 1954–55 as the world's best bowler but returned unable to command a place in the England team. He played only one more Test, as a late replacement for the injured Statham at home to South Africa a few months later. The root cause of the problem was ill health – he was handicapped by shingles early in the tour, played in the first Test at Brisbane while still unfit and spent the rest of the tour making a full recovery – but he was dropped from the second Test at Sydney as much for tactical reasons as indifferent form.

Hutton hankered after a potent pace attack and, by choosing to dispense with his old ally in conditions that would have suited him, arrived at one in Tyson and Statham. Fitter for the third Test in Melbourne, Bedser learned of his omission there when he saw his name crossed off the team sheet pinned up in the dressing-room, and Hutton, whose treatment of him caused uproar in the press, later conceded he handled the matter badly. Bedser greatly respected Hutton's ability as a batsman, but felt he was easier to keep quiet than Compton, whose unorthodoxy made him difficult to contain. Hutton, he thought, was the harder to dismiss.

Bedser, who did not fail to notice that three batsmen – Bradman, HOBBS and Hutton – were all knighted during his own playing days, became the second bowler after Richard Hadlee to be so honoured, on 1 January 1997.

Bedser's first-class record: 485 matches, 1,924 wickets, average 20.41. **Test record:** 51 matches, 236 wickets, average 24.89.

Bedser's Coopers & Lybrand ratings 1951–54: 4, 4, 2, 2.
Other leaders: 1951–52: W.A. Johnston (Aus). 1953–54: R.R. Lindwall (Aus).

Record against Number One batsmen:
v Hutton 1951–54: 5 matches, Hutton 10 innings, 646 runs, average 64.60 (four centuries, highest score 151); Bedser took his wicket four times.

PETER BARKER HOWARD MAY (England)

Number One: 1955–60

Born: Reading, Berkshire, 31 December 1929; died: Liphook, Hampshire, 27 December 1994. Career: 1948–63.

Peter May was the last English amateur who could be convincingly held up as the world's best batsman. Temperamentally he would have been more at home in the amateur's Edwardian heyday than his own time, but May applied to his cricket a hard-edged professionalism that took him to the pinnacles of achievement as batsman and captain. It made a stark contrast to his mildness off the field, and in the end the harsh realities of the modern world contributed to his decision to leave the game early. It was appropriate that in the year in which he effectively retired, 1962, the distinction between amateur and professional was abolished.

May thrived on the big, demanding occasion, regularly scoring runs when they were needed and usually in the most advantageous manner: for a post-war English batsman, he was unusually aggressive. Though he preferred, like HUTTON, to play slow bowling from the crease, BEDSER, writing in 1961, felt that it did not restrict May in the same way: 'Because of his great strength of wrist and forearm, he can force the ball where Hutton could not . . . Among present-day English players, Peter May alone ranks among the greats of all time.'

May faced up to adversity with a determination that was, as one England team-mate observed, 'so much a part of his temperament'.

Tyson said of him that, 'more than any other batsman I have met, he possesses a terrific power of concentration and application . . . Inwardly he is driven by a dynamic compelling force.' Cowdrey simply believed him to be tougher than Hutton, 'more resilient, so more powerful in a crisis'.

May's remarkable self-possession was undoubtedly the key to his success. It had been instilled by his parents – who were cousins and staunch Methodists – and was never more apparent than when he heard the news of his mother's death when he was sixteen. Bordering on coldness, it worked its spell on team-mates and opponents alike. It helped him become an integral member of two of the most successful teams in history. From 1952 to 1958, Surrey won the championship seven times in a row, while in the same period, England never lost a series. May captained Surrey for the last two of those years and England for the last four. At his peak, his mental strength was absolute and won the admiration of every player, amateur and professional.

It was Hutton's own unexpected retirement, early in the summer of 1955, that enabled May to inherit both the England captaincy and his position as the world's best batsman. He was then twenty-five years old and had been moving serenely towards greatness for years.

May, who like Bedser was born in Reading but to a family of considerably more means (they were builders' merchants), was a natural games-player and it was at cricket that he made the greatest strides. Though there was no sporting tradition in the family, his parents encouraged their two sons to play and by the time he was thirteen, Peter had been marked out for the highest honours, George Geary, his coach at Charterhouse, predicting that he had the technique and temperament to go on and play for England. Geary was more adviser than coach to May, who, though classical in method, was not ashamed of unorthodoxy. One of his habits during his best years was to eschew net practice, and watching play, on a day he was to bat.

May made a successful entry into first-class cricket during national service. When he then went up to Cambridge, he spent his first summer, 1950, as a junior member of a formidably strong university batting side and was capped by Surrey at the age of twenty. The following year he made his first appearances for the Gentlemen and England and scored hundreds for both, his 138 against South Africa at Headingley being hailed as the most significant flowering of English batsmanship since Hutton's 364 in 1938.

May had a great admiration for Hutton and under his leadership scored two further hundreds in the next four years. The first of these was vital to England drawing in the Caribbean in 1953–54, the second to their winning in Australia a year later. By the latter tour, he was among the best batsmen in the game. In his tall, upright manner – he stood 6ft 1in – he hammered Australia's fast bowlers off the front foot, confirming that they had been right to identify him as a threat in England eighteen months earlier and single him out – with some success – for special treatment. They had less joy now: he was near the finished article, a complete batsman with rare powers to score on the on side.

When Hutton went, who were May's rivals? There was Colin Cowdrey, three years younger and even more precocious in his rise to the top, who first played for England in Australia at the age of twenty-one and scored a century in testing circumstances at Melbourne. Cowdrey was still relatively unproven but had time to play the ball and timed it with the beauty of a true artist. But at this stage a modest and diffident man, he perhaps lacked the firmness and confidence to score as many Test runs as his ability warranted. As one team-mate recalled, he lacked the killer instinct that was so apparent in his close friend May.

Tom Graveney, who first played for England in 1951, was perhaps even more elegant, but played almost everything off the front foot and took time to convince doubters of his ability against the best fast bowlers and under pressure. He was inclined to rashness and his bad patches forever tested the faith of the selectors. And even on one leg, Compton remained a force to be reckoned with until 1956.

Several West Indian players were scoring heavily on their own benign pitches. When Hutton retired, Walcott had just completed a phenomenal Test series at home in which he scored 827 runs and five centuries against Australia, but even by Caribbean standards it was a batsmen's series. Weekes scored 469 runs and pounded three centuries off the reel in New Zealand a year later. Two years after that, the young SOBERS took merciless toll of a depleted Pakistan attack at Kingston, breaking Hutton's Test record with an unbeaten 365; he followed up with twin centuries in the match at Georgetown. But all accomplished little in England in 1957, when they were outshone by May.

Worrell's days as a consistently high run-scorer in Tests were behind him, as were those of Harvey, though the latter remained the most talented batsman Australia possessed. Pakistan had produced an outstanding defensive batsman in the tenacious Hanif Mohammad, who, in the same series in which Sobers made his record score, played the longest first-class innings on record, batting more than sixteen hours for 337 to save the Bridgetown Test after his side had followed on nearly 500 behind. Two years later, in January 1959, during a domestic match played on coir matting in Karachi, Hanif made the then world-record first-class score of 499.

None of them, however, consistently dominated Test series in the way May did. He was by some distance the best batsman on either side in four successive Test series at home between 1955 and 1958: versus South Africa, against whom he nearly scored a century in all five matches, Australia, West Indies and New Zealand. He was perhaps on his way to being so again against India in 1959 when his health gave way. His one overseas Test series during this period, in South Africa, saw him short of runs largely because he was on the receiving end both of a short-pitched barrage from Adcock and Heine and some outstanding catching; he scored heavily in other tour games.

His innings had large bearings on the outcome of Test series, none more so than his unbeaten 285 in the first Test against West Indies at Edgbaston in 1957, when he and Cowdrey batted together for over eight hours to save the game and break the power of Ramadhin. They did so in the most calculated manner, playing only his off-breaks and padding away everything else.

May was a superb player on bad wickets, as he showed in making a skilful, unbeaten 89 against South Africa at the Oval in 1955, but his supremacy was even more apparent in county cricket, much of which was played on dreadful pitches in the late 1950s. In 1957 he topped the English first-class averages by 10 runs per innings, the following year by a staggering 17. That year, on a fast, fiery pitch at the Oval, he made 165 against the New Zealanders. The next-highest individual score in the match was 25.

A whole generation of Englishmen held May in special regard. He was the first outstanding English batsman to emerge in the post-war era and this gave him a hold on the imaginations of many that could not be broken: many contemporaries, among players and public, even now maintain that he is the greatest batsman England has produced since 1945. 'No one was more determined,' said Benaud, who was perhaps May's greatest adversary in Test cricket. 'He was very awkward to bowl to, particularly when he and Cowdrey were batting together.' Benaud dismissed May nine times in first-class cricket, more than anyone except TRUEMAN, who faced May regularly and claimed his wicket on twelve occasions.

When England's unbeaten run under May came to an end, in Australia in 1958–59, the effect was marked. Team morale all but collapsed. Confronted by bowlers whose methods were highly questionable, England badly under-performed and May was criticized for his captaincy and for allowing his fiancée Virginia, a daughter of Harold Gilligan, to accompany him. With the boundaries between amateurs and professionals blurring, his style of leadership grated with some of the team (Tyson charged him with lacking the 'common touch'). His own batting did not suffer, but his appetite for the game waned.

Several months later he fell seriously ill with a digestive disorder, bringing his season to an early end in 1959. He underwent an operation and declared himself fit to lead England in the West Indies, but the wound reopened when he was in Trinidad. He struggled through two Test matches – finding the bouncers of Wes Hall and Charlie Griffith an ordeal, as he was a confirmed non-hooker – before being ordered home. Physically and mentally diminished – medical opinion cited stress as a factor in his condition – he was finished as the force of old. Sobers, meanwhile, established his right to supplant him.

May played little more. His return, delayed until 1961, was a disappointment, his dismissal in the Old Trafford Test – where Benaud bowled him round his legs – being instrumental in England's failure to regain the Ashes. Within weeks he had retired from international cricket, and his departure from county cricket soon followed, as he opted to devote himself to his business career as a broker and underwriter at Lloyd's. May was thus lost to the game as a player by the time he was thirty-three – an age at which Hutton had just embarked on his years of supremacy. Retirement also denied May the chance to become the second amateur after GRACE to score 100 hundreds – he finished with 85 – and parity in the eyes of many with HOBBS; and figures mattered more to May than might have been supposed.

May surprisingly renewed his high-profile involvement in the game in the 1980s, when he accepted an invitation to become chairman of selectors, but it was an episode that only widened his breach with the modern game.

May's first-class record: 388 matches, 27,592 runs, average 51.00.
Test record: 66 matches, 4537 runs, average 46.77.

May's Coopers & Lybrand ratings 1955–59: 2, 1, 1, 1, 2.
Other leaders: 1955: C.L. Walcott (WI). 1959: C.C. McDonald (Aus).

Record against Number One bowlers:
v Lindwall 1955–56: they did not oppose each other in first-class matches.
v Laker 1956–58: 1 match, May 2 innings, 13 runs, average 6.50 (highest score 8); Laker took his wicket once.
v Trueman 1959–60: 3 matches, May 6 innings, 133 runs, average 22.16 (highest score 54); Trueman took his wicket once.

◎ JAMES CHARLES LAKER (England)

Number One: 1956–59

Born: Frizinghall, Bradford, Yorkshire, 9 February 1922; died: Putney, London, 23 April 1986. Career: 1946–65.

Jim Laker was the first genuine off-spinner to merit serious consideration as the world's Number One bowler. SHAW, eighty years earlier, was a slow roundarmer who turned the ball gently from the off, but the craft was then in its infancy. The new leg-before law of 1935, which broadened the scope for appeals, offered encouragement to the slow, attacking off-spinner, but only those with immense skill and control – and few met the conditions. Laker, 6ft tall and strong, possessor of a model action and a prodigious spinner of the ball, was one who did.

Even so, it took him time to overcome the prejudices of those who felt that his style was of limited value. It was not until the 1950s that it was generally accepted that off-spin could trouble world-class batsmen on good pitches, which may explain why one immature performance – at Headingley in 1948, when Australia humiliated England by scoring 404 in the fourth innings to win – was held against him for so long by the selectors.

He had begun his career promisingly and appeared to establish himself as an England player in the space of two years. But between making his debut in the Caribbean in 1947–48 – where his performances in the most testing conditions ought to have convinced anyone of his capabilities – and the start of the home series with Australia in 1956, Laker played in 24 Tests and was passed over for 50 more. He was rarely taken on tour and paid the price for HUTTON's personal loss of faith in spin. Throughout this period Laker's record in county cricket was consistently excellent, and he returned statistically the most remarkable analysis in the game's history on a sticky wicket in a Test trial in 1950: eight for two from fourteen overs. He played series-deciding roles at the Oval in 1951, 1953 and 1955, and did the hat-trick four times.

In the end, though, Laker convinced many that he was not only the best off-spinner of his day but the best there had ever been. The turning point was the 1956 season and his sensational success against the Australians, who were neither experienced at coping with Laker's type of bowling nor an assertive batting side.

By now a mature campaigner of thirty-four, Laker took ruthless advantage, making the ball 'fizz' as few of his kind had before. He signalled the start of his period of domination by taking all ten (for 88) in the first innings of Surrey's match against the Australians in May, and his thirteen wickets in the match condemned them to their first defeat by a county in forty-four years.

He then proceeded to claim 46 wickets – an Ashes record – in the five Tests, at the paltry average of 9.60, as Australia were drubbed 3–1 (it would have been 4–1 but for the weather). This included his historic return of nineteen for 90 in the fourth match at Old Trafford – nine for 37 in the first innings and ten for 53 in the second – which gave him, in the words of *Wisden*, 'all the more important bowling records in the history of cricket'. Though he switched ends a number of times, Laker took all his wickets from the Stretford End on a pitch that turned – controversially – from the first afternoon. Remarkably, none of the other spinners bowled well on it. Laker thought he himself bowled better in taking all ten for Surrey, when the pitch gave only limited assistance; here, Australia compounded their troubles by trying to attack him.

Laker was immediately and widely accepted as the best spin bowler in the world and, inevitably, the attitude of the England selectors changed. He became an automatic choice for the rest of his Test career and aroused great interest when he finally visited South Africa and Australia. His figures overseas were obviously not as impressive as in England, where he played a central role in defeats of West Indies and New Zealand, but he was particularly proud of his performances in Australia in 1958–59, when, with almost everything against him, he was easily England's best bowler and proved to opponents intent on revenge for what they considered his successes on 'cooked' pitches that they could not punish him. He had many of them caught in the deep perishing in the attempt. Laker joined the tour only with reluctance, following disagreements with MAY, who unwisely accused him of not trying.

This proved to be Laker's last Test series, as his spinning finger, which he repeatedly tore and patched up with balsam, developed severe arthritis. Within a few months he had retired, although he returned to play a few matches for Essex as an amateur before embarking on a successful career as a journalist and broadcaster. He finished with 193 Test wickets at 21.24, a lower average than any other England bowler with 150 wickets managed except BARNES.

It was hardly surprising that Laker, by nature moody and introverted, was cynical at his treatment by the cricketing authorities and, like Barnes, viewed them with disparagement. He aired grievances in an autobiography shortly after he retired from playing, which led to a temporary breach with Surrey and MCC.

Laker was temperamentally well suited to his job. By keeping a mental distance from events, he could read a game astutely and stay unruffled by the heat of battle. He would detect changing circumstances and act accordingly, attacking with variations of flight and spin when the pitch was in his favour and opting for containment with his unremitting accuracy when it was not. At his height, he was the complete master of his trade. 'A craftsman in a great tradition,' wrote Cardus, 'a classic exponent of off-spin – the most classic of all kinds of bowling.'

Laker's detachment suggested boredom, but was usually nothing of the sort. Nor was it confined to his cricket: he was by nature an observer of life, a boy who lost his father when he was only two years old and whose mother was also dead by the time he returned from the Second World War at the age of twenty-three.

Laker's best years came at a time when there was a great depth of bowling talent and pitches generally favoured the ball. England possessed greater riches than perhaps at any other time in their history, with competition so severe that they rarely fielded a settled attack.

The fast bowling was chiefly in the hands of Statham and TRUEMAN, one accurate and endlessly hard-working, the other on his day magnificently destructive. Both were fast, with opinions varying as to their relative speeds. Trueman's stormy-petrel disposition meant he was erratic and mistrusted; full maturity, and his best days, were still to come. Statham was more reliable and was his country's first fast-bowling choice from 1954 to 1962, but his immaculate line and length removed an important element of surprise; nor did he greatly swing the ball, unlike Trueman. Statham took five wickets in an innings only nine times in 70 Tests, though he briefly held the Test record for most wickets before being over-taken by Trueman in 1963.

Laker's slow-bowling support came from Lock and Johnny Wardle. Both were left-armers (though dissimilar in method) and competing for the same place. Generally, Lock found preferment at home and Wardle overseas. Wardle was a maverick as bowler and man who, like Laker, paid the price for putting his thoughts into print – more seriously in his case, as it cut short his Yorkshire and England careers in 1958. He was more dextrous with ball than pen, enjoying his greatest success in South Africa in 1956–57, when he turned, as he sometimes did on the harder surfaces of the southern hemisphere, to left-handed off-breaks and googlies – a rare, risky but sometimes profitable means of attack.

Lock, like O'REILLY a spinner with a fast bowler's temperament and like Laker a prodigious spinner of the ball, was another member of Surrey's all-conquering side and he and Laker caused frequent devastation at county level, where the under-prepared pitches often broke up early. They fought each other for scalps – Lock was morti-fied that his share of the spoils from the Old Trafford Test of 1956 was one wicket in 69 overs – but in the process formed a spin part-nership to rival those of Briggs and Peel, Blythe and Woolley, Parker and Goddard, and GRIMMETT and O'Reilly. Lock's early success was achieved with bowling of brisk pace, but the legality of his quicker ball came into question and he was no-balled for throwing several times before tempering his methods in 1960.

In South Africa and on the Indian subcontinent, the mat posed new challenges to visiting teams. Given the new ball for Australia for the first time, Alan Davidson started making a name for himself in South Africa in 1957–58, as did Benaud, who took 106 first-class wickets on the tour and emerged as the next high-class Australian googly bowler. SOBERS rated another googly bowler, Subhash 'Fergie' Gupte of India, even more effective, if less accurate, and Laker concurred, ranking Gupte as the 'best of the modern leg-spinners' alongside Bruce Dooland, an exceptional bowler whose Test career was thwarted by Benaud's presence. But Gupte achieved most of his success on the subcontinent, as did Fazal Mahmood, the Pakistan fast-medium bowler, who cut the ball sharply on the mat.

South Africa possessed a pair of tall and menacing fast bowlers in Neil Adcock and Peter Heine, who extracted bounce from even lifeless pitches, but their success was intermittent. Tayfield, a master of flight and accuracy, persuaded some that he was a better off-spinner than Laker on hard pitches by taking 37 wickets at 17.18 against England in 1956–57, but was primarily a defensive bowler who looked less convincing against batsmen who got after him. Not many did – he drove many a great batsman to his wit's end – but the Australians managed it in South Africa in 1957–58. The verdict of Cowdrey, who scored a fine hundred against him in Cape Town the previous winter, was that he was 'not a bowler who ever frightened you'.

'I believe Jim Laker to be the finest off-spinner I have ever seen and, probably, in the entire history of the game,' Bailey wrote in 1997. 'On some overseas pitches Tayfield and GIBBS were as deadly, and on occasions more so, but neither was as complete a bowler as Laker.' In including him in an imaginary World XI at around the time of his own retirement, Benaud said that Laker was the best of his craft he had seen. Comparisons were harder for the fact that Australia did not stage a home series between England's visits in 1954–55 and 1958–59. What stood in Laker's favour was that he was a member of sides that won regularly.

Laker came to off-spin and Surrey by an unlikely route. There was no history of cricket in the Yorkshire family into which he was born the only son after four daughters. It was not until he settled in Catford, after awaiting demobilization there after the war, that he took to the game seriously, having previously played for pleasure as a batsman for Saltaire (a club for whom Barnes played) and in wartime matches in North Africa, where his ability as a slow bowler first manifested itself.

He was spotted playing for Catford by Andrew Kempton, a friend of HOBBS, who recommended him to Surrey (Kempton later discovered Lock as well). Laker gave up his job as a bank clerk when Surrey offered him a contract, the club having first checked that his native county – who remembered him only as a batsman – did not want him. Hutton later tried to lure him back, but by then it was too late.

Laker's first-class record: 450 matches, 1,944 wickets, average 18.41. **Test record:** 46 matches, 193 wickets, average 21.24.

Laker's Coopers & Lybrand ratings 1956–58: 1, 2, 2.
Other leaders: 1957: H.J. Tayfield (SA). 1958: G.A.R. Lock (Eng).

Record against Number One batsmen:
v May 1956–58: 1 match, May 2 innings, 13 runs, average 6.50 (highest score 8); Laker took his wicket once.

⟪ FREDERICK SEWARDS TRUEMAN (England)

Number One: 1959–64

Born: Stainton, Yorkshire, 6 February 1931. Career: 1949–69.

Fred Trueman had always wanted to be top dog. Long before he first played for Yorkshire at the age of eighteen, against the 'jazz-hats' of Cambridge University at Fenner's, he harboured ambitions to be the best bowler in his county, country and – though this was less important than the first two – the world. Ambition ultimately fulfilled, he prided himself on the notion that people around the globe talked about him, and he espoused the view that he was the 'finest fast bowler that ever drew breath'. Some critics agreed with him.

But Trueman's road to the top was a bumpy one. By the time he got there, in 1959, he was twenty-eight years old and not as fast as in his first flush of youth. He was born – at an unfeasible 14lb 1oz – the fourth of seven children, to a father who worked in the mines of south Yorkshire and played cricket for his local club. Fred followed him in both pursuits, his enthusiasm for cricket not dimmed by a blow in the groin while facing a fast bowler in a school match; the injury was so serious that he did not play again for two years and, according to his biographer John Arlott, 'at one point dire consequences were feared'. Trueman worked in the pit after leaving school and throughout his early days with Yorkshire, a matter that he viewed, wrote Arlott, 'as a disadvantage – and as a social handicap too'.

Yorkshire quickly identified his talent for fast bowling – he was strongly built at 5ft 10in, had a classic side-on action and fast arm – but were less impressed than he was with his speed, use of the bouncer and long run-up. The club were more concerned about his inaccuracy, and he was originally dubbed 'Fiery Fred' through an element of mockery. Behind a façade of brash self-confidence, the talkative Trueman craved reassurance, but Yorkshire could not immediately provide it – and nor could England, even though they were desperate for a hostile new-ball bowler to rival LINDWALL and Miller. Fortunately, his father constantly did.

Trueman undoubtedly struck fear into the Indians during his first Test series in 1952, in which he took 29 wickets at 13.31, but his verbal aggression during the tour of the Caribbean eighteen months later briefly alienated HUTTON, who jettisoned him in favour of Tyson in Australia the following winter. Trueman enjoyed a successful series at home to West Indies in 1957, but by the time he returned from Australia two years later, he had still been left out of more Tests than he had played in: 27 as against 26.

By then, though, he had fully learned his trade, a task Trueman himself said took him six or seven years from the time he first played for Yorkshire. The coaching he received at the club from Bill Bowes and others, and his own hard work, were about to have their rewards.

He was no longer solely concerned with speed. Having learned from watching Lindwall, among others, he now appreciated the benefits of pitching the ball up and allowing it to swing late. He possessed a big natural outswinger but could also bring the ball back. His control of the yorker almost equalled that of Lindwall, whom he never rivalled for accuracy but had the advantage over in one important respect: by reducing his pace, he commanded a deadly off-cutter. And to his great ability, Trueman now harnessed what Bowes described as a 'shrewd, calculating assessment' of opposing players. Despite Yorkshire's strictures about economy, he was never afraid to encourage a batsman to play shots if he thought it might bring a wicket.

For five years, starting with the home series against India in 1959, Trueman sustained a consistently high level of achievement. Eight consecutive full series brought him anything from seventeen to 34 wickets and he showed that he was no longer just an 'English' bowler, performing well on all manner of surfaces all over the world. His second tour of West Indies, in 1959–60, when he first revealed his full abilities away from home and constantly caused trouble with his swinging yorkers, arguably saw him at his best, and he gave Australia many uncomfortable moments on their own pitches three years later. But two of his most skilful and successful performances occurred at home. At Headingley in 1961 he destroyed Australia with five-wicket bursts in two innings, bowling off-cutters into worn patches, and at Edgbaston two years later – when it had been feared he was past his best – he routed West Indies with a spell of six wickets in twenty-four balls, on a pitch from which Hall and Griffith extracted nothing.

These were Trueman's years of 'pomp', years of hard work sustained by a durable physique – he had, according to Hutton, 'shoulders like a battleship' – and the sheer determination to fulfil his ambition. It was sheer determination that carried him through to become the first bowler to take 300 Test wickets with what appeared at the time to be his last spell of bowling for his country, at the Oval in 1964. During this period, Benaud described him as 'more craftsman than an express bowler', while Bailey wrote that, 'on all wickets, and in all conditions, it is doubtful whether there has been a more complete fast bowler'. Compton thought Trueman the best English bowler he saw. 'Batting against him held some of the terrors of picking a path through a minefield,' he said. 'You dreaded the unexpected.'

Trueman's desire to play the part of the fiery fast bowler, and his ability to raise his game for the big occasion, captured the public imagination and he was one of the most popular cricketers of his generation, certainly the most popular among Englishmen. He loved to involve himself as bowler, batsman or fielder – or conversationalist, a talent he satisfied in retirement at some length as a radio summarizer.

But Trueman never completely absorbed his lessons. Even in his heyday he was sometimes incapable of suppressing the urge to use – over-use – the bouncer, and it cost England dear at Headingley in 1964, when Burge kept hooking him for four and Australia came back from the dead to win. He was dropped for the next Test. (An earlier display of indiscipline, in 1961, had also resulted in temporary demotion.) Compton thought his preoccupation with the bouncer was 'a gesture of defiance to the world at large' – which it may well have been: Trueman never lost his loathing of the 'jazz-hats' of Oxford and Cambridge, whom, it was said, he would threaten to 'pin' against the sightscreen. 'He showed up mediocrity in an opponent in a manner no other bowler of his time could equal,' Bowes wrote. Sometimes, though, his threats only stiffened the enemy's resolve.

When England toured the Caribbean in 1959–60, it was clear that the encounters between SOBERS and Trueman would be central to the result. Their first meeting took place before the first Test, when Barbados played MCC in Bridgetown. 'When it was obvious that Fred and Gary were going to come up against each other,' Ted Dexter said, 'we asked Fred what he was going to do. He was very much in his pomp and Sobers was very much on the way up. The first chance he got, Fred dropped one short and Sobers pulled it way back into the stand. Fred gave him another one and Sobers did it again. Fred did not bother bouncing him after that.'

Sobers scored 154 for Barbados and played three innings in excess of 140 during the Test series, but the only Test that produced a definite outcome was the second in Trinidad, where Trueman dismissed him for 0 and 31. England won. Trueman took Sobers's wicket four times on that tour – going round the wicket to the left-hander, he bowled him twice in succession out of the rough – but it did not come cheaply and when the teams met in England in 1963, Trueman was notably less successful. His overall record against Sobers was unexceptional, but Sobers rated him the best of his type in England, ahead of Statham.

Trueman's stature was enhanced by the fact that, with one exception, he often led attacks for England and Yorkshire with little new-ball support. The exception was Statham, who, by tirelessly maintaining the pressure, assisted him in many England triumphs; between them they carried their country's attack in the early 1960s. Some critics argued that Davidson was briefly the most dangerous new-ball bowler, and his record in three successive Ashes series between 1958 and 1963 was statistically marginally superior, but Trueman proved himself in a broader range of conditions. Another Australian, Benaud, decided the destiny of the Ashes with his bowling at Old Trafford in 1961, but his success was more sporadic. Perhaps the best off-spinners were Titmus, for England, and the rapidly improving GIBBS.

More credible rivals were three Barbadians: Hall and Griffith, both operating off long run-ups and definitely a degree up in pace, and Sobers, who took up bowling fast-medium seam and swing bowling in Australia in 1961–62. This proved to be the most successful of Sobers's three styles – he also purveyed high-risk left-arm wrist spin in the 1960s, having begun as an orthodox left-arm spinner. Hall also swung the ball but he gave the batsmen plenty to score off; Griffith, at his best, was a real handful, persevering and mixing testing bouncers with yorkers. Against that, he did not swing the ball.

Sobers started as back-up to Hall and Griffith but by the mid-1960s was doing more with the ball than either, moving it late and cutting it back sharply. His quicker ball was extremely sharp and some rated him almost as good as Davidson among left-arm seamers.

The presence of Hall and Griffith in England in 1963 fired up Trueman, who responded by taking 34 wickets at 17.47, an England record against West Indies. Statistically Griffith did marginally better with 32 wickets at 16.21, but his was much the stronger side; Trueman virtually operated alone. Trueman's new-ball partner for most of the series was Shackleton, a wonderfully accurate bowler of slow-medium pace who swung the ball either way, but whose opportunities at Test level were restricted by England's strength: he had last played twelve years earlier. Shackleton was the leading wicket-taker in England in each year from 1962 to 1965 and claimed 2,857 victims in his career, more than any other exclusively post-Second World War bowler.

Trueman's first-class record: 603 matches, 2,304 wickets, average 18.29. **Test record:** 67 matches, 307 wickets, average 21.57.

Trueman's Coopers & Lybrand ratings 1959–64: –, 5, 3, 5, 3, 2. *Leaders*: 1959: G.A.R. Lock (Eng). 1960, 1961 and 1963: A.K. Davidson (Aus). 1962: W.W. Hall (WI). 1964: L.R. Gibbs (WI).

Record against Number One batsmen:

v May 1959–60: 3 matches, May 6 innings, 133 runs, average 22.16 (highest score 54): Trueman took his wicket once.

v Sobers 1960–65: 16 matches, Sobers 25 innings, 1667 runs, average 72.47 (eight centuries, highest score 226); Trueman took his wicket seven times.

GARFIELD ST AUBRUN SOBERS (West Indies)

Number One: 1960–70

Born: Bay Land, Bridgetown, Barbados, 28 July 1936. Career: 1953–74.

Gary Sobers, the first West Indian to attain Number One status, was a superbly gifted athlete who would have succeeded in almost any circumstances, but his phenomenal career was arguably shaped by two personal tragedies. The first was the drowning of his father while serving on a merchantman torpedoed in January 1942, when Sobers was five years old. The second was the death of Collie Smith in a car accident in September 1959. Smith was his closest friend within the West Indies team, and Smith, Sobers and Rohan Kanhai were talked of as natural successors to Worrell, Weekes and Walcott. Sobers was at the wheel when the accident occurred.

Like the three Ws born in or around Bridgetown, Sobers recalled his early childhood with nostalgia. The fifth of seven children, he belonged to an underprivileged but content family. His father and two elder brothers were sports fanatics and Sobers was instilled with an immediate love of cricket. These were happy days and Sobers, though imbued with a competitive spirit, never forgot the importance of giving pleasure through his play. His father's death also forced on him maturity beyond his years and, as far as cricket was concerned, an ice-cool temperament capable of handling any situation.

Smith's death sparked a more dangerous response. It encouraged Sobers to live for the day with frightening gusto. He drank, partied and deprived himself of sleep. He undertook a phenomenal workload, playing round the calendar for years on end, seasons with English league clubs, South Australia and Nottinghamshire melding into his commitments with Barbados and West Indies. Taking risks – gambling on the sports field and in the bookmakers – already held an attraction; now it became an essential ingredient to life.

The miracle was that Sobers not only survived but flourished spectacularly. He did not miss a Test between 1955 and 1972 and at his height arguably achieved as much in a concentrated period as any all-round player in history; his various bowling styles surely made him the most versatile. Towards the end of his career, he sometimes looked an ordinary player in county cricket and his knees gave out under the strain, but for a long time his batting showed no adverse effects. He remained a master craftsman and the biggest star of an age in which the ease of air travel first made playing twelve months of the year a tempting possibility.

Sobers was indebted to several advisers, among them Worrell, Weekes and BRADMAN, who was instrumental in taking him to South Australia in the early 1960s in an attempt to rekindle interest in a game struggling to maintain its appeal. Sobers went as indisputably the world's best batsman, with bowling a minor string to his bow – though state cricket soon changed that.

His ascent to the top of the batting tree had appeared pre-ordained. First chosen as a teenager for Barbados and West Indies as a spin bowler, his batting developed so rapidly that he was not yet nineteen when he opened the innings against Australia in 1955 and larruped LINDWALL and Miller for 43 runs ('cricket hell broke loose,' Miller said, 'that one innings set Sobers alight as a batting wizard'). In England two years later Sobers reached maturity, the one West Indian who maintained the fight through a losing series and refused to be shackled by LAKER. A few months later he broke HUTTON's world Test record with 365 not out against a threadbare Pakistan attack in Jamaica, launching a hot streak of six centuries in as many Tests.

It was in the Caribbean in 1959–60, though, that Sobers convincingly demonstrated that his defences were virtually impregnable. It was on this foundation that he was able to make the fiercest assaults on almost any bowler. In his first match against the visiting England team, he scored 154 for Barbados and hooked TRUEMAN – who had given him problems with the bouncer in the Caribbean six years earlier – with such murderous efficiency that Trueman quickly gave up the tactic as a dead loss.

Sobers's return from the Test series was 709 runs at 101.28, 226 of them in the opening match at Bridgetown, where he and Worrell narrowly failed to eclipse the then world-record Test partnership of 411 by MAY and Cowdrey. May was greatly relieved when

Trueman removed Sobers's middle stump with the stand worth 399, but this innings might be seen to mark the start of Sobers's reign. He was twenty-three years old and the first left-handed batsman with a persuasive claim to be the best in the world. 'The Englishmen seemed resigned to big innings from him,' reported *Wisden.*

They were not the only ones. In a practice match among the West Indies players during that season, Sobers batted against Hall and treated him as mercilessly as he had Trueman. The following winter Sobers cemented his position by taking brilliant centuries off Australia in Brisbane and Sydney. Many who saw his 132 in two hours in Brisbane said it was the greatest innings they had seen.

A year later, in his first season for South Australia, he struck 251 against New South Wales, whose attack contained Davidson and Benaud. The consistency of Sobers's run-making was to be affected by the demands of his bowling, which he seriously took up again, and the burden of the West Indies captaincy; but year in, year out, he remained the batsman for the big occasion. If his form dipped, as it did in his first series as captain against Australia in 1964–65, he invariably came back quickly and strongly.

'There is no question Gary was the best batsman of the sixties,' said Dexter, who was himself among the world's best at the time. 'You never saw him in the slightest trouble against any kind of bowling. Obviously, he got out now and then – just as Bradman got out in the end – but, while Gary was in, there was never any doubt he was in charge.

'I never saw him hit by a short ball or hit on the hands. Nor was he hit on the pads very often. I never heard anyone say, "What you do to Sobers to keep him quiet is . . ." Your only hope was to pitch up the ball to him early on before he played himself in. But we usually got fed up and gave him one to lose the strike.' There was a theory that Sobers had a tendency to play at off-side outswingers with his bat away from his body, a weakness that Cardus felt BARNES would have worked on. Sobers said that the best fast bowlers he faced were Hall, Griffith, Trueman and LILLEE; the fastest, Roy Gilchrist.

Sobers received no formal coaching – he learned by watching others and practical experience – but his technique was basically orthodox, though he would improvise as the need arose. He had synthesized forward and back play so completely that the process appeared as natural as breathing. His footwork was superb, taking him into the right positions and enabling him to make vital late adjustments of stroke: Benaud said that if Sobers did not pick a googly, he still had time to alter his shot. He rarely missed the ball and eschewed pads as a second line of defence.

But the key to his batting was its aggression. By means of a high backlift, he struck the ball with wonderful timing and power – Bradman said Sobers hit the ball harder than anyone he could remember – so that he was looking to score off even good-length deliveries. A forward defensive was the only stroke he did not play. Once, when West Indies were chasing runs at Bridgetown in 1965, Bob Simpson, the Australia captain, put eight men on the boundary when Sobers arrived at the crease, because he felt it was the only way of cutting off his strokes. Trueman described him as 'the most devastating batsman I encountered in Test cricket . . . He had the ability to hit the really good ball to the boundary with a perfectly straight bat.'

Sobers liked nothing more than to carry the fight back into the enemy camp. At Lord's in 1966 – during a series in which he topped 700 runs for the third time – he supervised a partnership of 274 with his young cousin David Holford, after West Indies had been in desperate trouble. England were left some uncomfortable moments before achieving a draw. Sobers described it as his greatest innings. Eighteen months later, at Kingston, he struck a magnificent century in the follow-on to avert an innings defeat, but, not content to accept an easy draw, declared to put England under pressure. They finished the match on 68 for eight.

Many other successful batsmen in the game were technically accomplished players dedicated to making runs at the sedate tempo then prevailing in Test cricket. Among them were Simpson and Bill Lawry of Australia, and Ken Barrington, Geoff Boycott and John Edrich of England. Despite their preoccupation with run-making, only Barrington bettered Sobers's Test average. Barrington had been first chosen for England as a fluent strokemaker at the age of twenty-four, but he was not ready and waited four years for another chance. The experience coloured his attitude and made him permanently over-defensive. Cowdrey remained an accomplished player of the highest quality of bowling, and was now more brooding, more of an accumulator. After switching counties, Graveney enjoyed his most productive period for England.

A few played with the panache of Sobers, if not his all-encompassing skill. Kanhai, blessed with the technique and the talent and like Ramadhin an East Indian, was one; Dexter another. The latter, reviving the spirit of Compton, was a superb and positive player of fast bowling who dominated many of the best bowlers in the world, and would have achieved more had he not retired in his prime.

Doug Walters scored centuries in his first two Tests and was hailed as the 'next Bradman', but never stopped mixing brilliance with inconsistency and failed to master English conditions. He also ran into difficulties against the bouncer in the early 1970s. Graeme Pollock of South Africa was another precocious left-hander blessed with power, artistry and a wonderful eye. When South Africa were excluded from international sport, his average in Test cricket stood at 60.97, a figure second only to that of Bradman, who was among his admirers. But unlike his countryman Barry RICHARDS, Pollock felt little desire to take himself abroad and test his talents against the best in the world. He declined offers to play county cricket, and when a strong Rest of the World side filled the void created by South Africa's cancelled 1970 tour of England, Pollock and Kanhai were mainly (though not always) eclipsed by Sobers. Pollock, a predominantly front-foot player, remained a prolific run-maker through to the 1980s (testimony to his insatiable appetite), but his lack of exposure made worthwhile comparisons difficult. Richards described him in 1996 as 'the best player I have seen' – but Pollock was one of those who, in his quest for strokes, always gave the bowler a chance.

In the late 1960s, Sobers's form became more erratic. After the home series against England in 1967–68, he struggled to make the same impact as of old – and it may have been no coincidence that this coincided with West Indies's first sustained period of failure since he began playing. He was distracted by the captaincy, a job that did not come naturally to him and must have been an unwelcome chore as West Indies embarked on a period in which they won only two Tests in six years. The demand of continuous playing was also finally taking its toll on him.

It was noticeable, too, that for Sobers, the flame of inspiration burned brightest when he was playing not for West Indies or in county cricket but for strong representative sides. He showed brilliant all-round form for the Rest of the World against England in 1970 – his last great series – and it was while playing for a World

XI against Australia at Melbourne in January 1972 that he played an innings of 254, breathtaking in its power and aggression. The spur was the World XI's rout for 59 all out in the previous game at Perth; Sobers, the captain of the side, had been out for 0 – one of eight victims for Lillee, who then removed him for 0 again in the first innings at Melbourne. Lillee took the brunt of the second-innings whirlwind. 'I believe Gary Sobers's innings was probably the best ever seen in Australia,' said Bradman. 'The people who saw Sobers have enjoyed one of the historic events of cricket; they were privileged to have such an experience.' But by then, Barry Richards had made his own persuasive case for being regarded as Number One.

As with other Caribbean cricketers, cricket provided Sobers, who left school at thirteen, with a means of acquiring a good living. By the late 1960s, in fact, he was easily the world's best-paid cricketer and it was with reluctance that he announced his retirement, at the age of thirty-eight, in 1974. He had given up the captaincy two years earlier, having recently survived a heated row following an ill-advised visit to Rhodesia for a double-wicket competition. Sobers was accused by Caribbean politicians of betraying Africans and obliged to make a public apology. Fatigue also played its part in his final decision, though he would have played in the first World Cup in 1975 but for an injury.

Having retired from the game, Sobers had no obvious alternative means of earning a living, though a brief liaison with Kerry Packer – an Australian entrepreneur who, in defiance of the authorities, signed up many of the world's leading players for lucrative fees to appear in highly competitive 'exhibition' matches – staved off the need. His most regular employment was working as a consultant for the Barbados tourist board. A divorce and high spending ensured he lived in modest circumstances. To celebrate the fortieth anniversary of his Test debut, the Barbados government organized a benefit fund for him in 1994, which raised around £100,000 and was placed in trust; and in 1997 he won about £200,000 in the island's lottery, thus, perhaps, recouping something of his invest-ment in horses.

At the time he retired, Sobers had scored more runs in Test cricket than anyone else. He was knighted for his services to cricket – not the least of them his impeccable sportsmanship – on 1 January 1975.

Sobers's first-class record: 383 matches, 28,315 runs, average 54.87. Test record: 93 matches, 8,032 runs, average 57.78.

Sobers's Coopers & Lybrand ratings 1960–70: 1, 1, 1, 1, 1, 3, 1, 1, 1, 5, 4.
Other leaders: 1965: K.F. Barrington (Eng). 1969: K.D. Walters (Aus). 1970: R.G. Pollock (SA). Sobers was also top in 1971 and 1973.

Record against Number One bowlers:
v Trueman 1960–65: 16 matches, Sobers 25 innings, 1,667 runs, average 72.47 (eight centuries, highest score 226); Trueman took his wicket seven times.
v Gibbs 1965–68: 3 matches, Sobers 4 innings, 404 runs, average 101.00 (two centuries, highest score 204); Gibbs took his wicket once.
v Snow 1968–69: 9 matches, Sobers 16 innings, 812 runs, average 62.46 (two centuries, highest score 152); Snow took his wicket twice.

ⓦ LANCELOT RICHARD GIBBS (West Indies)

Number One: 1965–68

Born: Georgetown, British Guiana, 29 September 1934. Career: 1954–76.

The mid-1960s was an unexceptional period for bowlers, and an undistinguished one for cricket. Test cricket undersold itself badly, locked for the most part in negative tactics and unimaginative play. Between September 1963 and April 1966, 39 of the 57 Tests staged ended in draws. With batsmen holding the game in their restraining grip, few bowlers shone and none dominated the scene.

Inspired by the genius of SOBERS, West Indies played by far the most enterprising cricket. They beat England in 1963 and 1966, Australia in the Caribbean – for what was billed as the unofficial world championship – in 1964–65, and India in India in 1966–67. Their bowling attack centred on Hall and Griffith, Sobers and Lance Gibbs, unarguably the world's leading off-spinner. These four claimed 277 wickets between them in the four series: Gibbs 83, Griffith 70, Sobers 66 and Hall 58.

Hall and Griffith were past their best by the time of the home series with Australia, which took place a few months after it had become apparent – during the Ashes series in England in 1964 – that TRUEMAN was at the end of the road as a Test player. Hall brought West Indies victory in the first Test in Jamaica with an inspired performance – he took nine for 105 – but did virtually nothing afterwards and his form in England in 1966 was patchy even by his own standards. Griffith, who had taken 32 of his wickets in England in 1963, was even less effective, disconcerted by a growing debate over the legitimacy of his action. He was no-balled for throwing in a county match in England in 1966.

Sobers had enjoyed success with his lively seamers in England in 1963 and did so again in 1966 – when he alternated between styles and claimed 20 wickets in the Tests – but played only a minor part against Australia with the ball, taking just four wickets among specialist batsmen. He bowled in all his three styles against India, chipped in with valuable wickets and was the most successful bowler after Gibbs. It was transparent to most that, had he not had to concern himself with batting and captaincy, Sobers had the capacity to be an even greater bowler. As it was, Dexter felt that he was not at any time the world's Number One.

Less glamorous and controversial, the quiet, dignified but aggressive Gibbs attracted the least attention of the quartet, but it was he who provided the fulcrum on which the West Indies' attack operated: he always had first choice of ends. He was their most successful wicket-taker partly because he bowled so much, but he only bowled so much because he was the most dependable and durable, and sought to attack the batsman even while containing him. He was a proposition in all conditions: he could turn the ball on surfaces which offered him little help, as he demonstrated by bowling Australia to defeat in the third Test at Georgetown, and exploit a crumbling pitch, as he showed when England were beaten in the first Test at Old Trafford, and India in the third at Madras.

In the three series against Australia, England and India between 1965 and 1967, Gibbs averaged 58 overs per match, conceded fewer than two runs per over and finished top of his side's bowling averages twice and second once – reasonable justification, perhaps, for him being bracketed with Tayfield as the best non-English off-spinner since the Second World War. Some critics rate him as the finest hard-wicket bowler of his type of all time.

The keys to Gibbs's success were his height (he stood 5ft 11in); long, powerful fingers; and a high, quick action that was the climax to a short, springing run – one contemporary said Gibbs was the nearest to a human grasshopper he had seen. It was these character-istics, rather than a highly unorthodox chest-on action, that enabled him to get bounce and turn from even the most unresponsive pitches, which was essential if he was to survive on the hard-baked surfaces of the Caribbean. He was, in addition, a master of flight and pace.

'Gibbs had it all,' Dexter said. 'He gave the ball a real tweak and possessed flight, control and imagination. He was very intelligent and fiercely competitive. He was the equal of LAKER on dry pitches but, having had less exposure to them, was obviously not as good on rain-affected pitches or slow English turners.'

Gibbs, who began his career bowling leg-breaks interspersed with the occasional off-break but changed styles in order to improve his accuracy, made his debut against MCC on a true Bourda pitch in February 1954 and was swiftly appraised of the need for discipline. His first wicket was that of Compton and came quickly, but he was made to wait for his second as Willie Watson and Graveney put on 402 together.

Gibbs began his Test career well against Pakistan four years later, but did not establish himself until the tour of Australia in 1960–61, when he took three wickets in four balls at Sydney and performed the hat-trick in Adelaide. The following year, he completed India's spectacular rout at Bridgetown by taking eight wickets for six runs in 15.3 overs in one session. 'Gibbs looked a world beater,' *Wisden* reported. 'So masterly was his variation of flight that he appeared capable of succeeding on the truest pitches.'

Like Tayfield, Gibbs was more effective bowling over the wicket than round and, on entering county cricket, took time to master this line of attack, which was essential in view of the prevailing law governing leg-before decisions. But when he did, he did so conclu-sively, capturing 131 wickets at 18.89 in 1971 as Warwickshire narrowly failed to win the championship. They went on to win it the following year, again with his help.

Like every other bowler, Gibbs struggled to pose problems for Sobers, who did, however, treat him with greater deference in the Caribbean than when they confronted each other in county matches in England. In their only meetings between 1965 and

1968, Sobers scored 204 and 165 in inter-island matches but Gibbs took the honours when the Rest of the World played Barbados at Bridgetown in March 1967. Bowling beautifully, he spun Barbados to a heavy defeat, dismissing Sobers for 32 in the first innings and making him struggle for forty minutes for three runs in the second.

Outside the West Indies, perhaps the best bowler in the mid-1960s was Garth McKenzie, Australia's strong and willing new-ball bowler, who carried their attack manfully. He took 71 Test wickets in 1964 alone, and from then until 1967 Australia never won a match without a substantial contribution from him. Peter Pollock, Graeme's elder brother, ploughed a similarly lonely furrow for South Africa, with less conspicuous success, before help arrived in the shape of Mike Procter.

Gibbs was the last great Caribbean spin bowler, and his passing had a direct bearing on the move towards the all-pace attacks with which West Indies battered oppositions into submission for nearly twenty years. Two months after Gibbs played his last Test match (during which he edged ahead of Trueman's world Test record of 307 wickets), Clive Lloyd, his first cousin, lost a Test match to India in Trinidad after leaving them ten hours to survive or score 403 to win. His three spinners took only two wickets and failed to exercise Gibbs's control, setting Lloyd firmly on a more direct means of attack.

Gibbs, whose mother was born in Barbados, is the only Number One player born on the South American continent. British Guiana, a colony that was renamed Guyana on full independence in 1966, was highly cosmopolitan and the only country in the region where English was the first language and a serious interest in cricket was shown. Gibbs subsequently spent time pursuing business interests in the United States, became a sports administrator in Guyana, and managed the West Indies team in the early 1990s.

Gibbs's first-class record: 330 matches, 1,024 wickets, average 27.22. **Test record:** 79 matches, 309 wickets, average 29.09.

Gibbs's Coopers & Lybrand ratings 1965–67: 1, 1, 2.
Other leader: 1967: K. Higgs (Eng). Gibbs was also top in 1964 and 1968.

Record against Number One batsmen:
v Sobers 1965–68: 3 matches, Sobers 4 innings, 404 runs, average 101.00 (two centuries, highest score 204); Gibbs took his wicket once.

Ⓒ JOHN AUGUSTINE SNOW (England)

Number One: 1968–72

Born: Peopleton, Worcestershire, 13 October 1941. Career: 1961–77.

John Snow's stature as one of the great fast bowlers chiefly rests on his outstanding performances in three demanding Test series: in West Indies in 1967–68, in Australia in 1970–71 and at home to Australia in 1972. With Snow providing the flintiest of cutting edges, England won the first two rubbers and drew the third – considerable achievements, as few visiting teams win in the Caribbean and England had last held the Ashes in 1959. But there was more to it than that: England lost only once in 39 Tests between August 1966 and August 1971, and Snow, with 113 wickets at 26.08 in 28 of those matches (injuries kept him out of most of the others), was one of the key factors in their success.

If LILLEE outbowled him in England in 1972, no one could touch Snow in the two earlier series. He made his mark on each immediately. He destroyed West Indies in the first innings in the second Test at Kingston – he had begun the tour raggedly and been omitted from the first Test – with seven for 49, and maintained his speed and accuracy in the next match at Bridgetown, where he took eight wickets. Although he played little part in England's one victory, in Trinidad, he produced his best effort in the final Test in Georgetown, where his ten wickets helped ensure England's series lead was safeguarded. He finished the series with 27 wickets, a record for an England bowler in the Caribbean, and *Wisden* proclaimed him 'the fastest and most dangerous bowler of the West Indian season'. GIBBS remained West Indies' best bowler, but was overbowled and less effective than before.

In Australia, Snow's fire in the first Test at Brisbane filled the home side with an apprehension that was not lifted for the rest of the tour, and his superb bowling on an unresponsive Sydney pitch swung the series England's way in sensational fashion. He took seven for 40, at which point he had taken 27 wickets in four matches; he finished the series with 31 (24 of them top-order batsmen) and his haul might have been greater had he not injured a hand during the sixth and last match.

Snow could discomfort the best batsmen. He won selection for England in 1966 – having played two Tests the previous year – by taking eleven for 47 against the West Indies on a green pitch at Hove and dispatching them to a two-day defeat. He then dismissed SOBERS on the first occasion they met in the Test series and later, at the Oval, had him caught hooking at his first ball. Dramatically, Snow then repeated this feat the very next time he bowled to Sobers, eighteen months on, trapping him leg-before first ball with a shooter in the Kingston Test. During the 1970 season, he dismissed him four more times, on three occasions in England's series against the Rest of the World – for scores of 183, 114 and 59 – in which Snow was their leading wicket-taker against formidably strong opponents. That year Snow also accounted for Barry RICHARDS three times, once for a duck in a county match at Hove in which he bowled his fastest spell of the summer.

Snow picked out Sobers, Pollock, Barry and Viv RICHARDS as the best he bowled to. 'I have respect for all their abilities,' he said. 'They had flair. But I could not say which one was supreme. Lawry was also good: you needed to blow him out with a stick of dynamite. Boycott would bore you to death.' He also prized the wicket of Seymour Nurse, who could be savage but also grafted. Sobers at least offered hope with the extravagance of his strokeplay.

Snow was a nature boy, who ran wild around the sprawling grounds of the family's Worcestershire home. His father, like his grandfather, was a clergyman – and keen sportsman – who had come down from Scotland to take the living there. There was more than an echo of the romantic version of JACKSON's childhood in his early years. Snow's father had envisaged his only son – there were also three daughters – becoming a batsman, but at sixteen Snow was persuaded to take up fast bowling by Len Bates, who coached at Christ's Hospital, Horsham, which John attended after the family relocated to Sussex.

Though he was a superb athlete and obviously had pace, Snow took time to gain control. Nevertheless, he was taking 100 wickets in a season and playing for England by the age of twenty-three. In maturity, he possessed a superb off-cutter, and was, when motivated, always trying something. He could also swing the ball away and rarely wasted a bouncer, but, like many fast bowlers, much depended on him locating his rhythm. Fortunately for him, this came readily between 1967 and 1972. 'I place Snow out in front of all the quicks I've played with or against,' Lillee wrote in 1974. 'Temperament, the ability to place the ball with precision, to make it cut off the wicket in England and lift sharply in Australia, made him the champion that he was.'

Snow gained a reputation for unpredictability and moodiness, but Dexter, his first county captain, felt these were partly acquired traits. 'When John arrived at Sussex he almost had straw in his hair,' he said. 'He was a soft-spoken, quiet country boy, but his character changed because, I think, he resented the pressures of captains going up to him, as they do to fast bowlers, and asking for a bit extra. He acquired meanness and a distinct quirkiness. When Greg Chappell was being written up in 1968, John thought he ought to make an impression. He hit him on the head third ball at Hove.' Two years later, though, he was indifferent to Barry Richards scoring 224 against MCC in Adelaide: 'I saw no point in busting myself to score a point over Barry.'

Snow was difficult. He had interests beyond sport, and advertised them. He published two volumes of verse, and when Basil d'Oliveira announced at a team meeting that 'the ultimate thing in life is to play for England', Snow replied: 'The ultimate thing in life is death.' He was suspended for one Test for barging Sunil Gavaskar to the ground as both ran up the pitch at Lord's in 1971 – Snow insisted it was not deliberate – and unashamedly saved himself for big matches, which once led to him being dropped by his county for not trying. But he knew that he could not bowl fast all the time, and was determined to preserve his ability to bowl the genuinely quick ball. 'Snow's mean streak was only the same one every great fast bowler has,' Dennis Amiss said. 'He bowled at pace on off stump, on a mean length, firing the ball into the rib area.'

In the months before Snow's triumph in the Caribbean, Erapally Prasanna, India's pocket-sized off-spinner, emerged as a great bowler on a tour of Australia and New Zealand, capturing 49 wickets in eight Tests at 23.20 and convincing the Australian players that he was now the world's best off-spinner. He gave the ball a big loop and varied the flight masterfully, engaging the batsman in deadly mind games, and turning the ball when few others could. When India next played Test cricket two years later, he claimed 46 wickets in successive home series with New Zealand and Australia, but gained a reputation for being more effective at home. He became locked in competition for a Test place with Srinivas Venkataraghavan, a taller, less adventurous but highly capable off-spinner.

India in fact possessed four outstanding spin bowlers who were about in their prime, the other two being Bishen Bedi, a left-armer, and Bhagwat Chandrasekhar, who bowled fastish top-spinners and googlies, with the occasional leg-break thrown in. Though inconsistent, Chandrasekhar was potentially the most dangerous of the four because of his novelty and desire to attack. Gavaskar would later describe Bedi as 'the finest left-arm spin bowler I have seen'. Bedi, who perhaps had the greater control, and Prasanna made a fine combination and engaged Australia's batsmen – the best of them Ian Chappell – in a magnificent battle in 1969–70, when Ashley Mallett, another fine off-spinner, returned better figures for Australia against a weaker batting side. Chandrasekhar, who could make the ball bounce, had excelled in his early appearances for India, but fell away around 1968 and did not regain his place until 1971, when he bowled his country to their first victory in England.

If Bedi was the best left-arm spinner, Derek Underwood was not far behind. Underwood was unorthodox, having begun as a medium-pacer and retained an unusual degree of speed for one of his type, though it was also his brisk run-up that gave him his wonderful rhythm. He was a natural – so natural that he claimed over 100 wickets in his first season of county cricket at the age of eighteen and had taken 1,000 wickets by the time he was twenty-five. He was virtually unplayable on rain-affected pitches and so accurate that he could tie up an end on good ones, without entirely switching to defence. But he was not as dangerous on good pitches as Bedi and enjoyed limited success against good opposition in the early years of his Test career. Norman Gifford was sometimes preferred to him as England's left-armer in the early 1970s and, despite many meetings, Underwood did not take the wicket of Sobers in a first-class match until 1974.

With Snow often keeping something in reserve, perhaps the most feared fast bowler in county cricket was Procter, who allied late inswing to searching pace and was also capable of switching effectively to off-spin. From 1968, Procter took more than fifty wickets in each of his first five full seasons with Gloucestershire, before his knee gave way and he pared his workload for three years. In his last Test series before cricketing relations with South Africa were severed, he claimed 26 wickets at 13.57 against Australia in 1969–70, a series that marked the beginning of the end for McKenzie, who had just taken 30 wickets against West Indies and 21 against India.

Snow's reputation, his own disenchantment with county cricket and a developing back problem meant that he did not tour with England again after the triumph in Australia. His last Test was in 1976 and the following year he was one of the first players to sign for Packer. This briefly renewed Snow's interest in the game. He had spent three years studying to teach, but after retiring as a player he set up his own sports travel agency; he had received a benefit of £18,000 in 1974. He also remained involved in the game, advising England bowlers and joining the Sussex committee in 1997.

Snow's first-class record: 346 matches, 1174 wickets, average 22.72. **Test record:** 49 matches, 202 wickets, average 26.66.

Snow's Coopers & Lybrand ratings 1968–71: 5, –, –, 2.
Leaders: 1968: L.R. Gibbs (WI). 1969–71: D.L. Underwood (Eng).

Record against Number One batsmen:
v Sobers 1968–69: 9 matches, Sobers 16 innings, 812 runs, average 62.46 (two centuries, highest score 152); Snow took his wicket twice.
v Barry Richards 1970–71: 3 matches, Richards 5 innings, 312 runs, average 62.40 (one century, highest score 224); Snow took his wicket twice.

BARRY ANDERSON RICHARDS (South Africa)

Number One: 1970–76

Born: Durban, Natal, 21 July 1945. Career: 1964–83.

It would be easy to recite reasons why Barry Richards might not have been the best in the world. He failed to appreciate the value of his own wicket and perhaps knew too well the value of the rand, which, with crushing lack of diplomacy, he conveyed to more people than was wise. He admitted he did things to please himself and so sometimes jeopardized the fortunes of his teams. And, of course, chiefly – though not only – because of the ostracization of apartheid South Africa, he was condemned to make only four Test appearances. This, in turn, consigned him to a life groping for motivation at lower levels, another subject on which he spoke a little tactlessly and damagingly.

But when he wanted to – and it was more often than might be supposed – Richards batted like a god. He had so much time to play his shots that he was almost never ruffled. Bowling of extreme pace did not worry him – he was a fearless and effective hooker – and the few times he was hit on the head were due to his own miscalculations. He once gashed his temple misjudging a hook against Procter in a county match, but Procter was no bogeyman: despite bowling to Richards hundreds of times in junior matches and in the nets, Procter was twenty-one before he got him out. And when Richards faced Jeff Thomson at his height, at Southampton in 1975, he played exhilarating innings of 96 and 69. A few spinners tested him – he singled out Bedi, Raymond Illingworth and Underwood – but he was more likely to get into trouble in a bout of extravagance against an anonymous medium-pacer. 'He appears not to move at all, yet his feet twinkle,' Cowdrey once said. There was a touch of TRUMPER about him.

Every indication was that he would have coped with the special demands of Test cricket. He jumped at the chance to play for Packer, and not just because of the money. He wanted to show what he could do against the world's best bowlers – and did so as impressively as everyone thought he would. Like every other batsman, Richards was shocked by the barrage of bouncers, but he emerged with an outstanding record, scoring two hundreds – one of them a double – in Supertests against attacks containing LILLEE. He also coped serenely with the likes of Sylvester Clarke when rebel teams began to visit South Africa in the early 1980s, though Richards was then in his late thirties.

Opponents feared him, knowing that he could be impossible to bowl to. 'Barry was the best player I ever saw, the batsman I would choose to play for my life,' Procter wrote after both had retired. 'If Barry felt like it, he could bat all day and there was little the bowler could do, unless it was hope for an unplayable delivery. His technical mastery was complete – there was no weakness I could ever see . . . All he wanted to do was prove himself against all the other great players of his time, year after year. Those of us who saw him at close quarter had no doubts of his superiority.'

'He naturally had this laissez-faire attitude but there was no flaw in his technique,' Mike Denness said. 'He would have done consistently well at Test level.' Lillee thought him the 'personification of batting perfection'. Cowdrey judged him the best batsman of the 1970s, ahead of Greg Chappell and Boycott.

Richards's talk of boredom and disaffection could be misleading. He complained of being bored by the grind of continuous cricket, but played it continuously for years on end. He claimed to need the challenge of a good bowler and bad pitch to inspire him, yet his long career yielded an average which few have bettered – and of which he was quietly yet inordinately proud. He indulged in extraordinary improvisations, but his game was firmly founded in first principles. As with SNOW, it was in his nature to be contrary.

At the end of his first season with Hampshire in 1968, Richards complained of the strain of county cricket but made a bigger impact that year than any other overseas player bar SOBERS and stuck with the county game for the next eleven years. He played eighteen seasons in South Africa, one in Australia and two with Packer, and was one of the early masters of the fast-growing form of one-day cricket. For years on end he played all year round – in the demanding role of opener – and reeled off runs at an astonishing rate. He was no less of a jet-age cricketer than Sobers.

Unable fully to realize his worth in playing terms, Richards resolved to do so financially, and arguably earned more than he would have done in a career devoted to Test cricket. He was prepared to withdraw his services if the rewards were insufficient – as he demonstrated when an International Wanderers team visited Cape Town in 1976 – and it was no coincidence that he gave up county cricket in 1978, a year after his benefit season and the start of his involvement with Packer. He went off to play lucrative club cricket in Australia and Holland instead. In retirement, he took up an administrative post with the Queensland Cricket Association.

His mercenary streak was not simply an emotional bolt-hole in the darkest days of South Africa's isolation. It was branded on him by the bitter experience of his father, who was made redundant from a good job as a salesman. Many years later, having acquired some wealth, Richards – an only child – took his father into business with him, letting property in Durban.

Richards gave an eloquent demonstration of his extraordinary abilities during his first full season in England in 1968, a wet summer in which his aggregate of 2,395 was the highest of any player and his average of 47.90 second only to Boycott, who had far more experience of the conditions. But it was Richards's performance in his one and only Test series, at home to Australia in 1969–70, that revealed his class to the world. He scored two centuries, averaged 72.57 and South Africa won all four games. 'It was hard to imagine how another mortal could approach such perfection,' Procter said of Richards's breathtaking century in his native Durban, which arrived in the over after lunch on the first day. 'Barry was the only player who could handle Gleeson's leg-spin with comfort during that series.'

Several months later, after some subdued performances for the Rest of the World in England, Richards again touched sublime heights during his one season for South Australia. He averaged 109.85 and scored 325 runs in a day (356 in all) in Perth against a Western Australia side containing Lillee, who ranked the innings alongside Sobers's 254. The bat was beaten only once – by the first ball he faced. Richards, who was on a dollar a run during that season, frequently stole the limelight from the tour by MCC, off whom he took a magnificent double century, Snow conceding 166 runs in 29 eight-ball overs. By now, Sobers's form was patchier than of old and although he did well against India in the Caribbean in 1970–71, it was a high-scoring series which West Indies lost.

During the next five years, Richards played innings which dominated games to an almost farcical extent. He scored 189 out of a score of 249 for six for Hampshire v MCC at Lord's in 1974; a double century at Trent Bridge the same year came in a match in which only two other batsmen passed 30. When he scored 240 against Warwickshire at Coventry in 1973, the next-highest individual score was 56. In one-day matches he took on, and sometimes virtually beat, teams single-handed.

By the end of the English season of 1976 – the summer in which he was eclipsed by Viv RICHARDS – Barry Richards had scored 14,975 runs in English first-class cricket, 5,868 runs in limited-overs matches, 9,516 in South Africa and 1,538 in Australia. Between 1970 and 1976, he helped Natal win the Currie Cup twice, South Australia the Sheffield Shield once and Hampshire the county championship once. The most serious squandering of talent came later.

A handful of players scored more runs than Richards, but few did so to better purpose. In the first-class averages in England between 1971 and 1975, Richards finished seventh, seventeenth, seventh, second and fourth; of those who appeared ahead of him, Boycott and Kanhai did so four times, Sobers not once. Lacking the natural talent of many free-scoring players, Boycott devoted long hours to honing his technique and stockpiling runs – more than any other exclusively post-war player – but in the process, according to BEDSER, then chairman of England's selectors, 'smothered some of his innate gifts'. Indeed, Boycott placed such a strain on himself that he opted out of Test cricket for three years from 1974. Lillee felt he rarely threatened to dominate the bowler.

Gavaskar, a tiny, quick-footed player from Bombay who tempered his aggressive instincts with a strong defence, made a spectacular start to Test cricket with 774 runs against modest attacks in the Caribbean in 1970–71, but did little more until he returned to the West Indies five years later. Then, against more hostile bowling, he exhibited the courage and application that were to be his hallmarks. Glenn Turner, a New Zealander hardened by playing county cricket from a young age, also scored massively in the Caribbean but batted excruciatingly; only much later did he develop into an expansive strokemaker, by which time he had fallen out with his cricket board and was playing virtually no Test cricket. Amiss was prolific in Tests in 1973 and 1974 – during which he scored two-thirds of his career output – before his technique was ruthlessly exposed by Lillee.

The pugnacious Ian Chappell made invaluable runs for his side after inheriting the captaincy of Australia, and never sold his wicket cheaply. He was rated highly by players but less so by the public, more captivated by the elegance of his younger and less forceful brother Greg, a masterly, orthodox craftsman whose on-drive drew comparison with MAY's. Greg was the leading batsman in the crushing defeats of England in 1974–75 and West Indies a year later. His discomfort against the short-pitched ball – brutally revealed by Snow – did not become a serious problem until later.

Perhaps the most cultured batsman was Lawrence Rowe, the best produced by Jamaica since Headley. He built his reputation on the serene pitches of home, as did Alvin Kallicharran, a left-handed Guyanan in the mould of Kanhai. Rowe won many admirers in the West Indies, some of whom placed him ahead of Viv Richards, but his temperament and health were fallible and he soon fell away. Majid Khan, the best of a generation of Pakistan batsmen inspired by Hanif Mohammad, played wonderfully before his exceptional reflexes slowed; and on his day, Gundappa Viswanath, Gavaskar's brother-in-law, was as infuriating to bowl to as Barry Richards. With flicks of the wrists, Viswanath could play similar deliveries to either side of the wicket; Gavaskar described his innings of 97 not out against a rampaging Andy Roberts on a bouncy pitch at Madras in January 1975 as 'the best innings I have seen'.

Another exceptional player was Gordon Greenidge, a hard-hitting Barbadian who, like Clive Lloyd, loved to attack and would become more reliable with age. Greenidge was Barry Richards's opening partner at Hampshire, and, though six years his junior, good enough to excite a sense of competition in his illustrious partner.

Richards benefited from South Africa's white educational system and its investment in sport. He worked hard at the game during his schooldays, honing his technique by hitting a golf ball against a wall in the style of the young HOBBS and BRADMAN. Among those who coached Richards in Durban was HAMMOND, to whom he was briefly sent as a nine-year-old by his father. Richards's strength on the off side prompted comparisons with Hammond, but Richards himself remembered little of the encounters and a stronger influence was HUTTON, whose technique he studied. Early in his career, opponents learned to attack Richards's leg stump, but his on-side play grew stronger, as did his placement. He hit the ball tremendously hard, a fact disguised by his exquisite timing.

He was an awesome player even before he was out of his teens. While captaining a South African schools side to England in 1963, he scored 79 against Hampshire's second XI; the county coach described him as the best young batsman he had seen. By then he had made his debut for Natal. Two years later, he spent a season with Gloucestershire's second XI and made 59 against the touring South Africans.

It was only a matter of time before cricket became Richards's profession. He was not academic and subsidized himself by working as an insurance clerk, a job that was found for him by a cricketing acquaintance. A long Test career also appeared certain, and when he scored a superb century against the touring Australians in East London in 1966–67, his moment seemed to have arrived. But although mature as a cricketer, he was in other respects still untamed. During the stay in East London, he was among a group of players denied late-night entry to a hotel cabaret – Richards's response was to demolish a large vase outside the foyer with his foot. He only escaped a night in jail through the intervention of a national selector, but the incident cost him selection for the Tests. Two years later, his Test debut was further delayed when the d'Oliveira affair led to the cancellation of MCC's tour and set in train events that swiftly led to a boycott of sporting links with South Africa.

Richards's first-class record: 339 matches, 28,358 runs, average 54.74. **Test record:** 4 matches, 508 runs, average 72.57.

Richards's Coopers & Lybrand ratings 1971–75: did not qualify (insufficient matches).
Leaders: 1971 and 1973: G.S. Sobers (WI). 1972 and 1974: G.M. Turner (NZ). 1975: G.R. Viswanath (Ind).

Record against Number One bowlers:
v Snow 1970–71: 3 matches, Richards 5 innings, 312 runs, average 62.40 (one century, highest score 224); Snow took his wicket twice.
v Lillee 1972–76: 3 matches, Richards 6 innings, 271 runs, average 45.16 (highest score 80); Lillee took his wicket once.

⦿ DENNIS KEITH LILLEE (Australia)

Number One: 1972–83

Born: Subiaco, Perth, Western Australia, 18 July 1949. Career: 1969–88.

Like most great fast bowlers, Dennis Lillee extended what might otherwise have been a short career by turning himself from a tear-away into the most intelligent of technicians. Mastering the arts of swing through the air and movement off the pitch, and possessed of incredible determination, courage and devotion to the team cause, he became the leading figure in an era blessed with more outstanding fast bowlers than any other. He inspired fear in opponents and admiration in the fast-bowling fraternity, for whom he set demanding standards among the next generation.

Not that Lillee was an inconsiderable tearaway. His childhood idol may have been Hall, and his run-up and action sprawling in his early days with Western Australia, where his first captain was Lock, but his pace was slippery enough to override every other consideration and gain him selection for Australia at the age of twenty-one, only six years after his first Perth club match.

Eleven months later, in December 1971, as he applied the lessons learned during a season of league cricket in England, and matured by his recent marriage, he sent shock waves round the globe by routing a strong World XI on his home ground. Fighting off a virus, he bowled downwind to claim eight for 29 in 57 balls – the last six for no runs – as the World team, led by SOBERS, crashed to 59 all out. Paul Sheahan, Lillee's team-mate, described it as 'one of the most destructive pieces of speed bowling imaginable . . . His awesome pace either exposed weaknesses in the techniques of some of the world's best batsmen or had them so terrified that they capitulated.'

Then, on his first tour, Lillee went to England in 1972 and took 31 Test wickets at 17.67 (then a record for an Australian there), his best performance coming on a beautiful batting pitch at the Oval. Lillee's heroic efforts were rewarded with ten wickets and Australia deservedly taking a share of the series. SNOW, with 24 wickets at 23.12, was left straggling in his wake. Ironically, Snow was the man who had passed on to Lillee the fundamentals of the leg-cutter; more predictably, LINDWALL had helped modify his run-up – indeed, was his closest adviser.

During that tour, Lillee's tearaway action was diagnosed as having damaged vertebrae. He played on, overcoming the fear of what further harm this might do, and did so again at home a few months later, when he bowled a long unchanged spell to pull a Test out of the fire against Pakistan at Sydney. A few weeks later, he broke down in the West Indies. The resultant operation left him in a plaster corset for six weeks and he did not bowl for a year. Some doubted whether he would play for Australia again, but Lillee was passionately intent on doing so and put himself through a punishing process of rehabilitation.

He returned in November 1974 and it was immediately clear, from the hostility of his body language and bowling against England at Brisbane, that he was capable of touching his former heights. Initially, his thunder was stolen by his new-ball partner Thomson – a powerful, extremely supple and highly unorthodox slinging fast bowler, whose one previous appearance for Australia had been a disastrous failure. Thomson's bounce and extreme pace, which was bracketed with Tyson's, swept England to defeat in the first Test, but as the series went on, Lillee grew in confidence and speed.

Lillee was the match-winner in the fifth Test at Adelaide, but his contribution to England's destruction – 'the greatest battering in the history of the sport', *Wisden* called it – was not truly reflected in the figures. He took 25 wickets in the series to Thomson's 33, but bearing in mind his recent injury, Lillee's was arguably the more remarkable performance. There was general agreement that Australia had found a pair of fast bowlers as terrifying as GREGORY and McDonald, or Lindwall and Miller. Thomson was perhaps the more dangerous on his day, but Lillee was the more complete bowler. He had the full armoury – his trademark rising ball on off stump was deadly – while Thomson, lacking control and movement, relied solely on pace.

Over the next eight years, Lillee scarcely had a bad Test, let alone a bad series – nor a bad 'Supertest' during the two years he spent with Packer. He was easily the leading bowler when Australia retained the Ashes in England in 1975, ahead of Thomson, Snow and Max Walker, his inexperienced but capable stand-in while his back was mending. Thomson took 29 wickets to Lillee's 27 when in 1975–76 West Indies were routed as thoroughly as England had been a year earlier, but Lillee was the more economical and penetrative of the two.

The following Australian season, Lillee carried all before him in Tests against Pakistan, New Zealand and England, whose defeat in the epic Centenary Test was almost entirely due to his tireless endeavour. Thomson, meanwhile, was badly injured in a collision in the field and was never quite the same explosive force again, though he took another 120 Test wickets. In April 1976, Lillee had underlined his versatility by flying to Johannesburg with an International Wanderers side and putting a strong South African team, containing Graeme Pollock and Barry RICHARDS, on the rack. He took seven for 27, with Richards, his first victim, leg-before for 0. Five years earlier, when Lillee was setting out on his career, Richards had scored 356 against him.

Lillee was one of the first players to join Packer and as a result played no Test cricket between March 1977 and December 1979 – Packer's players were barred from Test cricket on an ad hoc basis. But with so many of the world's leading players also signed up, there was no question which was the tougher environment: Viv RICHARDS remembered Packer cricket as 'some of the hardest, meanest cricket that I have ever played in'. But even here, among the army of fast bowlers working together closely, Lillee was supreme.

In fifteen 'Supertests' he took 79 wickets at 23.91 (including Viv Richards seven times), far better figures than his nearest rivals, Roberts and Michael Holding, achieved. Roberts, menacing and armed with some deadly variations, had been among the most feared bowlers since 1974. He had excelled in India, and provided West Indies with the one weapon with which they could respond in Australia in 1975–76; Lillee described him as the most complete fast bowler he saw. Holding was perhaps the most natural fast bowler, and finest athlete, of his generation. He could swing the ball, move it off the pitch and propel it at speeds to rival Thomson. This inspired Holding to give his all in the most unpromising conditions, as happened when he blasted out fourteen England batsmen at the Oval in 1976.

But Lillee's domination survived well into the post-Packer era. Those who had benefited from the relatively easy pickings on offer in 'official' Test matches during the hiatus found it hard when this arena again sported its full complement. They included Ian Botham and Bob Willis, both of whom had taken over 100 Test wickets for England, and Kapil Dev of India. Willis, who emerged as a force on the 1974–75 tour of Australia, had worked hard on the physical and mental sides of the game, drawing on Lillee's example as inspiration, and continued to do well. Botham and Kapil Dev could prodigiously swing the ball at pace and did so for another couple of years before their immense workloads took their toll. Like Willis, Botham's record against West Indies was unimpressive. Roberts was ageing and his success sporadic up to his retirement in 1984.

Holding remained the best of the rest. He returned better figures than Lillee when West Indies toured Australia in 1979–80, and again two years later when the Boxing Day Test at Melbourne in 1981–82 became a duel for supremacy between the two: Holding took eleven wickets, Lillee ten, but it was Australia who won the match. In the same game, Lillee passed GIBBS as the leading wicket-taker in Test history and took ten or more wickets in a Test for the seventh and last time, equalling the records of BARNES and GRIM-METT. On his day Holding was the fastest in the world – as Boycott famously had confirmed for him at Bridgetown in March 1981 – but Holding did not work at his fitness as he ought and was usually fighting one injury or another.

Holding also operated within one of the most powerful attacks in history, West Indies having found, once they reassembled their forces, that they possessed more top-class fast bowlers than they could accommodate. By religiously picking four of them for every match, regardless of conditions, they made the best use of them that they could and papered over their lack of worthwhile spinners. Easily capable of destroying most opponents, this co-operative countered the occasional resistance it met with unprecedented use of the bouncer and sluggardly over-rates. Even so, a disproportionate burden fell on the steepling, metronomic Joel Garner, capable of genuine speed but deployed by Lloyd to bottle up one end while attacks were made from the other. In Tests between 1979 and 1982, Garner took 86 wickets at 19.50 and conceded runs at barely two per over.

No such luxury was available to bowlers in other sides. Imran Khan, who by hard work had turned himself into a bowler of considerable pace and hostility by the early 1980s, virtually carried Pakistan's attack single-handed, as did Richard Hadlee with New Zealand. Hadlee, who also set out as a tearaway, had learned much from a close study of Lillee. He had cut his pace markedly in the late 1970s, embraced seam-and-swing wholeheartedly and was nearing his peak. Two South Africans were isolated for another reason. Like Imran, Garth le Roux had emerged from Packer cricket a far better bowler, while the giant Vintcent van der Bijl was perhaps the best bowler of the modern age never to play Test cricket.

By comparison, Lillee received strong support from Rodney Hogg, Geoff Lawson, Len Pascoe and Thomson, but he remained the cutting edge, and totally dedicated to the cause. He bowled long spells even when he got nothing out of the pitch – as he did magnificently against England at Melbourne in February 1980 – and, though no longer bowling at extreme pace, was at the peak of his technical powers. In the calendar year of 1981 alone he took a record 85 Test wickets at 20.95, 39 of them in a six-match series in England in which Terry Alderman, his Western Australia protégé whose style was perfectly suited to the conditions, took 41.

'He would try anything to take wickets,' Imran wrote of Lillee in his autobiography. 'He was always attacking, and trying to think of ways to get the batsman out . . . Lillee's greatest asset was that he would rise to the occasion, especially in front of those huge crowds at the Melbourne Cricket Ground.' Lillee took 82 wickets in fourteen Tests there, a record for a bowler on any ground. Imran rated him the best of all contemporary bowlers, while David Gower said he was the best he faced. Viv Richards, while not in the business of praising fast bowlers, also held Lillee in high regard, while MARSHALL said: 'He was surely the best of all fast bowlers.'

In an attempt to channel his aggression, Lillee – like SPOF-FORTH, Barnes and TRUEMAN – cultivated an intense dislike of batsmen. 'I was like a bull terrier – I would not let go if I had a batsman by the throat,' he said. 'I made sure he knew that.' He made unashamed use of the bouncer, could be verbally aggressive and, like Snow, contrary. Nor was he averse to controversy, indulging in some shabby behaviour late in his career, which was alien to his off-field persona and may have reflected the pressures of constantly occupying centre stage in a sport attracting ever-increasing media attention. Sobers saw the connection with Trueman: 'They were very similar as people – great triers, cussers and generous-hearted men who would applaud batsmen who got the better of them.'

Much earlier in his career, Lillee's nearest rivals were spinners. 'Gibbs was a very fine bowler but I do not think he was in the same class as Bedi, Prasanna and Chandrasekhar,' Keith Fletcher said. 'I would put only them behind Lillee, who was comfortably the best I faced. Snow was good, but not quite in his class.' But the tide had turned against slow bowlers. Inside Packer cricket they were targeted by batsmen grateful for respite – Underwood perhaps suffered most – and elsewhere by the legislators, who sanctioned the universal covering of pitches and limitations on the number of leg-side fielders, which threatened the prosperity of the off-spinner.

These developments contributed to England's decline as a bowling power.

Lillee's original intention was to retire after the World Cup in 1983. He had broken down a few months earlier, during a home series with England, and undergone a knee operation, and felt that, at the age of thirty-three, he was near the end. But in what proved to be his last game of the competition, in front of a big crowd at Lord's, his bowling was mauled by Viv Richards. He stayed on for a home series with Pakistan, and took his bow in glory.

In retirement, he went into business as a fast-bowling coach and soon established himself as the leader in the field. He ran clinics in Australia, New Zealand, India and England, and partly as a result was persuaded to come out of retirement after three years and play seasons for Tasmania and Northamptonshire. He did not let himself down.

Lillee grew up in a family for whom sport was a central part of life. His father, who earned his living as a truck driver, played Australian Rules football and Dennis, who was not academically minded, vied for sporting supremacy with his younger brother.

Lillee's first-class record: 198 matches, 882 wickets, average 23.46.
Test record: 70 matches, 355 wickets, average 23.92.

Lillee's Coopers & Lybrand ratings 1972–82: 2, –, –, 1, 1, 1, –, –, –, 4, 4.
Other leaders: 1972: D.L. Underwood (Eng). 1973: G.G. Arnold (Eng). 1974: M.H.N. Walker (Aus). 1978–79: I.T. Botham (Eng). 1980: Botham and J. Garner (WI). 1981: C.E.H. Croft (WI). 1982: M.A. Holding (WI).

Record against Number One batsmen:
v Barry Richards 1972–76: 3 matches, Richards 6 innings, 271 runs, average 45.16 (highest score 80); Lillee took his wicket once.
v Viv Richards 1976–83: 7 matches, Richards 12 innings, 610 runs, average 50.83 (one century, highest score 140); Lillee took his wicket four times.

ISAAC VIVIAN ALEXANDER RICHARDS (W. Indies)

Number One: 1976–90

Born: St John's, Antigua, 7 March 1952. Career: 1972–93.

Like many Number One batsmen before him, Vivian Richards came from a small, remote community. He and his childhood friend Andy Roberts, who made his debut for West Indies eight months before Richards in 1974, were the first Test cricketers to come from Antigua, an island with a population of fewer than 70,000, though for some years Richards had been a local hero. King of a small stage, Richards sought to dominate bigger ones in the same way. He did so with a swagger which no one has matched.

Richards took to games effortlessly. His father, who represented Antigua, and two elder half-brothers (he also had a younger brother) all played cricket well and he quickly developed into an exciting and uninhibited strokemaker. He was naturally balanced and timed the ball well. His progress was delayed by two years when he was banned for disputing an umpire's verdict in an inter-island match against St Kitts – his actions caused a large crowd to disrupt the game and overturn the decision – but the episode did not damage his prospects.

He was sent with Roberts by public subscription to Alf Gover's coaching clinic in London for six weeks – one of the few spells of technical advice he received – and was still only nineteen when he played his first match for Leeward Islands. Within a few weeks, he had struck an attractive 82 against the touring New Zealanders and been taken to Barbados to watch a Test, where he met SOBERS and Rowe, two of his heroes and whose attacking instincts he shared. Rowe gave him a pair of his batting gloves.

By then, Richards had left school, worked as a waiter and come under pressure from his father, who worked as a prison officer, to move to New York, where he had relations, and study electrical engineering. Before that could happen, Richards's own vague hopes of pursuing cricket as a career were boosted by an offer from Len Creed, the Somerset vice-chairman, to play for the Lansdown club in Bath by way of preparation for playing for the county in 1974. Creed, in Antigua with an English club side, was acting on an inspired hunch, Richards's name having been drawn to his attention by a favourable report from Colin Cowdrey, whose Kent side had visited the island the previous year.

Richards's rise was then swift. Some excellent performances in inter-island matches in 1973–74 gained him an unexpected place on the West Indies tour of India and Pakistan ('to say it was a shock would be an understatement,' he said) and the intervening five months with Somerset, under the captaincy of Brian Close, toughened him up mentally and tightened his defence. In India he had problems with Chandrasekhar – the only bowler, he said, who ever instilled fear in him – but scored an unbeaten 192 in the Delhi Test and helped his side win the series 3–2.

His second tour, to Australia, was less happy. West Indies were annihilated by LILLEE and Thomson but Richards, after running himself out at Brisbane through nerves, coped better than anyone. Moving up from his customary number-three position to open for the only time in his career, he scored 289 runs in the last two Tests through a combination of his superb eye and surges of adrenalin; his team-mate Kallicharran said Richards was 'like a man on drugs'. He followed up with centuries in three successive Tests at home to India and 829 runs in four Tests in England in 1976, 232 in his first innings at Trent Bridge and 291 at the Oval.

In eleven Test appearances in 1976 he scored 1,710 runs, a record for a calendar year, and within two years had gone from obscurity to centre stage in world cricket. As he had risen, expert opinion appeared divided as to the identity of the world's best batsman: it was known his name was Richards, but there was uncertainty as to whether it was Viv Richards or Barry RICHARDS. This avalanche of runs swung it in favour of the Antiguan.

Over the next nine years, Richards stood unrivalled, his sheer weight of runs in all forms of the game almost enough to put the question beyond doubt. By 1985, he had scored nineteen centuries in 77 Tests and was averaging 54, and that took no account of the runs he made in Packer matches between 1977 and 1979, when he was at his absolute peak. In the first season of 'Supertests', he scored four hundreds and averaged 86.20, a phenomenal achievement bearing in mind the quality and hostility of the bowling. One of the few things that shook his supreme confidence was West Indies's defeat by India in the 1983 World Cup final. Until then, those who knew him believed that he 'felt himself to be immortal'.

It was while he was engaged in captaining West Indies between 1986 and 1991 the Richards became less capable of scoring runs in the same volume as before. During this period, he scored 2651 Test runs at an average of 43 but frequently raised his game when the situation demanded it, weighing in with destructive innings that would change the tone of a match. It was only after the tour of Australia in 1988–89 – during which he scored 446 runs and passed 50 five times in nine innings – that his batting became a disappointment, perhaps worn down by endless travel and over-exposure. 'He was less consistently effective than he can be,' John Woodcock wrote in *Wisden*, 'more through a lack of patience than any apparent loss of ability.'

It was always the manner in which Richards made runs, and the times at which he made them, that set him apart. He so hated being tied down that he flouted the textbooks to escape restraint, frequently playing the ball through his favourite leg-side region, so that it was virtually impossible to stop him scoring. He also hated losing, which made him especially dangerous on the big occasion, such as those at Lord's, a stage on which this little-islander loved to strut. He scored 145 in his first Test match there, and in eight one-day cup finals on the ground for West Indies and Somerset he finished on the winning side in six. His scores in those games were 5, 44, 138 not out, 117, 132 not out, 51 not out, 51, 33; in the first game, the 1975 World Cup final against Australia, he executed three brilliant run-outs. At his best, he batted as few have ever done.

Just as GRACE had turned the tide against the fast bowlers in the 1870s, so, too, did Richards a century later, by tackling them head on and showing that they could be tamed. It was an audacious policy and one which few, if any, other players from any age could have accomplished. His desire to duel may have stemmed from his passion for boxing, which he had practised as a youth during his ban. He possessed a boxer's powerful shoulders and quickness of foot, and he liked to punch the ball hard. He timed his entrances into the 'ring' as dramatically as any heavyweight and kept sharp his instincts for self-preservation by refusing to wear a helmet – the second line of defence for every other batsman from the late 1970s. Richards viewed fast bowlers as 'basically bullies' and his jousts with them as 'the survival of the psychologically strongest'. He cultivated his own aura of intimidation and invincibility, which was so effective that it had the unintentional effect of disconcerting all but the steeliest of team-mates, too, contributing to his controversial release by Somerset in 1986.

Richards learned a lot from those first encounters with Lillee and Thomson in 1975–76. They gave him a torrid time, Lillee dismissing him five times and Thomson smashing his box and hitting him on the jaw, which swelled up 'as if I had the mumps'; but Richards learned to stare them down (a technique he would use to good effect against countless other bowlers) and finished the series strongly. When next they met in meaningful contests, he greeted them with withering strokeplay. He came across Lillee in a Packer 'Supertest' in December 1977: Richards played dazzlingly for 79 and 56 and Lillee finished wicketless. Though Lillee landed a blow on his face, Richards hooked him in front of square for six. Three months later, he caught up with Thomson in an official Test in Bridgetown: Richards pulled him through midwicket for six, but his fusillade was cut short when he holed out to backward short-leg for 23. In his next Test series in Australia, his scores were 140, 96, 76 and 74, as West Indies avenged their drubbing of four years earlier. Lillee played in all three Tests, Thomson in the first.

Richards also launched murderous assaults on many other great fast bowlers in their primes, including Procter (when Richards was in only his second week with Somerset), Roberts, Hogg, Willis, Imran Khan and Hadlee. He also engaged in less hostile duels with MARSHALL, against whom he occasionally played in inter-island and county matches.

Imran, who said that Richards treated him as though he were a medium-pacer, felt that Richards's approach played a big part in the supremacy of West Indies. It smoothed the path for the likes of Lloyd and Larry Gomes and lifted the whole side. 'This attitude makes it much easier for the following batsmen,' Imran wrote in 1988, 'who realize that the bowlers are only human: and the bowlers' confidence is shattered when their best deliveries are carted about.' It also helped Greenidge and Desmond Haynes, the regular West Indies openers for over ten years, to give free rein to their aggressive instincts, secure in the knowledge of what was to come. Imran said that, of all the cricketers he had played with or against, Richards 'stands head and shoulders above everyone else'. It was an opinion universally shared.

Other batsmen tended to dominate only when facing lesser

opponents or when the conditions were in their favour, though Mohinder Amarnath was a superbly fearless player of fast bowling, to whom India's selectors gave fickle support, and Allan Border played for Australia for fifteen years and never missed a Test through injury; in that time he ground out a record 11,174 runs at 50.56, though only three of his 27 hundreds were against West Indies. Javed Miandad, who worked tirelessly at eroding an opponent's confidence, scored a disproportionate number of his runs on good pitches, as did Dilip Vengsarkar, who failed to make a century in 49 Tests outside India and England, and Zaheer Abbas, a skilful player of spin and the first Pakistani to score 100 hundreds.

Graeme Hick, a prodigiously gifted young Zimbabwean with a liking for getting on the front foot, attracted great media attention over his phenomenal scoring in county and provincial matches – he was the youngest man to score 10,000 runs and in 1990 his career average stood at 64 – but his unease against aggressive fast bowling was ruthlessly exposed after he qualified for England in 1991.

Some possessed the talent to do what Richards did, but lacked his killer instinct. Martin Crowe of New Zealand had a commanding physical presence and was technically efficient and versatile, but did not possess the confidence to be himself; Peter Roebuck said 'he was forever playing like someone else'. Gower was technically and mentally flawed, though his eye and timing gave him a spark of genius that gained the approval of Compton, who cracked open a bottle of champagne the day that Gower overtook Boycott's Test aggregate. 'Gower bats as though he has never known fear,' Lillee said. Sobers, however, commented: 'If you call Gower a great player, you will have to invent a new word to describe the all-time great players like BRADMAN and Weekes.'

The best was Gavaskar, a technically superb player of fast bowling who rarely allowed attacks to dictate terms. He scored massively in Test cricket during the Packer period, but coped in tougher times also. Though only three of his thirteen hundreds against West Indies were taken off their strongest attacks, and he disliked the bouncier pitches in Australia and the Caribbean, he also played some brilliant, positive innings against high-class fast bowling. Imran described him as 'the most compact player I ever bowled to'. HUTTON said: 'I have a feeling that if he had been born English or Australian, many of the better judges would have been tempted to bracket him with Bradman . . . Certainly Gavaskar has a model technique. If I were to recommend a schoolboy to copy a modern master, I would go for Gavaskar rather than Viv Richards.'

Greg Chappell dealt well with the barrage of bouncers in Packer cricket, and scored more runs than Richards in its second season, but when the onslaught continued in Test cricket it eventually took its toll on him. His footwork became indeterminate and in 1981–82 his form collapsed completely for several weeks, prompting him to have his eyes tested. He also tended to brood over his responsibilities as batsman and captain. Hadlee, who disliked the intimidatory nature of West Indies cricket and only faced Barry Richards at the start of his career, deemed Chappell the best batsman he ever bowled to.

In three of his four Test series after February 1989, Viv Richards averaged less than 30, and in his three seasons for his second county, Glamorgan, his approach was often equally frenetic and ineffective. He had said he would retire before a bowler made him hurry his stroke, but he hung on too long and his frustration at his dwindling powers showed itself in some bizarre and unseemly behaviour. His final Test century, at Kingston in April 1989, ended with him disagreeing with the umpire's verdict; the mini-riot that followed producing an uncomfortable echo of the incident in his youth that had made him, he claimed, 'a wiser person'. Immense demands had been made of him for well over ten years and the strain took its toll on him no less than it did on Bradman and Hutton.

Outside cricket, too, Richards remained a small-town boy, although he saw himself as flying the flag for the black man in the world and did so far more overtly than RANJITSINHJI, GIBBS or Sobers. It was important to Richards that he never finished on the losing side in a Test series after the drubbing and abuse West Indies received in Australia in 1975–76.

Richards married his childhood sweetheart, Miriam, whom he had known since he was eight years old, in 1986, the celebrations turning a Test with England on Antigua into a personal party which Richards crowned with a century off 56 balls. In retirement, he coached the game in Arab countries and the United States.

Richards's first-class record: 507 matches, 36,212 runs, average 49.40. **Test record:** 121 matches, 8,540 runs, average 50.23.

Richards's Coopers & Lybrand ratings 1976–89: 1, 2, 2, –, 1, 1, 1, 1, 5, 3, 1, 3, 2, 3.
Other leaders: 1977–78 and 1984: C.G. Greenidge (WI). 1979: S.M. Gavaskar (Ind). 1985: D.I. Gower (Eng). 1987–88: D.B. Vengsarkar (Ind). 1989: Javed Miandad (Pak).

Record against Number One bowlers:
v Lillee 1976–83: 7 matches, Richards 12 innings, 610 runs, average 50.83 (one century, highest score 140); Lillee took his wicket four times.
v Marshall 1983–90: 5 matches, Richards 8 innings, 357 runs, average 44.62 (one century, highest score 186); Marshall took his wicket twice.

Ⓜ MALCOLM DENZIL MARSHALL (West Indies)

Number One: 1983–90

Born: Pine, Bridgetown, Barbados, 18 April 1958. Career: 1978–96.

Malcolm Marshall, who as a young cricketer was nothing if not over-archingly ambitious, desperately wanted to be West Indies's number-one bowler. There is no doubt he achieved his aim. Despite working within their fast-bowling collective, he finished with 376 Test wickets, well over 100 more than Garner, Holding or Roberts, and took them at a cheaper cost (20.94) than any out-and-out fast bowler of the twentieth century.

Teaming up with this trio a year after being dramatically drafted into the Test team during the Packer schism with only one first-class appearance behind him, Marshall was actually coached by them 'on site'. He could not have asked for better mentors, as he readily conceded. By his own admission, he was petulant and uncontrolled in his early days. He cried when he was first given out in a Test; was omitted from a Test in England in 1980 as a disciplinary measure; and broke down more than once in his over-enthusiastic attempts to rival Holding's speed. The advice of Roberts, in particular, was crucial. Marshall was not afraid to put questions – he asked LILLEE to show him how to bowl the leg-cutter – and quick to learn.

But to Marshall, his bowling colleagues were also his rivals. In his autobiography published in 1987, when his position was secure,

he charted in detail his climb up the West Indian ladder of preferment, reaching the top – in his view – in April 1981 with the fastest
spell of his life in a Test against England in Jamaica. But Marshall
was a proud competitor. More realistically, he did not reach the
summit until two years later, the final step delayed by a serious back
injury in Australia.

The turning point was a tour of the Caribbean by India early in
1983, a few weeks after Lillee had broken down against England.
With pressure for places relieved by Croft's decision to join a rebel
tour of South Africa (Marshall himself turned down the offer of a
large sum of money) and Garner and Holding weary after playing
state cricket in Australia, it was left to Marshall to spearhead the
West Indies attack. He did so superbly, with Roberts – who finished
with 24 wickets to Marshall's 21 – acting as the perfect foil.

Marshall generated tremendous speed and hostility, mainly from
around the wicket, to expose weaknesses in fragile Indian techniques. The previous summer, he had given an indication of his
growing maturity by capturing 134 wickets at 15.73 for
Hampshire, where he had arrived in 1979 charged with stepping
into the shoes of Roberts as overseas player. It was a record haul for
the county championship since its reduction in size in 1969.
Marshall was, by general consent, the quickest bowler in the
competition that year.

Six months later, on a return tour of India, Marshall was given
the new ball in a Test for the first time and with his opening spell, at
Kanpur, he took four wickets for nine runs in eight overs. Gavaskar
thought his speed 'amazing'; Viv RICHARDS described it several
years later as 'the best I have ever seen from him; his pace and accuracy were just mesmerizing'. It had been Holding's idea, and
Marshall remembered it as 'the finest compliment ever paid to me'.
In that series he took 33 wickets at 18.81, in the country in which
he had first learned, five years earlier, how to swing the ball.

Like Lillee, Marshall never had a bad series in his prime. Between
1982 and 1989, he played in thirteen out of fourteen Test series – he
was rested from the next tour of India – and was the leading wicket-
taker from either side in six and second-highest wicket-taker in five.
His 35 victims in England in 1988 – at the trifling cost of 12.65 –
was a series record for a West Indies player and a performance
tailored beautifully to slow, holding pitches. In these seven years, he
claimed 292 Test wickets at 19.23 and neither then nor at any other

time was he on the losing side in a series. His hold over opponents was almost hypnotic, as GOOCH and India's players – in whose dressing-room the urgent whisper 'Macko!' greeted the start of his spells – could testify.

At 5ft 10½ in, Marshall was small for a modern-day fast bowler, though only half an inch shorter than TRUEMAN and an inch shorter than LINDWALL. He was wiry but athletic, and it was his sprinting run-up and quick action, harnessed to a beautiful rhythm, that gave him his speed. He could be decidedly quick, and during an era in which greater demands were made of players than at any other time, he maintained his speed better than anyone.

Marshall's closest rival was undoubtedly Hadlee, who, though almost seven years older, was also now at his peak. Between 1982 and 1989, Hadlee claimed 227 Test wickets to Marshall's 292, and at a marginally cheaper cost, but if some easy pickings against Sri Lanka – admitted to Test cricket in 1982 – are deducted (West Indies never played Sri Lanka) Hadlee's figures are the less impressive. Marshall claimed a wicket every 43 balls against other Test teams; Hadlee required the equivalent of an extra over for each of his. Out of fifteen series, Hadlee was the leading wicket-taker from either side in eleven of them, although he bowled a disproportionate amount in a weak side.

In many ways the two were remarkably similar. They had terrific control, did more with the ball off the pitch than through the air (though they did that dangerously, too) and varied their attack endlessly. Marshall, who learned to move the ball very late, said that if Roberts, Holding and Garner taught him anything, it was to 'never bowl the same ball twice in succession: variation is the key to success'. Marshall perhaps concentrated more on the weaknesses of the batsmen, Hadlee on his own technique – the New Zealander was an introspective person who demanded a lot of himself and almost experienced a mental breakdown in 1983. They both bowled to get people out, collecting videotapes of batsmen from around the world and building up encyclopaedic knowledges of their methods, and had great stamina; Marshall, in particular, being willing to bowl in any conditions.

The difference was that Marshall had the greater pace, which gave him the edge when pitches had nothing in them. When West Indies and New Zealand met in the Caribbean in 1984–85, Hadlee, on his only tour there, took 15 wickets at 27.26 in the four Tests,

Marshall 27 at 18.00. Admittedly, they were playing in sides of vastly different strengths. A few months earlier, though, Marshall had bowled magnificently on a typical bowlers' graveyard at Adelaide and claimed ten for 107; four years later, he took eleven Indian wickets on a spinners' surface at Port-of-Spain. Hadlee was a master when the conditions offered him assistance, as Nottinghamshire's groundsman ensured they did when he played at Trent Bridge. Armed with a ferocious leg-cutter, he would bowl an unfailingly good line and length, and Australia will forever rue their foolishness in preparing green-tops at Brisbane and Perth late in 1985: Hadlee took fifteen wickets in the first game and eleven in the second. 'Marshall was the more persistently dangerous of the two,' said Roebuck, who frequently played against them both in county cricket.

Marshall's weakness was the bouncer, which he over-used, especially from round the wicket, though he was hardly the only fast bowler of his generation to make that mistake (Hadlee had his moments, too). At other times he was wonderfully self-disciplined as he bowled West Indies or Hampshire to victory against the clock. In mitigation, his natural style meant that he had only to pitch the ball fractionally short for it to skid through at head height to most batsmen; several received alarming injuries and there was a consensus that he was the bowler most players were afraid of.

Another experienced bowler now in his prime was Imran, who commanded a dangerous inswinger and boasted an outstanding record in his native Pakistan. There he took 40 wickets at 13.95 in six Tests against India a few weeks before Marshall first put them to the sword, but Imran soon after broke down with a stress fracture and barely bowled again for two years. His figures in the Pakistan–West Indies series of 1986–87 and 1987–88 were slightly better than Marshall's; Imran's eleven wickets at Georgetown in April 1988 – a game Marshall missed through injury – sealed the first Test win by a side visiting the Caribbean for ten years.

Garner was still the most reliable of the other West Indies bowlers and Holding, on his day, the most dangerous, before another back injury forced him into retirement in 1987. Courtney Walsh, who initially took over Garner's role, established himself with an heroic effort in India in 1987–88 and AMBROSE emerged a few months later with more immediate results. First Lawson and then Craig McDermott took over the leadership of Australia's attack after Lillee retired, though McDermott, who possessed genuine pace, lacked control and dropped out of the team for a time.

The most significant bowling success of the 1980s, though, was that of Abdul Qadir, a Pakistan leg-spinner of great variety, who capitalized on the general inability to play a type of bowling which most players now rarely encountered. Though he could be costly and temperamentally suspect, and had a poor record outside his own country, Qadir issued a reminder that spinners were not just there to keep an end tight – as Underwood had often done – but were capable of winning matches in their own right by giving the ball a real tweak. Most contemporaries, warned off by the demands for economy in one-day cricket, were unable to do that. Benaud said Qadir was the most talented leg-spinner he had seen for twenty years.

Marshall rarely bowled to Viv Richards in competitive situations, but theirs were meetings which both relished. 'Viv is always telling me how he is going to take me apart,' Marshall wrote in 1987, 'and I am always telling him how I am going to destroy a legend.' Neither established an ascendancy. Richards averaged 21 against Barbados during Marshall's time – when the island possessed a strong attack – but did better in county matches. At Southampton in 1990, by when Marshall had, admittedly, lost some of his pace, Richards took 14 off the last scheduled over from him to win the match, and Marshall described the six he hit in that over as the biggest he ever conceded.

Like many boys in Barbados, Marshall grew up with a passion for cricket. He idolized SOBERS, whom he had seen play in a Test in 1972 – a match also attended by the young Viv Richards – and from whom he cultivated the habit of wearing his collar raised and walking on the outside of his feet (his team-mates called him 'Sobey'). Marshall was brought up by his mother and grandparents after his father, a policeman, was killed in a motorcycle accident when Malcolm was a year old, and did not think of leaving the island until he was chosen for his first cricket tour. But his travels brought him wealth and he was able to return and build his own luxury home above the hotels and beaches of St James.

The first sign that Marshall's power was on the wane came in Australia in 1988–89, and it is a tribute to his skill that he was still easily the best bowler there. He did little in Test cricket for the next two years, but rediscovered his form against Australia in the Caribbean in 1990–91. Customizing his methods once more, he again did well in England a few months later, in what proved to be his last series (his last Test was Richards's last also).

Announcing his retirement from county cricket in 1993, Marshall spoke out against recent legislative changes. 'Bowling has become hard in recent years because the rules are now heavily weighted in the favour of batsmen,' he said. 'The one-bouncer-an-over ruling and smaller seams on the balls have helped make the reputations of some very ordinary batsmen in county cricket who are cruelly exposed when they step up into the Test team.' He continued as player-coach for Natal and took up coaching positions at Hampshire and with West Indies.

Marshall's first-class record: 408 matches, 1,651 wickets, average 19.10. **Test record:** 81 matches, 376 wickets, average 20.94.

Marshall's Coopers & Lybrand ratings 1983–89: –, 2, 1, 1, 2, 1, 1. *Other leaders*: 1983: Imran Khan (Pak). 1984 and 1987: R.J. Hadlee (NZ). Marshall was also top in 1991.

Record against Number One batsmen:
v Viv Richards 1983–90: 5 matches, Richards 8 innings, 357 runs, average 44.62 (one century, highest score 186); Marshall took his wicket twice.

GRAHAM ALAN GOOCH (England)

Number One: 1990–94

Born: Leytonstone, Essex, 23 July 1953. Career: 1973–97.

Graham Gooch did not dominate the best bowlers with the arrogance of Viv RICHARDS, nor did he possess the insolent range of strokes of Barry RICHARDS. There were times in his career when his methods were less than convincing and times when he went through baffling losses of form and periods of introspection. There were times, too, when his enthusiasm appeared qualified: he declined to go on several tours, preferring the company of his family.

But, for a period of four years, there was no doubt that Gooch was out on his own as a batsman. Between October 1989 and October 1993, he scored 3,569 runs in Test cricket at an average of 58.50, both figures unmatched during the period. His nearest rival, statistically speaking, was David Boon, a trenchant and unruffable run-scorer at number three for Australia, whose output was 3,017 runs at 51.13. Two other Australians, Mark Taylor and Allan Border, and the South African-born, England-qualified Robin Smith, also scored runs with impressive consistency.

Wristily elegant players from the Indian subcontinent, Salim Malik, Aravinda de Silva and Mohammad Azharuddin (who, in particular, evoked the style of RANJITSINHJI) were less often required to prove themselves in demanding circumstances. Nor was Martin Crowe. Richie Richardson's form – like that of his mentor Viv Richards – was now fragile and, in England, unexceptional. Javed Miandad had gone off the boil and Gower fallen out of favour – not least with Gooch himself, his successor as England captain, whose disenchantment with Gower's lackadaisical approach resulted in Gower playing only eleven Tests after 1989 (Gooch later admitted he erred in the way he handled Gower).

No one, though, could match Gooch for the authority with which he scored runs against all types of bowling or his ability to handle pressure. This was most apparent in his record against the modern might of the West Indies fast bowlers – the best of any player. In 26 matches, he took 2,197 runs off them at an average of 44.83, runs that needed chiselling out with infinite patience and under threat of physical harm. Gooch was an attacking player by instinct, and played some of the most exciting innings against West Indies in the early 1980s, but a decade later, in the search for greater efficiency, had tempered his methods. At home to West Indies in 1991, when England became the first team for fifteen years to beat them twice in a series, he spent twenty-three and a half hours at the crease for 480 runs. 'His record against us at our peak proves him to be ranked with the best batsmen of all time,' MARSHALL said.

The most remarkable aspect to Gooch's reign was how late in his life it came. He was thirty-six years old when it began and forty when it ended, an age at which most modern players had long since retired (the only other Number One batsman of the twentieth century to reach the top after the age of thirty was HUTTON, who was thirty-two in 1949 and shared Gooch's devotion to practice).

Gooch's career could not have been more different from that of Viv Richards, who was born only sixteen months earlier and whose talent took him to the summit by the time he was twenty-four. At thirty-six, Richards was running out of personal fields to conquer and chiefly motivated by a wish not to lose a series as West Indies captain.

There were several reasons for Gooch's late flowering. Having failed in fourteen years to succeed consistently at Test level, he was eager to do justice to his talents. He was acutely aware that his Test record was moderate and his form against Australia poor. He had been through distressing losses of form against the moving ball: Marshall, noticing that Gooch was not playing as straight as of old, dismissed him nine times in two series in the mid-1980s (five times for single-figure scores) and Alderman had him leg-before three times in nine innings in 1989, twice for ducks. Gooch had struggled so badly for Essex that he temporarily gave up the captaincy. Secretly, he had feared that his best days were behind him.

He had also missed a lot of Test cricket. Disenchanted with touring, he had opted to spend several winters at home, and partly for the same reason had joined a rebel tour of South Africa in 1982, which brought him a three-year ban from international cricket. The ban had surprised and shocked him, as had the criticism the tour drew, especially from his devoted father. This in itself wrought a profound and lasting change in his character: he withdrew his friendship from all but a select few and toughened up considerably, defending his stance on South Africa even when it played its part in the cancellation of an England tour of India.

Remedial action came in several forms. He made a number of technical adjustments, which helped reduce a tendency to play round his front pad, and one substantial revision of his mental outlook. Abandoning his natural insecurity, he put his faith in the power of positive thinking, a transformation he attributed to encouragement he received from SOBERS. 'There was no more waiting for the worst to happen, no more negative thoughts,' Gooch explained. 'I forced myself to recall the times when I had done particularly well against the bowlers I was due to face that day. None of this stuff about, "Oh God, it's Malcolm Marshall today – is he going to knock my off stump out of the ground for the tenth time on the trot?"'

Above all, though, it was the England captaincy that was the making of him. Given the post for a second and more permanent time late in 1989, Gooch found that the responsibility and power, which for many others were unwelcome distractions, provided him with important additional spurs to his desire to perform. Long devoted to a rigorous personal training programme, he now drove himself even harder as he strove to raise his team's fitness levels to those of the West Indies side he so admired. According to Keith Fletcher, Gooch believed that he was a potentially great batsman and that it was time he did something about it. One of Gooch's dictums was: 'I want to be the best, not one of the rest.'

Gooch's first Test series in charge was in the Caribbean in 1989–90. In the opening match in Jamaica, he led England to their first Test win over West Indies for sixteen years. Had his hand not been broken late on in the third Test in Trinidad, ending his active involvement in the tour, he might have taken them 2–0 up with two matches to play. In the first innings of that match, he had played England's longest innings of the series, batting six and a half hours for 84.

It was his 333 against India at Lord's in July 1990 – and his match aggregate of 456, a Test record – that many critics believed signalled his ascent to greatness. Alan Lee of *The Times* was among them, though not Hutton, who watched from the press box and insisted Gooch was good rather than great. Gooch batted for thirteen hours in the game, having two days before scored 177 for Essex. 'I was not tired at the end,' he said afterwards. 'My reactions are slowed, my arms tire – but that is why I train.'

That season, Gooch scored 2,746 runs at an average of 101.70; his aggregate was the highest in an English season for twenty-nine years and he emulated BRADMAN and Boycott by averaging in excess of 100. More than 1,000 came in six Tests against New Zealand and India, despite him being leg-before to the first ball he received in a Test that summer. The bowler was Hadlee, whom Gooch reckoned to be the best he faced, but Hadlee subsequently failed to exert the same sort of hold as Marshall and Alderman once had.

Such misleading starts became a habit. In Australia the following winter, Gooch was leg-before cheaply to Alderman in his first innings of the series but went on to total 426 runs in four matches, and in 1991 he began against West Indies by being out to the second ball he received from AMBROSE in the first one-day international.

Gooch's duels with Ambrose that summer played a central part in the outcome of a series drawn 2–2. Ambrose claimed Gooch's wicket twice in nine innings, but it was Gooch's monumental 154 in the second innings of the first Test at Headingley that set up an improbable England win. Carrying his bat through an innings lasting seven and a half hours against an attack that also contained Marshall and Walsh, he exhibited skill and defiance on a rare scale. 'Since World War II, no innings by an England captain has surpassed this,' John Woodcock wrote. 'It stands out not for artistic merit but for skill and courage against 'a very formidable attack in awkward conditions at a crucial time.'

'He is extraordinarily brave,' Dexter said of Gooch at the time. 'I give him great credit for his late development and clearly his self-confidence has grown enormously. There is a link between captaincy and major scores. I had always felt that Gooch hit the ball too far in front of him. The best players I saw, Sobers, Viv Richards and Hutton, hit the ball under their bodies. At the top level, players who have technical difficulties will be found out and Graham has had to modify the way he plays. He has technical frailties against pace bowling but can put his backlog of experience to good use.'

Like Hutton, Gooch found himself as captain carrying a batting side with a propensity to self-destruct. When he was temporarily absent – as occasionally occurred overseas when he was injured or ill – the side invariably struggled badly; conversely, when he was there, his defiant yet positive batting could inspire them. When he briefly struggled for runs in New Zealand in 1991–92, he soon pulled through, whereas in the past he might have taken much longer.

However, Gooch's ardent wish that his players should adopt his own high standards of discipline remained unfulfilled and, after a string of defeats in 1993, he resigned the England captaincy. His own form was unaffected – in his last series as captain he scored 673 runs against Australia, whose attack included WARNE. Many of these runs came from the middle order, as it was decided that Gooch could be best utilized in buttressing England's flagging batting. But he had decided before his resignation not to tour the West Indies the following winter. He returned to the England side with a double-century against New Zealand in 1994, but in the next eight months before announcing his international retirement made only one half-century in nineteen innings. He remained highly effective at county level, finishing as leading run-scorer in England in 1996, at the age of forty-three.

Though it took him a long time to get there, Gooch's years at the top could be seen as the culmination of a natural process. He had been a precocious talent. Introduced to the Ilford club by his father, who was a keen amateur player, Gooch played his first match for Essex's second XI at the age of fifteen, the county first XI at nineteen and England at twenty-one, the youngest England batsman since Cowdrey. Although he failed at first – he collected a pair on debut against Australia – by dint of hard work he established himself as a Test player three years later. He arrested a drop in his fitness by embarking on an ambitious training programme and tightened up his game by moving up to open for Essex, a role he filled – bar isolated exceptions – for county and country for the rest of his career. Within a further year he surprised critics by following the fashion for a raised-bat stance, the first Number One batsman to do so since WARD. It brought him great success and inspired many imitators.

He received little formal tuition in his early days: his first coaches at Essex were careful not to disrupt his impressive natural method. He had a wonderful eye, time to play the ball, and a powerful right arm that was ultimately the cause of his tendency to play around his front pad but also brought him countless runs on the leg side. Liking the ball to come on to the bat, he used very heavy bats – up to three pounds in weight – but this did not prevent him becoming a tremendous player of spin.

Gooch was also fiercely determined to succeed and better himself financially, though he remained loyal to his cultural roots, never allowing his involvement with England to dilute his affection for Essex. Born the first son and second child into a poor family and brought up in a council house in Leytonstone, he left school with modest qualifications and, before joining Essex, worked for two years as an apprentice toolmaker.

He pursued wealth with as much single-mindedness and success as he did runs. Before his sixteen-year marriage ended in 1992, he owned a six-bedroom house in Essex and a villa in Portugal, and had purchased another home for his parents. He gained a reputation for moroseness, but this was not an accurate reflection of his private self and was simply his method of dealing with the constant scrutiny of the media. In a touch of vanity, he also invested in hair replacements, something SHREWSBURY and GRIMMETT would have envied.

When his father – who with his mother attended every game he played in Essex – died in 1996, Gooch agreed to his last wish that he play one more season. He did, but his form was such that he retired mid-season.

Gooch's first-class record: 580 matches, 44,841 runs, average 49.11. **Test record:** 118 matches, 8,900 runs, average 42.58.

Gooch's Coopers & Lybrand ratings 1990–93: 3, 1, 1, 1.
Other leader: 1990: Javed Miandad (Pak).

Record against Number One bowlers:
v Ambrose 1990–93: 7 matches, Gooch 13 innings, 703 runs, average 63.90 (one century, highest score 154 not out); Ambrose took his wicket three times.
v Warne 1993: 6 matches, Gooch 12 innings, 673 runs, average 56.08 (two centuries, highest score 133); Warne took his wicket five times.

Ⓜ CURTLY ELCONN LYNWALL AMBROSE (West Indies)

Number One: 1990–93

Born: Swetes Village, Antigua, 21 September 1963. Career: 1986–.

Curtly Ambrose struck a familiar figure when he entered Test cricket in 1988. He was freakishly tall and, with his steepling bounce and arrow-like yorker, uncommonly accurate – and for West Indies, the temptation to press a bowler of wicket-taking potential into the defensive role once occupied by Garner was overwhelming, and more than Viv RICHARDS, the captain, could resist. During the first three years of Ambrose's international career, Richards heaped on him an immense workload. 'He's got the biggest heart of any bowler I've known,' Richards said in 1991. 'He always wants to bowl and always makes that extra effort. No matter what the position, he always feels he has the chance of a breakthrough.'

But whatever Richards might have said, Ambrose was not another Garner and did not always want to bowl, at least not in long spells. He was, at 6ft 7in, around the same height as Garner, but Garner was physically much sturdier; Ambrose was slim, gangling and seemingly liable to break down. Unlike Garner, who reluctantly accepted his lot under Lloyd, Ambrose protested at the danger of burn-out, though the risks were increased by his own decision to play county cricket for Northamptonshire from 1989 onwards. He bowled a fuller length than Garner and was faster off the pitch, making him, when fresh, a far more persistent threat to the batsman's survival.

Ambrose's own survival as the most consistently threatening fast bowler of the last ten years was a remarkable and unpredicted outcome. Somehow he kept the competitive spirit alive, confounding those who thought his interest in the game was qualified and interpreted his grumbling and lack of punctuality as evidence that he was not a trier. He was as unexpectedly durable, in his way, as SOBERS. In those ten years, he missed only six Tests through injury or illness and, despite sometimes hunting alone rather than in a 'pack', as had so many West Indian bowlers of late, managed – as Richards said – to make the breakthrough when his team really needed him to, turning matches and series time and again. His predatory instinct set him apart.

Among bowlers of genuine speed, Ambrose at his best was perhaps the most consistently accurate in the game's history – ahead of LINDWALL and LARWOOD at their peaks. While minding his ribs and fingers, the batsman had to play him. Imparting pace with a snap of his wrist, Ambrose would hit the seam from a great height and let the movement of the ball do the work; he did not swing it much, though he did vary his pace. 'He should be playable on a good wicket,' Nasser Hussain said, 'but the problem is that he doesn't bowl you any bad balls, so he never lets you off the hook no matter what the conditions. He also seems able to bowl with the same action for both short balls and yorkers.' Ambrose described himself as a rhythm bowler. 'Once I get my rhythm right, I know I can put the ball down where I want to,' he said.

He singled out key opponents with all the ruthlessness and intelligence of Richards with a bat in his hand. They might be newcomers trying to make their way at international level, or captains to whom team-mates looked for a lead. He gave Steve WAUGH a torrid time in his early career, preventing him from establishing himself at number three in the order, and inflicted similar misery on Hick in the latter's first Test series, dismissing him six times in seven innings before Hick was withdrawn from the England side. Ambrose's knack of removing Border, Australia's captain, at crucial times was vital to West Indies maintaining their unbeaten record. GOOCH, assisted by slow pitches in England in 1991, was one of the few whose performances against Ambrose bore scrutiny.

A key figure in Ambrose's success was his mother, a small woman with a big heart, who brought up her large family in difficult circumstances with an iron glove. Ambrose, who received little formal coaching, learned much about the psychology of bowling from Roberts, who did more than anyone to convince him he could make himself into an international cricketer. A chord must have struck with these two enigmatically expressionless men, both of whom grew up in remote villages on Antigua. Ambrose's taciturnity and self-discipline may have had similar cultural origins to HUTTON's: he was a regular attender at the Moravian church in Swetes, which remained his home. Ambrose had previously been more interested in basketball and, like the youthful Headley, considered emigrating to the United States. He had played cricket as a youngster at school and thought it a 'bore', and did not take it up until he was seventeen years old. He was twenty-two when he first represented Leeward Islands and twenty-four before he played for them again. By then, he had followed Richards's advice and spent the first of two seasons broadening his experience in league cricket in northern England. The benefits were immediate, as they had been with LILLEE.

In his first full season of inter-island cricket – during which he was inexplicably no-balled for throwing in his first match, though there was not a serious question about the legality of his action – Ambrose took a record 35 wickets at 15.51 in the Red Stripe Cup. His accuracy was striking: nine of his twelve wickets against Guyana were bowled. He was called up to play for West Indies against Pakistan, took the new ball in the absence of the injured MARSHALL in the first Test and, recovering from an indifferent start, improved enough to gain selection for the tour of England in 1988. There, leapfrogging other candidates, he provided the perfect foil for Marshall. During the subsequent tour of Australia, Ambrose's continued advance compensated for Marshall's decline.

Tired from over a year of intensive cricket, and fighting illness, Ambrose then struggled against India while Ian Bishop, a similarly tall and menacing bowler from Trinidad, began to look an equal prospect. Rejuvenated for England's tour of the Caribbean in early 1990, however, Ambrose teamed up with Bishop to form an awesome combination, and it was Ambrose's unforgettable spell with the new ball in the final session of the penultimate Test in Bridgetown that turned the series the way of West Indies. Bowling fast and straight, he took five wickets in five overs – one bowled and four leg-before, for innings figures of eight for 45 – to snatch a victory that had appeared to be slipping away from them. He followed up with six more wickets as the last match, in Antigua, was also won. He was now out on his own as a match-winning force.

He spent the following months playing for Northamptonshire during an English season hopelessly lopsided in favour of the bat, partly because of the reduced seams on the balls. This obvious handicap did not prevent Ambrose finishing fifth in the averages, with 58 wickets at 23.32, or taking five wickets in an innings more times than anyone but the highly experienced Neil Foster.

During the next three years, Ambrose, showing a maturity beyond his years, won Test matches for West Indies with bowling that was, literally, irresistible. He was the architect of their series-levelling victory at Trent Bridge in 1991, where his second-innings dismissal of Gooch, for the latter's only Test failure of the summer, triggered the decisive collapse. When, as the post-apartheid era dawned, West Indies met – and narrowly beat – South Africa in a Test for the first time, Ambrose's match analysis at Bridgetown read 60.4–26–81–8. And when they were one down with two to play in Australia the following year, he took ten for 120 at Adelaide – where West Indies won by one run – and nine for 79 at Perth to ensure they clinched the series. Bowling with Perth's familiar breeze at his back, just as Lillee had done when he destroyed a World XI twenty-one years earlier, Ambrose produced a similar historic spell, snapping Australian resistance like tinder on the first morning with a burst of seven wickets for one run in the space of thirty-two balls. Border went first ball, and six of the victims were caught either by the wicketkeeper or in the slips.

It would have been impossible to sustain such heights of concentrated ferocity, and Ambrose's form dipped when exhaustion took its toll, but he usually found the stamina to make breaches for others to exploit. With Bishop frequently laid low by back trouble after 1990, the durable, aggressive Walsh, responding to his growing responsibilities, now became Ambrose's chief ally – a versatile one, but not quite as accurate.

A key factor in Ambrose's success was his ability to remain unruffled almost whatever the pressure, although Waugh's tireless resistance in the Caribbean in 1994–95 got to him in the end. Here was an important difference between Ambrose and the Pakistan pair Wasim Akram and Waqar Younis, who went to the Caribbean in 1992–93 as potential conquerors, having frequently destroyed weaker opposition during the previous three years. They commanded genuine pace – Crowe was one of many who said Waqar was the fastest in the world in 1990 – and prodigious late swing either way with the old ball, far greater than had ever been achieved by Imran Khan, their mentor. But they showed themselves reluctant to bowl when West Indian blades were flailing during the first Test in Trinidad, and Pakistan slid to an embarrassingly one-sided series defeat. Though he was tired and his overall figures unimpressive, Ambrose's early incisions played an integral part in the outcome.

Wasim, a whippy left-armer with a wide repertoire, and Waqar made a formidable partnership. On some days, they could be as irresistible as Ambrose; on others, they were surprisingly mute. Their successes at this time were clouded in the eyes of the cricketing public because of the widely publicized rows about ball tampering in which the Pakistan national team was involved – a controversy which culminated in umpires changing a ball the Pakistan team was using during a one-day international at Lord's in 1992, allegedly because it had been interfered with. The Pakistanis strenuously denied the claim (the dispute was never satisfactorily resolved). Waqar and Wasim have risen above that unfortunate episode to continue very successful careers. When, after the rise of WARNE, Ambrose hit another 'hot streak' to destroy England at Port-of-Spain in March 1994 – he took six for 24 as they subsided to 46 all out – Atherton, the England captain, said that he rated Ambrose as more dangerous than either Wasim or Waqar.

Fast bowlers were still in the ascendant and Australia, growing in strength after a spell in the doldrums, possessed some of the best of them. McDermott and Merv Hughes were a lion-hearted pair, but they, like other countrymen before them, lacked the control and variety of Lillee. Arguably a better operator was Bruce Reid, a searching left-armer who was not dissimilar in build to Ambrose, but he was rarely fit and was forced into premature retirement.

Ambrose topped the English first-class averages in 1994, but his power showed the first signs of diminishing the following year in the series against Australia and England, as both he and West Indies struggled to come to terms with the end of their long domination. In thirty Tests between December 1993 and June 1997, he took 116 wickets at 21.50, making him barely more expensive than he had been in his prime. The unplayable and match-turning spells, though, were less in evidence.

Ambrose's first-class record: 201 matches, 800 wickets, average 20.53. **Test record:** 72 matches, 306 wickets, average 21.45.

Ambrose's Coopers & Lybrand ratings 1990–92: 3, 3, 1.
Other leaders: 1990: R.J. Hadlee (NZ). 1991: M.D. Marshall (WI). Ambrose was also top in 1994, 1995 1996 and 1997.

Record against Number One batsmen:
v Gooch 1990–93: 7 matches, Gooch 13 innings, 703 runs, average 63.90 (one century, highest score 154 not out); Ambrose took his wicket three times.

ⓒ SHANE KEITH WARNE (Australia)

Number One: 1993–

Born: Ferntree Gully, Melbourne, 13 September 1969. Career: 1991–.

There are times in history when a player comes along who changes the mood and culture of the game. Shane Warne did just that, restoring the spin bowler to the heat of battle after years of enforced idleness. Throughout the 1980s, fast bowling had dominated; but Warne's school coach, noticing his unusual ability to give the ball a rip, advised him to persevere rather than pursue ambitions to be a batsman or the next LILLEE. After all, the all-conquering West Indies were vulnerable to the turning ball, as Abdul Qadir and even Border, no more than a part-time left-arm 'roller', had shown.

West Indies were not the only ones to have a problem with leg-spin. Ignorance of the subject was so widespread that few could remember what effect a top-quality performer had. With the sometimes profligate Qadir and Chandrasekhar uppermost in the memory, there was a general misconception that leg-spin was an expensive art, its victories exclusively pyrrhic. Warne would remind everyone that the best leg-spinners – such as fellow Australians GRIMMETT, O'REILLY and Benaud – were effective *and* economical; control was a problem only for lesser lights. Thus, BRADMAN said that Warne was the best thing to happen to cricket for a long time.

A few years down the line, but still at unreasonably early stages, Warne's talent was identified by other Australians keen to turn the tables on the world's most powerful team. After just four Sheffield Shield appearances for Victoria, and having shown some form in Zimbabwe and – significantly – against the touring West Indians, Warne was fast-tracked into the Australia side to play India in January 1992. His captain was Border.

Warne failed, but earned an invitation to go back to the Australian cricket academy in Adelaide, from which he had been suspended two years earlier. There he came under the spell of Terry Jenner, a kindred spirit who, with his protégé's blessing, set about improving Warne's fitness and attitude. He also received guidance from Benaud, who would hail him as 'the greatest young leg-spinner I have seen'. Benaud told him to work on a big-spinning leg-break that he could deliver at will, thinking it would take him four years to accomplish; it actually took him two. Warne also spent a season playing club cricket in the west of England.

He was back in the Australia side the following year and within the space of eight months and nine matches had helped them win Tests against three countries. He turned finely balanced matches against Sri Lanka and West Indies – as history had suggested it would, Warne's dismissal of Richardson, the captain, caused a melt-down and he swept up seven wickets – and was arguably the player of the series on Australia's tour of New Zealand, where he took seventeen wickets at 15.05. He established himself as an integral cog in the team and an entertaining and consistent performer; his average concession of 1.61 runs per over was low even by top-quality leg-spinning standards. Crowe, the New Zealand captain, described him as the best leg-spinner in the world – not that there was then much competition.

Warne's next ball in Test cricket provided the defining moment of his career: with his first delivery in an Ashes Test, at Old Trafford in 1993, he dismissed Mike Gatting, recognized as a good player of spin, with a ball so unplayable that the media quickly dubbed it

'The Ball of the Century' – although, had visual comparisons been possible, it might have been run close by the one with which BARNES dismissed TRUMPER at Sydney in 1907. It was the big-spinning leg-break: it began on the line of Gatting's legs, dipped further away towards the leg side – seemingly harmlessly – before bouncing eighteen inches outside leg stump, turning and jagging across Gatting's body to clip the top of his off stump.

For the rest of the series, Warne held England's batsmen in thrall – and the cricketing world for a lot longer. His simple presence now preyed on the minds of opponents, and many could not cope. Before the series was complete – and Warne's final haul of victims reached 34, surpassing Valentine's record for a spinner visiting England – England had dropped Gatting, Hick and Robin Smith, who had made his reputation as a player of fast bowling but whose technical limitations in another area were now exposed. Warne dismissed GOOCH five times, twice with deliveries that turned almost as far as the one to Gatting.

The following winter, Warne was again the leading wicket-taker in all three series in which he played – and made life a misery for Dipak Patel, Daryll Cullinan and Brian McMillan among others. When he rounded off 1994 with a hat-trick against England in Melbourne, he had taken 70 Test wickets two years in succession and been asked by Border to get through nearly twice as much work as any other bowler in the international arena. Some critics, thinking of his control and ability to turn the ball feet rather than inches, concluded that he was now, at the tender age for the type of twenty-five, the greatest spin bowler in history. Certainly he was now one of the best-paid cricketers in the world, and without doubt the most easily recognized.

Warne was careful to maintain the aura of magic. He liked to talk of 'mystery' balls and expanding his repertoire, but in fact his range was not wide. Apart from his big-spinning leg-break, he commanded a good top-spinner, a deadly 'flipper' and a googly that was far from lethal, being slow and easy to spot. Salim Malik played him as well as anyone – he scored 557 runs without being out to him in three Tests in Pakistan in 1994–95 – and part of the reason was that Warne's repertoire was similar to Qadir's, and Malik had played alongside Qadir for years. Others were less well informed and the dangers for them were multiplied by Warne's accuracy and flight.

Warne could be immature but, unlike Qadir, was rarely so when it came to deploying his weapons: one of his strengths was that he instinctively worked to his strengths and covered his weaknesses. By repeatedly firing his leg-breaks into the batsmen's legs from around the wicket, he invited them to take unacceptable risks and drove many to messy and embarrassing ends. This was also a good defensive ploy if other approaches came under attack. In this respect he was more expert than his illustrious predecessors, to whom going round the wicket was not viewed as a genuine option. 'Leg-spinners never used to bowl quite like that,' Bailey said. Warne's wickets often came through a corrosive process rather than prolonged bursts of destruction in the way of AMBROSE. It was rare for Warne to take five wickets in an innings in any match, let alone a Test.

Apart from Malik and some left-handers – who posed special problems for Warne, as they had for O'Reilly – another batsman who successfully took the attack to him was Hansie Cronje of South Africa. The best players tended to use their feet to Warne when he bowled over the wicket, and stayed in the crease and used their pads when he went round.

Warne carried his workload well in the circumstances. Though his approach to the wicket was no more than a walk, his action put demands on his whole body, not just his immensely powerful hands, the power of which possibly stemmed from an accident he had as a toddler: he broke both legs and paddled around for a time in a cart (shades of HARRIS and his potter's hands). His massive shoulders required regular treatment, including daily massage, but in 1996 he underwent surgery on his main spinning finger, causing him to miss a short tour of India.

Warne made a cautious return and there were clear signs that his control had been affected. He did not turn the ball as much or as consistently, and a year later admitted that his finger grew tired more quickly, but he could still give it a rip when the situation demanded.

He modified his methods, but continued to hold centre stage. He was among Australia's leading wicket-takers as West Indies were beaten at home and South Africa and England away, and remained the player the opposition feared. They would try to neutralize him by preparing low, slow pitches that seamed (even though one of the hallmarks of Warne's greatness was that he was often a threat on unhelpful surfaces). But as England discovered in 1997, this only played into the hands of Australia's other bowlers, by far the best of whom was Glenn McGrath, who, perhaps benefiting from the spotlight shining elsewhere, emerged as their best and most intelligent new-ball bowler since Lillee. McGrath had a knack of targeting key opponents such as LARA and Atherton.

Warne enjoyed the material benefits of his position but had as much trouble as Lara handling the media frenzy he created, and soon discovered that there was a difference between celebrity and popularity. Although it was really a compliment about the threat he represented, Warne found himself the target of verbal hostility from the more aggressive crowds in South Africa and England. But he was also disliked because there was a perception that he was not very likeable and not much changed from the middle-class Melbourne suburban boy who had been struck on Australian Rules and the good life – and thrown out of the academy. He sported earrings, bleached blond hair and sometimes graceless manners. He sulked when he met resistance – whether from unco-operative umpires or from stubborn batsmen – and was vulgar in triumph, either towards unfortunate victims or disappointed foreign crowds, as he demonstrated at Trent Bridge in 1997 when he leaped off the players' balcony and cavorted on the pavilion roof.

'As a person I am confident and as a bowler I am cocky,' he reflected at the end of the tour of England in 1997. 'I don't think I am arrogant, though I don't suppose I'd get a unanimous vote of agreement on that . . . From 1992 to 1995 I was the favourite son, now for some reason I feel that they search for the opportunity to cut me down.' A few months earlier he had said: 'There is that much pressure, I don't know if I can stay at the right mental level for the next four to five years.'

By then, a few – a very few – questioned whether Warne was even the best leg-spinner in the game. Mushtaq Ahmed, who first played for Pakistan at the age of nineteen in 1989 but did not establish himself in Test cricket for another six years, cultivated a wide repertoire and won the admiration of Lara, but it took a back injury to force Mushtaq to unveil less often his favourite – and very effective – googly. When he did so, the rewards were immediate and he started winning matches for his country. In Australia in 1995–96, his virtuoso performances were at least the equal of Warne's.

Wasim Akram hailed Mushtaq as Warne's superior, and Ian Healy, Australia's wicketkeeper, did not quite refute the suggestion when he said in response: 'Mushtaq's got a well-disguised wrong 'un, he's got a flipper and a little rusher or skidder. But he does not rip the leggie like Warne does.' Mushtaq shared his thoughts with Warne, as did Qadir, who advised him about ways to bowl to left-handers.

Another in the leg-spinners' circle was Anil Kumble, although he was a different type. He set out as a medium-pacer but was persuaded to change by Chandrasekhar and the legacy was apparent: Kumble concentrated on googlies and flippers delivered at a brisk pace. India prepared pitches to suit him and he helped them win a string of Tests at home, but his lack of variety betrayed him and his returns fell away dramatically.

When another Indian, Kapil Dev, overhauled Hadlee as the leading wicket-taker in Test cricket with his 432nd victim in February 1994, he was acclaimed in his own country as the 'world's greatest ever bowler'. In fact, though as willing and durable as ever, Kapil had long since become no more than a reliable stock bowler, with only five 5-wicket hauls to his credit in the previous ten years.

Apart from McGrath, the other outstanding fast bowlers were Wasim and Waqar of Pakistan, and Allan Donald, easily the best of 'new' South Africa's bowlers. Waqar continued to be troubled by his fitness, and whereas Wasim improved on his earlier Test record, Waqar's figures deteriorated, his wickets proving harder to come by and far more expensive – though still cheap by most standards. He was still an occasional match-winner. Wasim, who put his bowling shoulder under as much strain as Warne, survived better and his greater variety stood him in good stead as he entered his thirties, fit to compare with the most complete fast left-armers of all time. Donald had some catching up to do after not starting his Test career until he was twenty-five. He could be devastating – he had pace and a dangerous outswinger – but suffered from being over-bowled.

Where bowling would end up in the post-Warne era was hard to divine. But if he, admittedly blessed with genius, could so thoroughly exploit long-standing ignorance, might not an off-spinner do the same?

Warne's first-class record: 109 matches, 471 wickets, average 24.44. **Test record:** 58 matches, 264 wickets, average 23.95.

Warne's Coopers & Lybrand ratings 1993–97: 5, 3, 4, 2, 4. *Leaders*: 1993: Waqar Younis (Pak). 1994–97: C.E.L. Ambrose (WI).

Record against Number One batsmen:
v Gooch 1993: 6 matches, Gooch 12 innings, 673 runs, average 56.08 (two centuries, highest score 133); Warne took his wicket five times.
v Lara 1994–95: 4 matches, Lara 8 innings, 308 runs, average 44.00 (highest score 88); Warne took his wicket once.
v Waugh 1995–97: 2 matches, Waugh 4 innings, 124 runs, average 31.00. (highest score 80); Warne failed to take his wicket.

BRIAN CHARLES LARA (West Indies)

Number One: 1994–95

Born: Cantaro, Santa Cruz, Trinidad, 2 May 1969. Career: 1988–.

A case could be made for Brian Lara being the world's best batsman by early 1993. Between November 1992 and April 1993 he scored more than 1700 runs in Australia, South Africa and the Caribbean, and took dazzling one-day centuries off Wasim and Waqar, and Donald. His *pièce de résistance*, though, was his 277 in a Test at Sydney that many judges considered among the finest displays of the modern era. It was a performance breathtaking in its range of strokes and marked the turning point of the series, so effectively did it draw the sting of Australia's attack, which included WARNE. Kanhai, then West Indies's assistant manager, described it as 'one of the greatest innings I have ever seen'; Richardson, who partnered Lara, said he found it difficult 'playing and being a spectator at the same time'. It remained Lara's favourite innings.

But Lara was still relatively unproven. He had previously played little for West Indies, having been kept waiting, rather uncomfortably, for a regular place in the team until Viv RICHARDS retired. (Richards later claimed to have kept Lara back 'because I knew he was so special and I wanted him to grow in his own space'.) The Sydney Test, only the fifth of Lara's career, suggested he might fill Richards's place at the hub of the side's batting, but time alone would tell.

The world did not have to wait long. Lara played little in what remained of 1993 (in one of his rare appearances, he scored 153 off 144 balls in a one-day match in Sharjah) but provided compelling evidence in the first half of the following year that he was now not only the best batsman in the world but potentially one of the greatest of all time. In a golden fifty-day spell, he scored an unprecedented seven hundreds in eight innings – his 1,551 runs occupied only 1,713 balls – in the course of which he claimed two of the most coveted records in the game: the highest innings in both Test cricket and all first-class cricket. He was the first man to hold the two simultaneously since BRADMAN. 'In 1994, Brian Lara was, beyond dispute, the greatest batsman in the world,' stated *Wisden*.

Lara began the year by scoring 715 runs in five Red Stripe Cup matches for Trinidad and Tobago, thus breaking the competition record for the second time in four years. In his most exceptional performance, he scored 180 against Jamaica while his partners contributed 21; David Holford said he 'reduced the game to a farce'. England were due to play a Test series in the Caribbean and before they arrived, Lara announced that it was his aim to score a triple-century against them. After getting as far as 167 at Georgetown, he duly accomplished his ambition in the final match at Antigua, eclipsing the 365 of SOBERS, a fellow left-hander and someone who had taken an early interest in Lara's career, by ten runs. A late signing for Warwickshire, Lara proceeded straight to England, where he scored centuries in each of his first five championship matches, culminating in a world-record 501 not out against Durham at Edgbaston, an astonishing 390 of them in one day, 45 more than any other player had ever managed.

Three weeks later, he made a sparkling 197 off 195 balls at Northampton, engaging in an enthralling duel with AMBROSE that was billed as a contest between the world's best batsman and fast bowler. Lara scored only twelve runs off the forty-five balls he received from Ambrose – who split Lara's helmet and had him dropped at slip – but maintained his record of never having been out to Ambrose in a first-class match (they had been opponents on four previous occasions).

Ambrose demonstrated the importance of bowling at Lara with metronomic precision. 'You almost have to bowl too straight at him,' Angus Fraser, England's most accurate bowler, said after Georgetown. 'Anything just outside off stump he throws the kitchen sink at.' Lara's lack of size (he stood only 5ft 8in) – something that had caused him tears at school – was an advantage. He was so quick on his feet that he was rarely out of position and capable of outrageous improvisations. His placement square of the wickets was a key factor in his swift scoring, as was his unusually high and rapid backlift – which did, however, have the potential to lead to difficulties when he was out of form.

'I don't think a better person could have broken the [Test] record,' Sobers said. 'To me, he is the only batsman around today who plays the game the way it should be played. He doesn't use his pads, he uses his bat.' Lara's attacking instincts ensured that he drew crowds like few others since the Second World War – Compton, Sobers and Viv Richards, perhaps. To some, he was a reminder of how Harvey, another left-hander, had played.

At this time, there was often an air of predictability after Lara had been at the crease an hour. This was the case with both his world records, when circumstances were heavily in his favour. At Antigua, West Indies had already won the series; while the Edgbaston match was dead as a contest when the final day began. Both pitches were ideal for batting. 'He was just so single-minded,' Bob Woolmer said of Lara's half-thousand. 'It was always inevitable, almost mystical.'

The inevitability may have been partly due to Lara's deep-seated ambition, which kept him focused. He was eight years old when he said that he wanted to be the world's greatest cricketer, and perhaps talked too readily during his many idle moments on the 1991 tour of England of comparisons between himself and Sobers (he was rebuked by GIBBS, the West Indies manager, for his impertinence). If there was a streak of arrogance, Lara also possessed an inbred pragmatism. After his 501, he said that he did not yet think himself 'a complete player'.

Lara's family quickly recognized that he had an aptitude for ball games. It was something they willingly nurtured. Though the second-youngest of eleven children, he never lacked for attention and despite his modest means, his father Bunty, a manager at a government agricultural station, took Brian at the age of six from their village in the Santa Cruz Valley to Port-of-Spain for cricket coaching. Lara absorbed himself in the game's tactics and improvised his own practice sessions. Trinidad did not have a tradition of producing great batsmen – Lara's hero and role model was Roy Fredericks, a Guyanan – but by the time he was attending Fatima College, a leading Catholic school in Port-of-Spain, and scoring centuries there, the die was cast. Though he left school with sufficient qualifications for accountancy to be a career option, it never became one.

At fourteen, Lara was making his debut in under-19 cricket; by seventeen, he was shining in the Caribbean youth championship. A year later he captained West Indies at the Youth World Cup. He made his first appearance for Trinidad and Tobago at eighteen and in his second match batted for five and three-quarter hours for 92 against a Barbados attack containing Garner and MARSHALL, whom he rarely encountered again. At twenty, Lara was captaining Trinidad – though the experiment was unsuccessful and not repeated for four years – and making his Test debut, at Lahore, as a stand-in for Richards. He waited seventeen months to play another Test, by which time he had made a name for himself at the 1992 World Cup and Richards had finally departed the scene.

But Lara, having touched dizzying heights in 1994, was soon struggling to live up to his lofty position. His spectacular achievements came so quickly upon one another that the media hype gained a dangerous momentum. It was out of proportion with anything most cricketers experienced, as were the commercial spin-offs. Lara's contract with Warwickshire, plus countless sponsorship deals in Trinidad and Britain, were estimated to have earned him £500,000 that year, but they also devoured his time and space off the field. When he boarded an aeroplane bound for his native island two days after his quintuple century – chiefly to fulfil sponsorship commitments – he was reported to have said: 'It's all happening so fast. This is scary. It's very scary.'

The next two years were turbulent. Seeking a respite from the constant demands, and finding motivation difficult, Lara frequently skipped fielding duties for Warwickshire in the second half of the 1994 season, and even delivered a doctor's note recommending rest. His special status, and his pleas for exceptional treatment, did not endear him to some team-mates. He was disciplined for reporting late for his next engagement with West Indies, a tour of India on which he was required to fulfil a punishing schedule of off-field engagements.

His form suffered there, too, though having come to terms with the conditions, he scored vital quick runs to set up a series-levelling victory in the final Test at Mohali. His series aggregate was less than half that of Sachin Tendulkar, India's precocious young batsman, who made the most of a slow surface at Nagpur to boost his tally to 402.

Tendulkar, who did not take up the game until he was ten but was playing Test cricket by the age of sixteen, had produced one or two exceptional innings for India – he captivatingly cut his way to 114 against Australia on a lively Perth pitch in February 1992 – but his opportunities had been seriously restricted by the vagaries of India's Test schedule: they rarely played the strongest countries, and their series with West Indies was one of only two between March 1994 and June 1996. Lara viewed him as a long-term rival, and in an interview in 1995, Lara's fiancee said that he talked a lot about Tendulkar. 'I remember Brian saying: "People call me the number one batsman in the world, but Tendulkar is a tremendous player too,"' she said. 'According to Brian, he [Tendulkar] is the real competitor.'

Lara's unorthodox life and behaviour began to affect his relationships within the West Indies team, a situation not helped by declining standards and morale as their fifteen-year domination of Test cricket came to an end at home to Australia in May 1995. It had been anticipated that the series would be close and decided by the duels between Lara and Warne. In the event, Australia reduced West Indies's batting to near impotency through the disciplined performances of their seam bowlers. Lara, having scored heavily in the one-day series, was a disappointment, scoring 308 in his eight Test innings and batting with brilliant but reckless abandon on the first morning of the deciding Test. He was completely overshadowed by WAUGH, whose double century in that game settled the outcome – and arguably marked the start of his own 'reign'.

The fall-out from this defeat was felt by Lara, who briefly walked out on the West Indies team three months later, following a row with senior officials during the tour of England. He contemplated retirement and was denounced by some as arrogant. He was fined for his behaviour and responded by withdrawing from the World Series Cup in Australia. By then, he had already pulled out of an agreement to return to Warwickshire in 1996. If his petulance was inspired by frustration at being made to wait for the West Indies captaincy, it only ensured that he waited longer. Yet despite all the brouhaha, he accumulated over 1,200 runs in his twelve Test appearances in 1995, 583 of them in three matches as he belatedly found his form in England.

'He is a young man who has been going very fast for two years,' Bryan Davis, a former Trinidadian Test player and friend, said in 1996. 'No one trains you to be a hero. I think he misses his family and friends. Today's press are not very supportive for his plight. Journalists tend to dampen the spirits of heroes. Years ago Sobers was the same way. He asked for a rest – but he got one.' Wes Hall, the West Indies manager, felt there was something wrong when such a gifted cricketer as Lara no longer wanted to play the game. 'He is always saying, "Cricket is ruining my life",' Hall said in December 1996. 'The commercial demand on his time is like an albatross round his neck.'

It was at this time, when he was lacking for good advice, that Lara particularly missed his father, who died in 1988. Up until his death, Bunty had attended all his son's matches and had a profound influence on his development. When he broke Sobers's record, Lara had expressed regret that his father had not been there to share the moment with him. 'He never really talked to me about his father's death,' said Joey Carew, a long-standing adviser. 'I never saw him cry, but he loved his father very much. I don't know if he has bottled it up. But Bunty would have been very proud.'

Lara's temperament was being sorely tested in another way, as a chink in his playing armour was exposed. He had developed a tendency to move to the off side early in his innings, leaving him vulnerable on leg stump. Dominic Cork, bowling wicket-to-wicket, used it to advantage in England in 1995, as did McGrath in Australia in 1996–97, when he went round the wicket to slant the ball into the left-hander's off stump: Lara's scores at Sydney and Melbourne were 2, 1, 2 and 2, all terminated by McGrath and crucial to Australia's series victory.

This was a crushing experience for Lara, who had been desperate for West Indies to make amends for their defeat eighteen months earlier, and anxious to reassert his claim to be the world's best batsman and display his mastery over Warne. He failed on all three counts. Australia won the series easily, and Lara played at his best only when it was decided – he scored a sparkling 132 in the final Test at Perth – and reacted rashly when confronted by Warne at a crucial stage of the fourth Test at Adelaide: he made an ungainly heave at his first ball and lobbed a catch to mid-on. West Indies were all out for 130 and lost the match.

However, Lara's overall record against Warne remained good: by

September 1997, he had scored 604 runs in nine Tests and 584 in ten one-day internationals in which they were opposed. He had been out to him five times.

Lara's first-class record: 128 matches, 10,978 runs, average 54.07.
Test record: 45 matches, 4,004 runs, average 54.10.

Lara's Coopers & Lybrand ratings 1994: 1.
Lara was also top in 1995.

Record against Number One bowlers:
v Warne 1994–95: 4 matches, Lara 8 innings, 308 runs, average 44.00 (highest score 88); Warne took his wicket once.

STEPHEN RODGER WAUGH (Australia)

Number One: 1995–

Born: Canterbury, Sydney, 2 June 1965. Career: 1984–.

Steve Waugh may have lacked the surfeit of talent possessed by LARA, Tendulkar and his twin brother Mark, to whom the game came a good deal easier, but he undoubtedly approached the business of maximizing his potential with greater determination. The others were held in greater affection by the public because of the more adventurous way they played; Steve, though admired, was viewed with a certain detachment. He often appeared taciturn and unsmiling, but his play was founded on the same rocks of ruthless efficiency and will to win as BRADMAN's. He was ideally suited to the demands of Test cricket, less well to those of the limited-overs game, in which the others excelled. He may not have been pretty to watch – but then often nor was Bradman, GRACE or HUTTON.

But the practical results in the greatest arena brooked little argument. Waugh was a key player at key times. When a match or series hung in the balance, he stepped forward to claim the winning of it time and again. In fourteen Test series between February 1993 and September 1997, he topped Australia's averages eight times, was second twice, third twice, fourth once and seventh once – this in a side acknowledged to possess the strongest batting line-up in the world. Of those series, Australia won nine and drew three.

It was Waugh's part in Australia's victory in the Caribbean in 1994–95 that arguably established him as the world's Number One batsman. He had been in rich form over the previous two years – averaging 67.44 in Tests against England, New Zealand, South Africa and Pakistan – but his monumental contribution to the first series defeat inflicted on West Indies in fifteen years revealed him as a cricketer of extraordinary quality. He took vital catches and wickets with his occasional medium-pace bowling, but most important were his granite-like innings from Australia's middle order: half-centuries in the first three Tests and an epic 200 in the fourth and deciding game in Jamaica.

Waugh judged his double century to be the best innings he had played, and with good reason. Involving nearly ten hours, 425 balls received – more than 150 of them short-pitched – and six painful bruises, it broke the back of the opposition so effectively that, frustrated and bewildered by the failure of tactics that had served them well for years, they slipped quietly to an innings defeat. He was dropped on 42, but needed no further acts of kindness.

Waugh's confidence received a terrific boost from his success in the Caribbean and laid the platform for the future. He had struggled badly in the past against West Indies: in his early Test career, he went in first-wicket down but was technically and temperamentally compromised by the movement of the new ball, and by deliveries fired into his ribs and on the line of off stump. The West Indies attack had not been slow to probe his weaknesses: AMBROSE dismissed him nine times and Walsh twice, and Waugh was given shelter in Australia's middle order.

But in the 1994–95 series, Waugh did not get out to either of them, evidence of his mastery over the bouncer and a triumph of positive thinking on a par with GOOCH's. 'One thing that has constantly amazed me during this series is just how relaxed and devoid of nerves I've felt when arriving at the crease,' he wrote in his tour diary, which was later published. 'I guess this feeling goes hand-in-hand with confidence and self-belief, two things I've tried to instil in myself.' Waugh's new-found confidence extended to staring matches: he had the audacity to interrupt one eyeball-to-eyeball confrontation with Ambrose by demanding to know: 'What the * * * * are you looking at?' and telling him to get back to his mark. He has stared down countless bowlers since. And he has never shirked a challenge. Indeed, he seeks out the best bowlers, relishing the confrontation.

Although he scored less heavily than in the previous series against West Indies, Waugh played some vital innings when Australia successfully defended the Worrell Trophy at home eighteen months later, his overall figures tarnished by a double failure in the final match at Perth, when the series was already won. It was also not until that game that he finally succumbed to Ambrose or Walsh.

Waugh played a central role in Australia's almost uninterrupted run of success that followed the win in the Caribbean, but two other series-turning performances stood out. One was in the first Test at Johannesburg in March 1997. Waugh came in with Australia wavering at 169 for three in reply to South Africa's 302. He immediately lost a partner and was joined by the relatively inexperienced Greg Blewett. They stayed together for 127 overs and shared a record-breaking stand of 385. But it was Waugh's 160 in nearly five hours that was decisive.

'He never looked like throwing his wicket away,' Cronje, South Africa's captain, said. 'He played a significant role in calming Blewett down and building a big partnership, session by session. He remains one of those players who believes too many players are in a hurry in Test matches, and is quite prepared to bide his time and grind the opposition into the ground.' Australia duly went on to win the series and Waugh to top their averages. In seven Tests against South Africa, he averaged 74.77 and was out to Donald only once.

The second crucial performance was at Old Trafford four months later, when on a pitch of low, uneven bounce, he scored unbeautiful but invaluable centuries in each innings. Conditions were easier for batting in the second innings, but by then he had a severely bruised hand – the result of repeated jarring – and could hardly hold the bat for a time. The steadiness of his progress never faltered; he batted in eight sessions during the match and scored fewer than 35 runs in seven of them. Waugh described his first-innings 108, in an innings total of 235, as the second-best innings of his life. Australia, 1–0 down, won the match and went on to win the series. When they did so, Mark Taylor, his captain, referred to him on the balcony at Trent Bridge as 'a champion batsman'.

The media had long been more enamoured of the idea that Lara and Tendulkar were fighting over the top spot. The position may yet be regained by Lara, who is nearly four years younger than Waugh, and will almost certainly be claimed at some stage by Tendulkar, who is almost eight years Waugh's junior. But it was Waugh that they needed to beat first, not each other – and faced with matching his extraordinary talents of organization and discipline, their chief failing was possibly the same one of impetuosity. Perhaps distracted by the sheer number of strokes at their command, neither chose as clinically as Waugh.

In the two and a half years after the series in the Caribbean, Waugh scored 1,520 Test runs at 58.46, compared to Lara's 2,029 at 50.72 and Tendulkar's 1,482 at 51.10. All but one of Waugh's fourteen career Test hundreds were in winning causes: only three of Lara's ten and three of Tendulkar's thirteen were, though admittedly they played for weaker sides.

While Lara failed to make the sort of impact he would have liked either at the World Cup in 1996 or in Australia several months later, Tendulkar's time appeared imminent. He had conducted his business affairs more sensibly (he had signed endorsements making him the richest cricketer in the world), had married, and learned to be unfazed by the fanatical adulation of tens of millions of his countrymen. He was the leading run-scorer at the World Cup and scored masterly centuries against England on an uneven pitch at Edgbaston and against South Africa at Cape Town when his side was in deep trouble – his first hundred as India's captain, a role which had threatened to be inhibiting. While with Lara it was his destructiveness that excited, with Tendulkar it was his technique: he played with such a beautifully straight bat – unless it suited him to improvise – and at 5ft 5in was another short player untroubled by the short ball. Bradman watched him on television and delivered high praise: 'He plays much the same as I played . . . his compactness, his stroke-production and technique.' During the World Cup, WARNE said that Tendulkar was a better player than Lara because Tendulkar was less forgiving – though Warne had then not bowled to Tendulkar in a Test for four years.

What was needed to reinforce Tendulkar's case was an eye-catchingly big score, but he let several golden opportunities slip through his fingers. In the game at Colombo in August 1997 in which Sri Lanka amassed a Test record of 952 for six (Sanath Jayasuriya 340, Roshan Mahanama 225), Tendulkar managed only 143, leaving his personal best in Tests standing at a modest 179. 'I am sure Sachin takes a close interest in how Lara gets on,' a friend said. 'I think he is slightly envious of him and his records. Lara has made a lot of big scores and played some great innings.' But Tendulkar, more phlegmatic and perhaps less motivated by the record books, believed comparisons should wait until both had retired. A series between West Indies and India in 1997 was badly affected by rain and left honours between the two even.

Waugh's durability had its origins in a naturally competitive nature and his early experiences in international cricket, into which he was thrust at the age of twenty. He was born into a family of modest means living in a Sydney suburb, one of four sports-mad boys of sports-mad parents. Steve and Mark were the eldest and, in a way reminiscent of LILLEE's upbringing, brothers became competitors. They shared a room throughout their childhood and fought out games of cricket, football and tennis in the back yard. Their personalities, though, developed differently, Steve – the eldest by twenty-four minutes – being the more serious and hard-working, Mark the more easy-going. Both found their fortes and futures in batting, neither with the aid of much coaching. Steve won early comparisons with McCabe; Mark consciously modelled himself on Walters, whose 'casual attitude' he admired.

Initially, Steve progressed the more rapidly, gaining a place in the New South Wales team at nineteen and with Australia a year later, after nine first-class matches and on promise rather than achievement. Australia were suffering from the retirement of a number of experienced players and the defection of many more on a rebel tour of South Africa. Waugh was identified and stuck with, and although his returns were unexceptional, he was learning and not slow to take responsibility. 'I wouldn't have had it any other way,' he said later.

He possessed a lot of strokes and played some brilliant counter-attacking innings against fast bowlers at lower levels, notably in his first Sheffield Shield final in 1985 – only his fifth first-class match – and while he was playing the first of two seasons for Somerset in 1987. But in the cauldron of Test cricket, he was uncertain against extreme pace on the fast, bouncy pitches found outside Sydney and England. The bouncers hurt, and so did the jibes, and his development at Test level was retarded.

In January 1991, five years into his Australia career, he was dropped in favour of Mark, who had been kept waiting perhaps too long for his chance but now looked more destructive than his brother and more capable than anyone of making the game look simple. Steve, who broke news of the swap to Mark, was left on the fringe for two years, a period that added extra steel to his character. But after one more difficult series against West Indies, he was dropped down the order from number three to number six – and the success story began. Mark's reward for usurping his brother was to watch him over the next four years almost double his previous average by scoring 3,635 Test runs at 66.09, while Mark himself, failing to tighten his own game and build on his earlier promise, averaged 43.92 compared with 34.60 earlier. Perhaps he felt intimidated.

Steve, meanwhile, like so many great batsmen in maturity before him, carefully pared down his game, jettisoning shots that involved undue risks. Perhaps the most important step was to cut out the hook stroke, which had cost him dear early in his Test career. He started to hit almost everything along the ground. 'The difference in my game between now and eight years ago is that I have greatly improved my concentration and tightened up my game,' he said at Old Trafford in 1997. 'I play the percentages more, I am more patient, but I think my placement has improved most of all.' His ability to find the gaps meant that he often kept the score moving in an unobtrusive way. 'It would be wrong to stereotype him as a grafter,' Carl Rackemann said. 'He has still got all the shots when the occasion demands.'

Though he was highly competitive, Waugh had a profound respect for, and interest in, the traditions and culture of the game. In August 1997, he bid £4,000 in a Melbourne auction – via telephone from England – for a cap worn by TRUMPER in 1902, but was unsuccessful. It fetched £15,000.

Waugh's first-class record: 237 matches, 15,568 runs, average 51.89.
Test record: 95 matches, 5,960 runs, average 49.66.

Waugh's Coopers & Lybrand ratings 1995–97: 2, 1, 1.
Other leader: 1995: B.C. Lara (WI).

Record against Number One bowlers:
v Warne 1995–97: 2 matches, Waugh 4 innings, 124 runs, average 31.00 (highest score 80); Warne failed to take his wicket.

SOURCES and
ACKNOWLEDGEMENTS

It would have been possible to fill several pages listing publications that were of assistance in the writing of this book; goodness knows how many there have been with 'opinions' in them since the sexagenarian John Nyren, working from his own recollections as a cricketer and those of another old player (whose manuscript was handed on to him by William Ward), set the ball rolling with *The Young Cricketer's Tutor* 166 years ago. But, to paraphrase A.G. Macdonell in his study of Napoleon, I will confine myself to the simple statement that the great majority of details in this book have been taken from one or other work of history, reference, reminiscence or biography.

Those that have not come from the many people whose assistance and memories I have, with their kind permission, co-opted. I must particularly thank Dennis Amiss, Benedict Bermange, Robert Brooke, Steven Coverdale, Brian Croudy, Mike Denness, Ted Dexter, Rob Eastaway (of Coopers & Lybrand), Keith Fletcher, David Foot, David Green, Stephen Green, Jeff Hancock, Alan Hill, Richard Hutton, Alan Moss, Derek Pringle, Carl Rackemann, Peter Roebuck, John Snow, Rob Steen, Ivo Tennant, John Woodcock and Peter Wynne-Thomas. My gratitude, also, to Caroline North and Ian Preece of Gollancz, and Charles Richards, for their kindness and patience – but above all to Gayle, for her tireless support.

INDEX TO PLAYERS